GENERAL
PRACTICE
COMPANION HANDBOOK

GENERAL PRACTICE
COMPANION HANDBOOK

JOHN MURTAGH AM
MBBS, MD, BSc, BEd,
FRACGP, DipObstRCOG

Professor of General Practice
Monash University

McGRAW-HILL BOOK COMPANY Sydney

New York San Francisco Auckland Bogotá
Caracas Lisbon London Madrid Mexico City
Milan Montreal New Delhi San Juan
Singapore Tokyo Toronto

**National Library of Australia Cataloguing-in-Publication
data:**

Murtagh, John.
General practice companion handbook

ISBN 0 07 470275 0

1. Medicine—Dictionaries. I. Murtagh, John.
General practice. II Title. III. Title : General practice.

610.3

Published in Australia by
McGraw-Hill Book Company Australia Pty Limited
4 Barcoo Street, Roseville NSW 2069, Australia
Publisher   John Rowe
Production editor Sybil Kesteven
Designer   George Sirett, Asymmetric Typography
Illustrator   Lorenzo Lucia
Typeset in 8/9 pt Cheltenham Light by Midland Typesetters
Printed in Australia by McPherson's Printing Group

Contents

G

H

N

O

P

V

W

Z

Preface

This companion is a summary of the content of the major text *General Practice*. It was written in response to requests from several hundred practitioners who considered that it would be very useful to have a pocket-sized condensation of *General Practice* which could be carried around during work hours. The companion gives an alphabetical presentation of the vast majority of problems—especially nitty-gritty problems—presenting in routine practice.

It focuses on management so that detailed information about clinical features, investigation and whole person management will be lacking. Such details can be found in *General Practice*. Detailed references are also found in *General Practice*. The main references used for this companion are the Drug Guideline series published by the Victorian Medical Postgraduate Foundation Therapeutics Committee.

ABOUT THE AUTHOR

John Murtagh AM

MBBS, MD, BSc, BEd, FRACGP, DipObstRCOG
Professor of General Practice and Head of the
Department of Community Medicine,
Monash University.
General Practitioner, East Bentleigh
Murrumbeena Medical Group.

John Murtagh was a science master teaching chemistry, biology and physics in Victorian secondary schools when he was admitted to the first intake of the newly established medical school at Monash University. He practised in partnership with his medical wife, Dr Jill Rosenblatt, for ten years in the rural community of Neerim South, Victoria.

He was appointed Senior Lecturer (part-time) in the Department of Community Medicine at Monash University and eventually returned to Melbourne as a full-time Senior Lecturer. He was appointed to a professorial chair in Community Medicine at Box Hill Hospital in 1988 and subsequently as chairman of the extended department and Professor of General Practice in 1993. He was medical editor of *Australian Family Physician* from 1986 until 1995.

In 1995 Professor Murtagh was awarded the member of the Order of Australia for his service to medicine, particularly in the areas of medical education, research and publishing.

Laboratory reference values

These reference values and ranges are given in the system of international units (SI) and may vary from laboratory to laboratory. An asterisk (*) indicates that paediatric reference ranges differ from the adult range given

Electrolytes/renal

Sodium	(135–145 mmol/L)
*Potassium	(3.5–5.0 mmol/L)
Chloride	(95–107 mmol/L)
Bicarbonate	(23–32 mmol/L)
Urea	(2.5–6.7 mmol/L)
Creatinine	(M40–130. F40–110 µmol/L)
*Calcium	(2.10–2.60 mmol/L)
Phosphorus	(0.90–1.35 mmol/L)
*Magnesium	(0.65–1.30 mmol/L)
*Uric acid	(M170–480. F120–450 µmol/L)

Liver function/pancreas

*Bilirubin (total)	(< 19 µmol/L)
(direct)	(< 3 µmol/L)
*AST	(< 40 U/L)
*GGT	(F < 45; M < 65 U/L)
*Alkaline phos	(< 120 U/L)
Total protein	(60–80 g/L)
Albumin	(38–50 g/L)
Amylase	(30–110 U/L)

Therapeutic drugs

*Digoxin	(Ther. 1.3–2.6 nmol/L)
*Phenytoin	(Ther. 40–80 µmol/L)
*Valproate	(Ther. 300–700 µmol/L)
*Carbamazepine	(Ther. 10–50 µmol/L)
Gentamicin (pre)	(< 2.0 µg/mL)
(post)	(< 12.0 µg/mL)
Lithium	(Ther. 0.5–1.0 mmol/L)

Cardiac/lipids

*AST	(< 40 U/L)
CK (total)	(F < 200; M < 300 U/L)
CK-MB	(< 25 U/L)
*Cholesterol	(< 5.5 mmol/L)
*Triglycerides	(< 2.0 mmol/L)
HDL cholesterol	(> 1.00 mmol/L)
LDL cholesterol	(< 3.5 mmol/L)

Thyroid tests

Free T-4	(10.0–20.0 pmol/L)
*Ultra sens TSH	(0.3–5.0 mU/L)
Free T-3	(3.3–8.2 pmol/L)

Other endocrine tests

s Cortisol 8 am	(130–700 nmol/L)
4 pm	(80–350 nmol/L)
FSH adult	(1–9 IU/L)
ovulation	(10–30 IU/L)
post menopausal	(4–200 IU/L)
Oestradiol menopausal	($<$ 200 pmol/L)
Testosterone	(M 10–35 F $<$ 3.5 nmol/L)

Tumour markers

PSA	(0–4.0 µg/L)
CEA	($<$ 7.5 µg/L)
AFP	($<$ 10 µg/mL)
CA 125	($<$ 35 U/mL)

Iron studies

Ferritin	(20–200 µg/L)
Iron	(14–30 µmol/L)
Iron binding capacity	45–80 µmol/L

Blood gases/arterial

*pH	(7.38–7.43)
*pO$_2$	(85–105 mmHg)
*pCO$_2$	(36–44 mmHg)
*Bicarbonate	(20–28 mmol/L)
*Base excess	(−3 to +3 mmol/L)

Glucose

Glucose (fasting)	(3.5–5.9 mmol/L)
Glucose (random)	(3.5–9.0 mmol/L)
Hb A1c	(4.7–6.1%)

Haematology

*Hb	(F 11.5–16.5 M 13.0–18.0 g/dL)
*PCV	(F 37–47 M 40–54%)
*MCV	(81–98 fl)
Reticulocytes	(0.5–2.0%)
*Leucocytes	(4.0–11.0 × 10⁹/L)
Platelets	(150–400 × 10⁹/L)
ESR	($<$ 20 mm)

Paul Bunnell (I.M. test)	%	Abs. values	Ranges
*Brand neutro			0.0–5 × 10⁹/L
*Mature neutro			2.0–7.5 × 10⁹/L
*Lymphocytes			1.0–4.0 × 10⁹/L
*Monocytes			0.2–0.8 × 10⁹/L
*Eosinophils			0.0–0.4 × 10⁹/L

Coagulation
Bleeding time   (2.0–8.5 min.)
Fibrinogen   (2.0–4.0 g/L)
Prothrombin time   sec.
Prothrombin ratio (INR)
APTT   sec.

Others
s Creatine (phospho) kinase   (< 90 U/L)
s Lead   (2 µmol/L)
s C-reactive protein   (< 10 µg/mL)

Abbreviations used in this text

AAA	aortic abdominal aneurysm		**CPR**	cardiopulmonary resuscitation
ac	before meals		**CRFM**	chloroquine-resistant falciparum malaria
ACE	angiotensin-converting enzyme			
ACTH	adrenocortico-tropic hormone		**CSFM**	chloroquine-sensitive falciparum malaria
ADT	adult diphtheria vaccine			
ALT	alanine aminotransferase		**CT**	computerised tomography
ALTE	apparent life threatening episode		**CXR**	chest X-ray
			DABC	defibrillation, airway, breathing, circulation
AOM	acute otitis media			
APF	Australian pharmacy formulary		**DIC**	disseminated intravascular coagulation
APTT	activated partial thromboplastin time		**drug dosage**	bd—twice daily tid, tds—three times daily qid, qds—four times daily
BMI	body mass index			
CABG	coronary artery bypass grafting			
CDH	congenital dislocation of hip		**DS**	double strength
			DRE	digital rectal examination
CDT	combined diphtheria/tetanus vaccine		**DTP**	diphtheria, tetanus, pertussis
CLL	chronic lymphocytic leukaemia		**DUB**	dysfunctional uterine bleeding
CMC	carpometacarpal		**DVT**	deep venous thrombosis
CNS	central nervous system		**EAR**	expired air resuscitation
co	compound		**EBM**	Epstein-Barr mononucleosis (glandular fever)
COAD	chronic obstructive airways disease			
COC	combined oral contraceptive		**ECG**	electrocardiogram
			ECT	electroconvulsive therapy

ELISA	enzyme linked immunosorbent assay	**IR**	internal rotation
esp.	especially	**IUCD**	intrauterine contraceptive device
ESR	erythrocyte sedimentation rate	**IUD**	intrauterine device
FBE	full blood count	**IV**	intravenous
FEV1	forced expiratory volume in 1 second	**LA**	local anaesthetic
fl	femto-litre (10^{-15})	**LDLC**	low density lipoprotein cholesterol
FSH	follicle stimulating hormone	**LFTs**	liver function tests
FUO	fever of undetermined origin	**LIF**	left iliac fossa
GABHS	group A beta-haemolytic streptococcus	**LRTI**	lower respiratory tract infection
GGT	gamma glutamyl transferase	**mane**	in the morning
GI	gastrointestinal	**MAOI**	monamine oxidase inhibitor
GIT	gastrointestinal tract	**MCU**	micro and culture of urine
Hb	haemoglobin	**MCV**	mean corpuscular volume
HDL	high density lipoprotein	**MRI**	magnetic resonance imaging
HDLC	high density lipoprotein cholesterol	**MTP**	metatarso-phalangeal
HIDA	hepatobiliary iminodiacetic acid	**nocte**	at night
HIV	human immunodeficiency virus	**NR**	normal range
HMG	hydroxymethyl-glutaryl	**NSAIDs**	non-steroidal anti-inflammatory drugs
HRT	hormone replacement therapy	**(o)**	taken orally
IA	intra-articular	**OA**	osteoarthritis
IM/IMI	intramuscular/intramuscular injection	**OTC**	over the counter
INR	international normalised ratio	**PA**	posterior-anterior
IOFB	intraocular foreign body	**Pap**	Papanicolaou
		PFT	pulmonary function test
		PID	pelvic inflammatory disease
		POP	progestogen-only contraceptive pill
		PR	per rectum
		PSA	prostate specific antigen
		PUO	pyrexia of undetermined origin

RAP	recurrent abdominal pain	**SUFE**	slipped upper femoral epiphysis
RIB	rest in bed	**TA**	temporal arteritis
RICE	rest, ice, compression, elevation	**TENS**	transcutaneous electrical nerve stimulation
RIF	right iliac fossa	**TG**	triglyceride
RSD	reflex sympathetic dystrophy	**TIA**	transient ischaemic attack
RSV	respiratory syncytial virus	**TMJ**	temporomandibular joint
SAH	subarachnoid haemorrhage	**TORCH**	toxoplasmosis, rubella, cytomegalovirus, herpes virus
SC/SCI	subcutaneous/ subcutaneous injection	**URTI**	upper respiratory tract infection
SCC	squamous cell carcinoma	**UT/UTI**	urinary tract/ urinary tract infection
SL	sublingual	**WBC**	white blood cells
SLE	systemic lupus erythematosus	**WCC**	white cell count
SSRI	selective serotonin reuptake inhibitors	**WHO**	World Health Organization
STD	sexually transmitted disease		

ABC of general practice

Its nature and content

General practice is a traditional method of bringing primary health care to the community. It is a medical discipline in its own right, linking the vast amount of accumulated medical knowledge with the art of communication.

Definitions

General practice can be defined as that medical discipline which provides 'community-based, continuing, comprehensive, preventive primary care', sometimes referred to as the CCCP model.

The RACGP uses the following definitions of general practice and primary care:

General practice is defined as the provision of primary continuing comprehensive whole-patient care to individuals, families and their communities.

Primary care involves the ability to take responsible action on any problem the patient presents, whether or not it forms part of an ongoing doctor-patient relationship. In managing the patient, the general/family practitioner may make appropriate referral to other doctors, health care professionals and community services. General/family practice is the point of first contact for the majority of people seeking health care. In the provision of primary care, much ill-defined illness is seen; the general/family practitioner often deals with problem complexes rather than with established diseases.

The practitioner must be able to make a total assessment of the person's condition without subjecting the person to unnecessary investigations, procedure and treatment.

Unique features of general practice

The features that make general practice different to hospital or specialist based medical practices include:

- first contact
- diagnostic methodology
- early diagnosis of life-threatening and serious disease
- continuity and availability of care

- personalised care
- care of acute and chronic illness
- domiciliary care
- emergency care (prompt treatment at home or in the community)
- family care
- palliative care (at home)
- preventive care
- scope for health promotion
- holistic approach
- health care co-ordination

Apart from these processes the general practitioner has to manage very common problems including a whole variety of problems not normally taught in medical school or in postgraduate programs. Many of these problems are unusual yet common and can be regarded as the 'nitty gritty' or 'bread and butter' problems of primary health care.

A diagnostic perspective

The basic model

The use of the diagnostic model requires a disciplined approach to the problem with the medical practitioner quickly answering five self-posed questions. The questions are contained in Table 1.

Table 1 *The diagnostic model for a presenting problem*

1. What is the probability diagnosis?
2. What serious disorders must not be missed?
3. What conditions are often missed (the pitfalls)?
4. Could this patient have one of the 'masquerades' in medical practice?
5. Is this patient trying to tell me something else?

1. The probability diagnosis

The probability diagnosis is based on the doctor's perspective and experience with regard to prevalence, incidence and the natural history of disease.

2. What serious disorders must not be missed?

To achieve early recognition of serious illness the general practitioner needs to develop a 'high index of suspicion'. This is generally regarded as largely intuitive, but this is probably not so, and it would be more accurate to say that it comes with experience.

The serious disorders that should always be considered 'until proven otherwise' are listed in Table 2.

Table 2 *Serious 'not to be missed' conditions*

Neoplasia, esp. malignancy

HIV infection / AIDS

Asthma

Severe infections, esp.
• meningoencephalitis
• septicaemia
• epiglottitis
• infective endocarditis

Coronary disease
• myocardial infarction
• unstable angina
• arrhythmias

Imminent or potential suicide

Intracerebral lesions e.g. SAH

Ectopic pregnancy

Myocardial infarction or ischaemia is extremely important to consider because it is so potentially lethal and at times can be overlooked by the busy practitioner. Coronary artery disease may also manifest as life-threatening arrhythmias which may present as palpitations and/or dizziness. A high index of suspicion is necessary to diagnose arrhythmias.

3. What conditions are often missed?

This question refers to the common 'pitfalls' so often encountered in general practice. This area is definitely related to the experience factor and includes rather simple non-life-threatening problems that can be so easily overlooked unless doctors are prepared to include them in their diagnostic framework. Some important pitfalls are given in Table 3.

4. The masquerades

It is important to utilise a type of fail-safe mechanism to avoid missing the diagnosis of these disorders. Some practitioners refer to consultations that make their 'head spin' in confusion and bewilderment, with patients presenting with a 'shopping list' of undifferentiated problems. It is with these patients that a checklist is useful.

Table 3 *Classic pitfalls*

Allergies
Abscess (hidden)
Candida infection
Chronic fatigue syndrome
Domestic abuse inc. child abuse
Drugs
Herpes zoster
Faecal impaction
Foreign bodies
Giardiasis
Lead poisoning
Menopause syndrome
Migraine (atypical variants)
Paget's disease
Pregnancy (early)
Seizure disorders
Urinary infection

Table 4 *The seven primary masquerades*

1. Depression
2. Diabetes mellitus
3. Drugs
   - iatrogenic
   - self-abuse
     alcohol
     narcotics
     nicotine
     others
4. Anaemia
5. Thyroid and other endocrine disorders
   - hyperthyroidism
   - hypothyroidism
6. Spinal dysfunction
7. Urinary infection

A century ago it was important to consider diseases such as syphilis and tuberculosis as the great common masquerades, but these infections have been replaced by iatrogenesis, malignant disease, alcoholism, endocrine disorders and the various manifestations of atherosclerosis, particularly coronary insufficiency and cerebrovascular insufficiency.

If the patient has pain anywhere it is possible that it could originate from the spine, so the possibility of spinal pain (radicular or referred) should be considered as the cause for various pain syndromes such as headache, arm pain, leg pain, chest pain, pelvic pain and even abdominal pain. The author's experience is that spondylogenic pain is one of the most underdiagnosed problems in general practice.

Table 5 *The seven other masquerades*

1. Chronic renal failure

2. Malignant disease
   - lymphomas
   - lung
   - caecum/colon
   - kidney
   - multiple myeloma
   - ovary
   - metastasis

3. HIV infection/AIDS

4. Baffling bacterial infections
   - syphilis
   - tuberculosis
   - infective endocarditis
   - the zoonoses
   - chlamydia infections
   - others

5. Baffling viral (and protozoal) infections
   - Epstein-Barr mononucleosis
   - TORCH organisms, e.g. cytomegalovirus
   - hepatitis, A,B,C,D,E
   - mosquito-borne infections
     malaria
     Ross River fever
   - others

6. Neurological dilemmas
   - Parkinson's disease
   - Guillain-Barré syndrome
   - seizure disorders esp. complex partial
   - multiple sclerosis
   - myasthenia gravis
   - space-occupying lesion of skull
   - migraine
   - others

7. Connective tissue disorders and the vasculitides
   - Connective tissue disorders
     SLE
     systemic sclerosis
     dermatomyositis
     overlap syndrome

(continues)

Table 5 *(continued)*

- Vasculitides
  polyarteritis nodosa
  giant cell arteritis/polymyalgia rheumatica
  granulomatous disorders

A checklist that has been divided into two groups of seven disorders is presented (Tables 4 and 5). The first list, 'the seven primary masquerades', represents the more common disorders encountered in general practice; the second list includes less common masquerades although some, such as Epstein-Barr mononucleosis, can be very common masquerades in general practice.

5. Is the patient trying to tell me something?

The doctor has to consider, especially in the case of undifferentiated illness, whether the patient has a 'hidden agenda' for the presentation. Of course, the patient may be depressed (overt or masked) or may have a true anxiety state. However, a presenting symptom such as tiredness may represent a 'ticket of entry' to the consulting room. It may represent a plea for help in a stressed or anxious patient. The author has another checklist (Table 6) to help identify the psychosocial reasons for a patient's malaise.

Table 6 *Underlying fears or image problems that cause stress and anxiety*

---

1. Interpersonal conflict in the family
2. Identification with sick or deceased friends
3. Fear of malignancy
4. STDs especially AIDS
5. Impending 'coronary' or 'stroke'
6. Sexual problem
7. Drug-related problem
8. Crippling arthritis
9. Financial woes
10. Other abnormal stressors

Abdominal pain

Key facts and checkpoints

- The commonest causes of the acute abdomen in two general practice series were: *Series 1* acute appendicitis (31%) and the colics (29%); *Series 2* acute appendicitis (21%), the colics (16%), mesenteric adenitis (16%). The latter study included children.

Diagnostic guidelines

General rules

- Upper abdominal pain is caused by lesions of the upper GIT.
- Lower abdominal pain is caused by lesions of the lower GIT or pelvic organs.
- Early severe vomiting indicates a high obstruction of the GIT.
- Acute appendicitis features a characteristic 'march' of symptoms: pain → anorexia → nausea → vomiting.

Pain patterns

The pain patterns are presented in the figure below. Colicky pain is a rhythmic pain with regular spasms of recurring pain building to a climax and fading. It is virtually pathognomonic of intestinal obstruction. Ureteric colic is a true colicky abdominal pain, but so-called biliary colic and renal colic are not true colics at all.

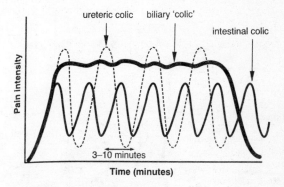

Characteristic pain patterns for various causes of 'colicky' acute abdominal pain

Abdominal pain in children

Abdominal pain is a common complaint in children, especially recurrent abdominal pain.

Infantile colic

Typical features

- baby between 2 and 16 weeks old esp. 10 weeks
- prolonged crying—at least 3 hours
- crying during late afternoon and early evening
- child flexing legs and clenching fists because of the 'stomach ache'

Management

Reassurance and explanation to the parents.

Medication

Avoid medications if possible but consider:

    simethicone preparations, e.g. Infacol wind drops

        or

    dicyclomine, e.g. Infacol-C syrup

Intussusception

Typical clinical features

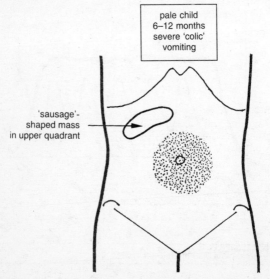

Typical features with pain distribution of acute intussusception

Diagnosis
• barium enema

Treatment
• hydrostatic reduction by barium enema under radiological control or hydrostatic reduction with oxygen
• surgical intervention may be necessary

Drugs

In any child complaining of acute abdominal pain, enquiry should be made into drug ingestion. A common cause of colicky abdominal pain in children is cigarette smoking (nicotine); consider other drugs such as marijuana, cocaine and heroin.

Mesenteric adenitis

This presents a difficult problem in differential diagnosis with acute appendicitis because the history can be very similar. At times the distinction may be almost impossible. In general, with mesenteric adenitis localisation of pain and tenderness is not as definite, rigidity is less of a feature, the temperature is higher and anorexia, nausea and vomiting are also lesser features. The illness lasts about five days followed by a rapid recovery.

Recurrent abdominal pain

Recurrent abdominal pain (RAP) occurs in 10% of school-aged children. (RAP = 3 distinct episodes of pain over 3 or more months.) In only 5–10% of children will an organic cause be found so that in most the cause remains obscure.

Investigations
• stool microscopy and culture
• urine analysis
• full blood count and ESR

Specific causes of acute abdominal pain

Abdominal aortic aneurysm (AAA)

The risk of rupture is related to the diameter of the AAA and the rate of increase in diameter.

Investigations

• ultrasound (good for screening in relatives >50)
• CT scan (clearer imaging)
• MRI scan (best definition)

Refer all cases.

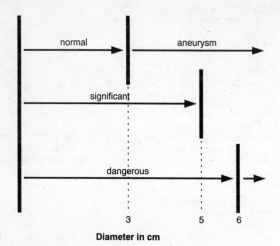

Diameter in cm

*Guidelines for normal and abnormal widths of
the abdominal aorta in adults (to exact scale)*

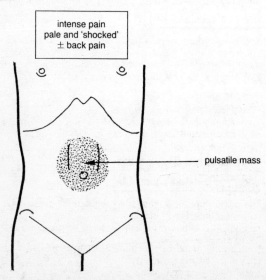

*Typical pain distribution of a ruptured aortic
abdominal aneurysm*

Mesenteric artery occlusion

Acute intestinal ischaemia arises from superior mesenteric artery occlusion.

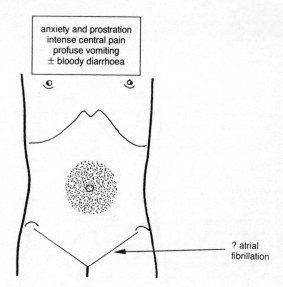

anxiety and prostration
intense central pain
profuse vomiting
± bloody diarrhoea

? atrial
fibrillation

Typical pain distribution of mesenteric arterial occlusion

Management

Early surgery may prevent gut necrosis but massive resection of necrosed gut may be required as a life-saving procedure. Early diagnosis (within a few hours) is essential.

Acute retention of urine

Management

- Perform a rectal examination and empty rectum of any impacted faecal material.
- Catheterise with size 14 Foley catheter to relieve obstruction and drain.
- Have the catheter *in situ* and seek a urological opinion.
- If there is any chance of recovery, e.g. if the problem is drug-induced: withdraw drug, leave catheter in for 48 hours, remove and give trial of prazosin 0.5 mg bd.

Acute appendicitis

Acute appendicitis is mainly a condition of young adults (esp.
20–30 years) but affects all ages (although uncommon under
3 years). It is the commonest surgical emergency.

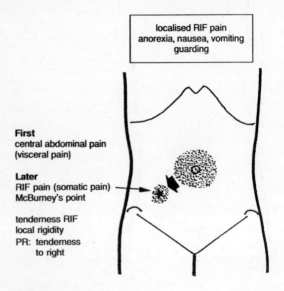

localised RIF pain
anorexia, nausea, vomiting
guarding

First
central abdominal pain
(visceral pain)

Later
RIF pain (somatic pain)
McBurney's point

tenderness RIF
local rigidity
PR: tenderness
to right

*Typical pain distribution for acute
appendicitis*

Management

Immediate referral for surgical removal.

Small bowel obstruction

The symptoms depend on the level of the obstruction. The
more proximal the obstruction the more severe the pain.

Management

- IV fluids and bowel decompression with nasogastric tube
- laparotomy (not for Crohn's disease)

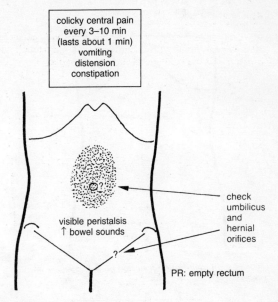

colicky central pain
every 3–10 min
(lasts about 1 min)
vomiting
distension
constipation

check
umbilicus
and
hernial
orifices

visible peristalsis
↑ bowel sounds

PR: empty rectum

*Typical pain distribution for small bowel
obstruction*

Large bowel obstruction

Management
Surgical referral.

Perforated peptic ulcer

The clinical syndrome has three stages:
1. prostration
2. reaction (after 2–6 hours)—symptoms improve
3. peritonitis (after 6–12 hours)

X-ray: chest X-ray may show free air under diaphragm (in
75%)—need to sit upright for prior 15 minutes.

Management
• drip and suction (immediate nasogastric tube)
• immediate laparotomy after resuscitation

colicky pain (sudden)
distension ± vomiting
constipation

↑ bowel sounds

rigidity

PR: empty rectum
? carcinoma
? impaction

Typical pain distribution for large bowel obstruction

sudden severe pain
anxious, still, 'grey', sweaty
deceptive improvement
nausea & vomiting (delayed)

pain radiation

board-like rigidity
guarding
silent abdomen

PR: pelvic tenderness

Typical features of perforated peptic ulcer

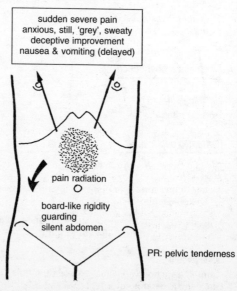

- conservative treatment may be possible, e.g. later presentation and gastrografin swallow indicates sealing of perforation

Ureteric colic

Renal colic is not a true colic but a constant pain due to blood clots or a stone lodged at the pelvic-ureteric junction; ureteric colic, however, presents as severe true colicky pain.

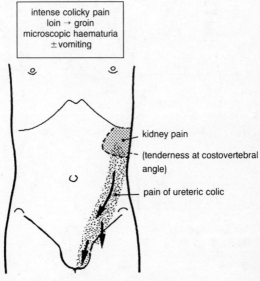

intense colicky pain
loin → groin
microscopic haematuria
± vomiting

kidney pain
(tenderness at costovertebral angle)
pain of ureteric colic

Ureteric colic: typical radiation of pain in left ureteric colic

Diagnosis

- plain X-ray: most stones (75%) are radio-opaque (calcium oxalate and phosphate)
- intravenous pyelogram: confirms opacity and indicates kidney function
- ultrasound: to locate calculus and exclude obstruction

Management

- pethidine 100 mg (IM) or 50 mg (IV)
(average size adult)
       and
metoclopramide 10 mg IM or IV

- liberal fluids and exercise
- indomethacin suppositories for further pain (limited to 2 a day)

Biliary pain

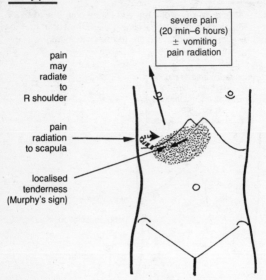

pain may radiate to R shoulder

pain radiation to scapula

localised tenderness (Murphy's sign)

severe pain (20 min–6 hours) ± vomiting pain radiation

Typical site of pain of biliary 'colic' and acute cholecystitis

Diagnosis

- abdominal ultrasound/HIDA

Management

- gallstone dissolution or lithotripsy
- cholecystectomy (main procedure)

Treatment of acute cholecystitis

- rest in bed
- IV fluids
- nil orally
- analgesics
- antibiotics: amoxycillin IV or IM
              and
          gentamycin IV
              or
          cephalosporins IM or IV
- cholecystectomy

Acute pancreatitis

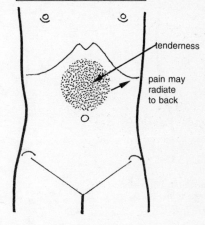

severe pain (hours to days)
nausea & vomiting
relative lack abdominal signs
weak, pale, sweaty

tenderness

pain may
radiate
to back

Typical pain distribution of acute pancreatitis

Diagnosis
- WCC—leucocytosis
- serum amylase (usually 5-fold increase)
- plain X-ray, may be senital loop
- CT scan

Management
- Arrange admission to hospital.
- Basic treatment is bed rest, nil orally, nasogastric suction (if vomiting), IV fluids, analgesics (pethidine, not morphine) and anti-emetics IM or IV.

Acute diverticulitis

This occurs in less than 10% of patients with diverticular disease.

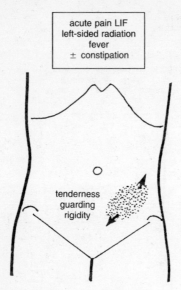

acute pain LIF
left-sided radiation
fever
± constipation

tenderness
guarding
rigidity

Typical pain distribution of acute diverticulitis

Investigations

- leucocytosis
- pus and blood in stools
- abdominal ultrasound/CT scan

Treatment

- nil orally
- analgesics
- antibiotics: amoxycillin IV + gentamicin IV
                           + metronidazole IV
- surgery for complications

Lower abdominal pain in women

A UK study of chronic lower abdominal pain in women showed the causes were adhesions (36%), no diagnosis (19%), endometriosis (14%), constipation (13%), ovarian cysts (11%) and PID (7%).

Ectopic pregnancy

Diagnosis

- pregnancy tests may be positive
- vaginal ultrasound can diagnose at 5–6 weeks (empty uterus, tubal sac)
- laparoscopy (the definitive diagnostic procedure)

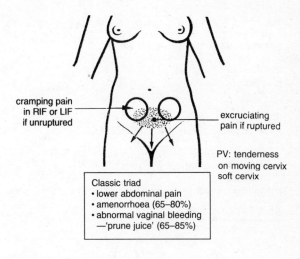

cramping pain in RIF or LIF if unruptured

excruciating pain if ruptured

PV: tenderness on moving cervix soft cervix

Classic triad
- lower abdominal pain
- amenorrhoea (65–80%)
- abnormal vaginal bleeding —'prune juice' (65–85%)

Clinical features of ectopic pregnancy

Management

Treatment may be conservative (based on ultrasound and β-HCG assays); medical, by injecting methotrexate into the ectopic sac; laparoscopic removal; or laparotomy for severe cases. Rupture with blood loss demands urgent surgery.

Ruptured ovarian (Graafian) follicle (mittelschmerz)

Typical clinical features

- onset of pain in mid cycle
- deep pain in one or other iliac fossa (RIF>LIF) (average 5 hours)
- often described as a 'horse kick pain'
- pain tends to move centrally
- heavy feeling in pelvis

Management

- explanation and reassurance
- simple analgesics: aspirin or paracetamol (acetaminophen)
- 'hot water bottle' comfort if pain severe

Ruptured ovarian cyst

The cysts tend to rupture just prior to ovulation or following coitus.

- sudden onset of pain in one or other iliac fossa
- may be nausea and vomiting
- pain usually settles within a few hours

Signs

- tenderness and guarding in iliac fossa
- PR: tenderness in rectovaginal pouch

Management

- appropriate explanation and reassurance
- conservative
  —simple cyst < 4 cm
  —internal haemorrhage
  —minimal pain
- may need needle vaginal drainage or laparoscopic surgery

Acute torsion of ovarian cyst

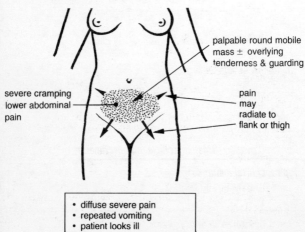

palpable round mobile mass ± overlying tenderness & guarding

severe cramping lower abdominal pain

pain may radiate to flank or thigh

- diffuse severe pain
- repeated vomiting
- patient looks ill
- exquisite pelvic tenderness

Typical clinical features of acute torsion of an ovarian cyst

Diagnosis
- ultrasound

Treatment
- laparotomy and surgical correction

Pelvic adhesions

Pelvic adhesions may be the cause of pelvic pain, infertility, dysmenorrhoea and intestinal pain. They can be diagnosed and removed laparoscopically when the adhesions are well visualised and there are no intestinal loops firmly stuck together.

Acne

Some topical treatment regimens

Mild to moderate acne

1. Use isotretinoin 0.05% gel or tretinoin 0.05% cream, apply each night (especially if comedones).
2. After 2 weeks, add benzoyl peroxide 2.5% or 5% gel or topical clindamycin once daily (in the morning). That is, after 2 weeks, maintenance treatment is:
   - isotretinoin 0.05% gel at night
   - benzoyl peroxide 2.5% or 5%
     or
     clindamycin topical   } mane
     or
     erythromycin 2% topical gel
3. Maintain for three months and review.

Clindamycin regimen
Use clindamycin HCl in alcohol. Apply to each comedone with fingertips twice daily.

- A ready clindamycin preparation is Clindatech.
- Clindamycin is particularly useful for pregnant women and those who cannot tolerate antibiotics or exfoliants.

Oral antibiotics
Use if acne resistant to topical agents.
  Tetracycline 1 g per day or doxycycline 100 mg per day or minocycline 50 to 100 mg bd for four weeks (or up to 10 weeks if slow response) then reduce according to response e.g. doxycycline 50 mg for 6 weeks.

Other therapies
Severe cystic acne (specialist care)
- isotretinoin (Roaccutane)

Females not responding to first-line treatment

• combined oral contraceptive pill, e.g. ethinyloestradiol/
cyproterone acetate (Diane-35 ED)

A new agent for mild to moderate acne

• azelaic acid, apply bd

Facial scars

Injections of collagen can be used for the depressed facial
scars from cystic acne.

Acute allergic reactions

Multi-system
    —acute anaphylaxis
    —anaphylactic reactions
Localised
    —angio-oedema
    —urticaria

Treatment of anaphylaxis and anaphylactic reactions: adults

First line

• oxygen 6–8 L/min (by face mask)
• adrenaline 0.3–0.5 mg (1:1000) SC or IM (more severe)
best given in upper body e.g. deltoid
(mg = mL of 1:1000 adrenaline)

    If no rapid improvement
    adrenaline 1 in 10 000: (dilute 1 mL 1:1000 in 9 mL
    saline)
    5–10 mL IV over 2–5 minutes

    Repeat adrenaline every 10 minutes as necessary (IM or IV)
• insert IV line and infuse
colloid solution e.g. Haemaccel (500 mL → I L)
        or
crystalloid solution e.g. N saline (1.5 L → 3 L)
1 part colloid = 3 parts crystalloid (by volume)
• salbutamol aerosol inhalation (or nebulisation if severe)
• promethazine 10 mg IV slowly (or 25 mg IM)
        or
diphenhydramine 10 mg IV (or 25 mg IM)
• admit to hospital (observe at least 4 hours)

If not responding

Continue adrenaline every 10 minutes:

• hydrocortisone 500 mg IV
• establish airway (oral airway or endotracheal intubation) if
required

Treatment for children

- oxygen by mask
- adrenaline 1:1000 (0.01 mL/kg) IM or SC
  or
  adrenaline 1:10 000 slow IV infusion in dose 0.1 mL/kg of
      1:10 000 or less if the desired effect is achieved before
      full dose given
- hydrocortisone: 8–10 mg/kg IV

If necessary

- hypotension: colloid solutions IV e.g. Haemaccel
      stable plasma protein solution (SPPS) or Dextran 70
- bronchospasm: nebulised salbutamol
- upper airways obstruction: mild to moderate—inhaled adren-
      aline (0.5 mL/kg) 1:1000 (max 4 mL) dilute to 4 mL with
      saline or water if necessary
          severe—intubation may be necessary

Angio-oedema and acute urticaria

Acute urticaria and angio-oedema are essentially anaphylaxis
limited to the skin, subcutaneous tissues and other specific
organs. They can occur together.

Treatment

Uncomplicated cutaneous swelling—antihistamines
    e.g. diphenhydramine 50 mg (o) tds or 25 mg IM if more
severe
Upper respiratory involvement—adrenaline 0.3 mg SC
                              —antihistamine IM

Adolescent health

Adolescence is the name given to the psychosocial life stage
which starts around the time of puberty.

Hallmarks of the adolescent

The main hallmarks of the adolescent are:

- self-consciousness
- self-awareness
- self-centredness
- lack of confidence

Needs of the adolescent

Adolescents have basic needs that will allow them the optimal
environmental conditions for their development:

- 'room' to move
- privacy and confidentiality

- security (e.g. stable home)
- acceptance by peers
- someone to 'lean on' (e.g. youth leader)
- special 'heroes'
- establishment of an adult sexual role
- one good trustworthy friend

The clinical approach

Consider the mnemonic HEADS in the history:

H—home
E—education, employment, economic situation
A—activities, affect, ambition, anxieties
D—drugs, depression
S—sex, stress, suicide, self-esteem

During this process it is necessary to be aware of the fundamental development tasks of adolescence, namely:

- establishing identity and self-image
- emancipation from the family and self-reliance
- establishing an appropriate adult sexual role
- developing a personal moral code
- making career and vocational choices
- ego identity and self-esteem

It is necessary to conduct a physical examination and order very basic investigations if only to exclude organic disease and provide the proper basis for effective counselling.

Areas of counselling and anticipation guidance that are most relevant are:

- emotional problems/depression
- significant loss, e.g. breakdown of 'first love'
- sexuality
- contraception
- guilt about masturbation or other concerns

Depression, parasuicide and suicide

When dealing with adolescents it is important always to be on the lookout for depression and the possibility of suicide, which is the second most common cause of death in this group. Males successfully complete suicide four times more often than females while females attempt suicide 8 to 20 times more often than males.

It is important not to be afraid to enquire about thoughts of suicide as it gives teenagers a chance to unburden themselves; it is not provoking them to contemplate suicide.

Alcohol problems

Excessive and harmful drinking

People are said to be dependent on alcohol when it is affecting their physical health and social life yet they do not seem to be prepared to stop drinking to solve their problems.

For men, excessive drinking is more than four standard drinks of alcohol a day. For women, drinking becomes a serious problem at lesser amounts—two standard drinks a day. This level can also affect the foetus of the pregnant woman. High-risk or harmful drinking occurs at more than six drinks a day for men and four drinks a day for women.

Laboratory investigations

The following blood tests may be helpful in the identification of excessive chronic alcohol intake.

- blood alcohol
- serum gamma glutamyl transpeptidase (GGT): elevated in chronic drinkers (returns to normal with cessation of intake)
- mean corpuscular volume (MCV): >96 fl

Measuring alcohol intake

One standard drink contains 10 g of alcohol, which is in one middy (or pot) of standard beer (285 mL), two middies of low-alcohol beer or five middies of super-light beer. These are equal in alcohol content to one small glass of table wine (120 mL), one glass of sherry or port (60 mL) or one nip of spirits (30 mL).

1 stubby or can of beer   = 1.3 standard drinks
1 × 750 mL bottle of beer = 2.6 standard drinks
1 × 750 mL bottle of wine = 6 standard drinks

| 1 middy of standard beer (285 mL or 10 oz) | 1 glass of wine (120 mL or 4 oz) | 1 glass of sherry or port (60 mL or 2 oz) | 1 nip of spirits (30 mL or 1 oz) |

Standard drinks

Approach to management

The challenge to the family doctor is early recognition of the problem. Several studies have shown that early intervention and brief counselling by the doctor are effective in leading to rehabilitation. Some of the results are very revealing:

- Patients expect their family doctor to advise on safe drinking levels.
- They will listen and act on our advice.
- Treatment is more effective if offered before dependence or chronic disease has developed.

A brief practical management plan

A six-step management plan, which has been employed in a general-practice early intervention program, is as follows:
1. *Feed back* the results of your assessment and specifically the degree of risk associated with their daily alcohol intake and bout drinking. Emphasise any damage that has already occurred.
2. *Listen* carefully to their reaction. They will need to ventilate their feelings and may respond defensively.
3. *Outline the benefits* of reducing drinking:
   e.g. save money, better health.
4. *Set goals* for alcohol consumption which you both agree are feasible.
   For men: *no more than* 3–4 standard drinks 3–4 times per week (aim for less than 12 per week).
   For women: *no more than* 2–3 drinks 2–3 times per week (aim for less than 8 per week).
   For patients with severe ill effects and who are physically dependent on alcohol, long-term abstinence is advisable.
5. *Set strategies* to keep below the upper safe limits e.g.:
   - Quench thirst with non-alcoholic drinks before having an alcoholic one.
   - Switch to low-alcohol beer.
   - Take care which parties you go to.
   - Explore new interests—fishing, cinema, social club, sporting activity.
6. *Evaluate* progress by having patients monitor their drinking by using a diary. Make a definite appointment for follow-up and give appropriate literature such as *Alcohol and health*. Obtain consent for a telephone follow-up. A useful minimum intervention plan is presented in Table 7.

The use of disulfiram

In compliant patients, disulfiram 250–500 mg daily can be used—such treatment has hazards and the patient requires intensive supportive therapy.

Table 7 *Minimum intervention technique plan (5–10 minutes)*

1. Advise reduction to safe levels
2. Outline the benefits
3. Provide a self-help pamphlet
4. Organise a diary or other feedback system
5. Obtain consent for a telephone follow-up
6. Offer additional help, e.g. referral to an alcohol and drug unit or to a support group

Follow-up (long consultation one week later)

Review the patient's drinking diary. Explore any problems, summarise, listen and provide support and encouragement. If appointment is not kept, contact the patient.

Recommended treatment for early withdrawal symptoms

- diazepam 5–20 mg (o) every 2–6 hours (up to 120 mg (o) daily) titrated against clinical response (taper off after seven days)
- thiamine 100 mg IM or IV daily for 3–5 days, then 100 mg (o) daily
- vitamin B group supplement (o) or IM daily

Alopecia areata (patchy hair loss)

Potent topical corticosteroids (class III or IV).
Intradermal injections of triamcinolone
(Kenacort A10)
or
Minoxidil 2% (Regaine)
1 mL bd applied to dry scalp (for 4 or more months)

Anaemia

Anaemia is a label, not a specific diagnosis. Anaemia is defined as a haemoglobin (Hb) below the normal reference level for the age and sex of that individual.
Definition:
Hb < 13 g/dL (males)
Hb < 11.5 g/dL (females)

Classification of anaemia

The various types of anaemia are classified in terms of the red cell size—the mean corpuscular volume (MCV). (See Table 8.)

Microcytic anaemia—MCV ≤ 80 fL

The main causes of microcytic anaemia are iron deficiency and haemoglobulinopathy, particularly thalassaemia.

Iron deficiency anaemia

Iron deficiency is the most common cause of anaemia worldwide.

The most common causes are chronic blood loss and poor diet.

Table 8 *Causes/classification of anaemia*

Microcytic (MCV) < 80 fL
    Iron deficiency
    Haemoglobinopathy e.g. thalassaemia
    Sideroblastic anaemia (hereditary)
    Anaemia of chronic disease (sometimes microcytic)

Macrocytic (MCV > 98 fL)
a) With megaloblastic changes
        Vitamin B_{12} deficiency
        Folate deficiency
        Cytotoxic drugs
b) Without megaloblastic changes
        Liver disease/alcoholism
        Myelodysplastic disorders

Normocytic (MCV 80–98 fL)
    Acute blood loss/occult bleeding
    Anaemia of chronic disease
    Haemolysis
    Chronic renal disease
    Endocrine disorders

Haemological investigations: typical findings

- microcytic, hypochromic red cells
- anisocytosis (variation in size), poikilocytosis (shape)
- low serum iron
- raised iron-binding capacity
- serum ferritin low (NR: 20–200 µg/L) (the most useful index)

Treatment

- Correct the identified cause.
- Iron preparations
  —oral iron (preferred method)
  —parenteral iron is best reserved for special circumstances. It can cause a 'tattoo' effect.

Response
   —anaemia responds after about 2 weeks and is usually corrected after 2 months

—oral iron is continued for 3 to 6 months to replenish stores
—monitor progress with regular serum ferritin
—a serum ferritin > 50 µg/L generally indicates adequate stores

Thalassaemia

The heterozygous form is usually asymptomatic; patients show little if any anaemia. The homozygous form is a very severe congenital anaemia needing lifelong transfusional support.

The key to the diagnosis of the heterozygous 'thalassaemia minor' is significant microcytosis quite out of proportion to the normal Hb or slight anaemia, and confirmed by finding a raised Hb A2 on Hb electrophoresis. It must be distinguished from iron deficiency anaemia, for iron does not help thalassaemics and is theoretically contraindicated.

Macrocytic anaemia—MCV > 98 fL

Vitamin B_{12} deficiency (pernicious anaemia)

The clinical features are anaemia (macrocytic), weight loss and neurological symptoms especially a polyneuropathy. The serum Vitamin B_{12} is below the normal level.

Replacement therapy
• Vitamin B_{12} (1000 µg) IM injection
  body stores (3 to 5 mg) are replenished after 10–15 injections given every 2 to 3 days
• maintenance with 1000 µg injections every second month

Folic acid deficiency

The main cause is poor intake associated with old age, poverty and malnutrition, usually associated with alcoholism. It may be seen in malabsorption and regular medication with antiepileptic drugs such as phenytoin. It is rarely, but very importantly, associated with pregnancy.

Replacement therapy
Oral folate 1.5 mg/day, to replenish body stores (5–10 mg) in about four weeks.

Angina pectoris

Management of angina

• Attend to any risk factors.
• If inactive, take on an activity such as walking for 20 minutes a day.
• Regular exercise to the threshold of angina.
• Relaxation program.
• Avoid precipitating factors.
• Don't excessively restrict lifestyle.

Medical treatment

The acute attack

- glyceryl trinitrate (nitroglycerine) 600 µg tab or 300 µg (½ tab) sublingually (SL)

Alternatives

- isosorbide dinitrate 5 mg SL every 5 min (to maximum of 3)

                    or

- glyceryl trinitrate SL spray: 1–2 sprays to maximum of 3 in 15 minutes

                    or

- nifedipine 5 mg capsule (suck or chew) if intolerant of nitrates

Advise that if no relief after 3 tablets get medical advice.

Mild stable angina

Angina that is predictable, precipitated by more stressful activities and relieved rapidly.

- aspirin 150 mg (o) daily
- glyceryl trinitrate (SL or spray) prn
- consider a beta-blocker or long acting nitrate

Moderate stable angina

Regular predictable attacks precipitated by moderate exertion.

- as above

                +

- beta-blocker, e.g. atenolol 50–100 mg (o) once daily

                         or

                    metoprolol 50–100 mg (o) daily

- glyceryl trinitrate (ointment and patches) daily (12–16 hours only)

        or

    isosorbide mononitrate 60 mg (o) SR tablets mane (12 hour span)

Unstable angina

Add a dihydropyridine Ca channel blocker

- nifedipine 10–20 mg (o) bd

        or

- nifedipine controlled release 30–60 mg (o) daily

        or

- amlodipine 2.5–10 mg (o) once daily

If beta-blocker contraindicated use

- diltiazem SR 90 mg (o) bd (max 240 mg daily)

Refractory angina

Consider hospitalisation for stabilisation and further evaluation. The objectives are to optimise therapy, give IV trinitrate and heparin and consider coronary angiography with a view to a corrective procedure.

• perhexiline maleate—if unsuitable for angiography

Anorectal disorders

Anorectal pain

The patient may complain that defecation is painful or almost impossible because of anorectal pain.

Anal fissure

Anal fissures cause pain on defecation and usually develop after a period of constipation (may be brief period) and tenesmus.

Treatment

Milder cases

In a milder case of anal fissure the discomfort is slight, anal spasm is a minor feature and the onset is acute.

Conservative management
• Xyloproct suppositories or ointment.
• High-residue diet (consider the addition of bran or wheat preparations).
• Avoidance of constipation with hard stools (aim for soft bulky stools).

More severe chronic fissures

The feature here is a hyperactive anal sphincter, and a practical procedure is necessary to solve this painful problem.

Method 1: Digital anal dilatation
Under general anaesthesia, undertake four-finger (maximum) anal dilatation for 4 minutes. A most appropriate treatment for children with anal fissures.

Method 2: Lateral sphincterotomy
The spasm of the internal sphincter that occurs because of an anal fissure is relieved by the procedure of lateral sphincterotomy, allowing the fissue to heal in about two weeks. The procedure gives dramatic relief.

Proctalgia fugax

Main features:

- fleeting rectal pain
- varies from mild discomfort to severe spasm
- lasts 3–30 minutes
- often wakes patient at night
- a functional bowel disorder
- affects adults, usually professional males

Management

- explanation and reassurance
- salbutamol inhaler (2 puffs orally statim) worth a trial

Perianal haematoma

Within 24 hours of onset:

- simple aspiration of blood
                or
- surgical drainage under LA

Within 24 hours to 5 days of onset:

- express thrombus through small incision under LA (deroof skin)

Day 6 onwards:

- leave alone unless very painful or infected

Strangulated haemorrhoids

A marked oedematous circumferential swelling will appear if all the haemorrhoids are involved. If only one haemorrhoid is strangulated proctoscopy will help to distinguish it from a perianal haematoma. Initial treatment is with rest and ice packs prior to haemorrhoidectomy at the earliest possible time. Relatively urgent referral is recommended.

Perianal abscess

Careful examination is essential to make the diagnosis. Look for evidence of a fistula.

Treatment

Drainage via a cruciate incision over the point of maximal induration.

Anorectal lumps

Skin tags

The skin tag is usually the legacy of an untreated perianal haematoma. It may require excision for aesthetic reasons, for hygiene or because it is a source of pruritus ani or irritation.

Perianal warts

It is important to distinguish the common viral warts from the condylomata lata of secondary syphilis. Local therapy includes the application of podophyllin every two or three days by the practitioner.

Internal haemorrhoids

Haemorrhoids or piles are common and tend to develop between the ages of 20 and 50 (Fig. 18). The commonest cause is chronic constipation related to a lack of dietary fibre.

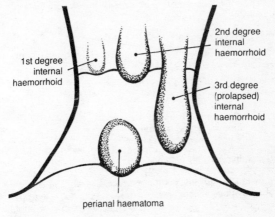

Classification of haemorrhoids

Treatment

The treatment of haemorrhoids is based on four procedures: namely, injection, rubber band ligation, cryotherapy and sphincterotomy. Surgery is generally reserved for large strangulated piles. The best treatment, however, is prevention, and softish bulky faeces that pass easily prevent haemorrhoids.

Anorexia (simple) in children and infants

Acid or alkaline gentian mixture (preferably alkaline)
   5–10 mL 30 to 60 minutes before meals, tds
Acid or alkaline gentian mixture (for infants)
   4 mL 30 to 60 minutes before feeds
      or
Incremin mixture
   < 2 years: 2.5 mL daily
   > 2 years: 5 mL daily

Anxiety

Anxiety is an uncomfortable inner feeling of fear or imminent disaster. The criterion for anxiety disorder as defined at the International Classification of Health Problems in Primary Care (ICHPPC-2-Defined) (WONCA, 1985) is:

generalised and persistent anxiety or anxious mood, which cannot be associated with, or is disproportionately large in response to a specific psychosocial stressor, stimulus or event.

Classification of anxiety

The following list represents approximately the categories of anxiety disorders recognised by the DSM-III-R:

- generalised anxiety disorder
- panic disorder
- phobic disorder
- obsessive compulsive disorder
- post-traumatic stress disorder

Generalised anxiety disorder

Generalised anxiety comprises excessive anxiety and worry about various life circumstances and is not related to a specific activity, time or event such as trauma, obsessions or phobias.

Important checkpoints
Five self-posed questions should be considered by the family doctor before treating an anxious patient:
- Is this hyperthyroidism?
- Is this depression?
- Is this normal anxiety?
- Is this mild anxiety or simple phobia?
- Is this moderate or severe anxiety?

Management of generalised anxiety disorder

The management applies mainly to generalised anxiety as specific psychotherapy is required in other types of anxiety. Much of the management can be carried out successfully by the family doctor using brief counselling and support.

- use non-pharmacological methods
- give explanation and reassurance
- promote stress management techniques including meditation
- advice on coping skills
- avoid the use of drugs if possible

Pharmacological treatment

Acute episodes

The following drugs are recommended for patients who have intermittent transient exacerbations not responding to other measures.

> diazepam 2–5 mg (o) as a single dose
> > repeated bd as required
> > > or
> diazepam 5–10 mg (o) nocte
> > > or
> oxazepam 15–30 mg (o) as a single dose
> > repeated bd as required

Special notes:

- Recommended (if necessary) for up to two weeks, then taper off to zero over next four weeks.
- Reassess in seven days.
- Consider beta-blockers in patients with sympathetic activation such as palpitations, tremor and excessive sweating, e.g. propranolol 10–40 mg (o) tds. They do not relieve the mental symptoms of anxiety, however.

Long-term treatment

If non-pharmacological treatment is ineffective for persisting disabling anxiety and benzodiazepines are undesirable, the drug of choice is:

> buspirone 5 mg (o) tds

- increase if necessary to 20 mg (o) tds
- continue for several weeks after symptoms subside
- mean effective dose is 20–25 mg daily
- response usually takes 7–10 days (may be 2–4 weeks)

Panic disorder

Patients with panic disorder experience sudden, unexpected, short-lived episodes of intense anxiety. These tend to be recurrent and occur most often in young females. Follow DSM-III-R guidelines for diagnosis.

Management

Reassurance, explanation and support (as for generalised anxiety).

Cognitive behaviour therapy

This aims to reduce anxiety by teaching patients how to identify, evaluate, control and modify their negative, fearful thoughts and behaviour. If simple psychotherapy and stress management fails then patients should be referred for this therapy.

If hyperventilating, breathe in and out of a paper bag.

Pharmacological treatment

Acute episodes:
diazepam 5 mg (o)
or
oxazepam 15–30 mg (o)
or
alprazolam 0.25–0.5 mg (o)

Prophylaxis

benzodiazepines
alprazolam 0.25–6 mg (o) daily in divided doses
or
clonazepam 0.5–6 mg (o) daily in divided doses

Note: Medication should be withdrawn slowly.
Medication for panic disorder may need to be continued for 6–12 months.

Phobic disorders

In phobic states the anxiety is related to specific situations or objects. Patients avoid these situations and become anxious when they anticipate having to meet them.

The three main types of phobic states are:

• simple phobias
• agoraphobia
• social phobias

The ten most common phobias (in order) are spiders, people and social situations, flying, open spaces, confined spaces, heights, cancer, thunderstorms, death and heart disease.

Management

The basis of treatment for all phobic disorders is psychotherapy that involves behaviour therapy and cognitive therapy.

Pharmacological treatment

This should be used only if non-pharmacological measures fail.

Agoraphobia with panic: use medications as for panic attacks. Consider antidepressants.

Social phobia with performance anxiety: propranolol 10–40 mg (o) 30–60 minutes before the social event or performance.

Obsessive compulsive disorder

Management

Optimal management is a combination of psychotherapeutic and pharmacological treatment, namely:

- cognitive behaviour therapy for obsessions
- exposure and response prevention for compulsions
- clomipramine 50–75 mg (o) nocte increasing gradually to 150–250 mg (o) nocte

An alternative agent to clomipramine (if not tolerated or ineffective) is fluoxetine.

Post-traumatic stress disorder

Treatment

This is difficult and involves counselling, the basis of which is facilitating abreaction of the experience by individual or group therapy. The aim is to allow the patient to face up openly to memories. Persistent symptoms are an indication for referral.

Pharmacological treatment

There is no specific indication for drugs but medication can have benefit in the treatment of panic attacks, generalised anxiety or depression.

Aphthous ulcers (canker sores)

Associations to consider:

blood dyscrasia, denture pressure, Crohn's disease, pernicious anaemia, iron deficiency

Minor ulcers: <1 cm in diameter—last 10–14 days.

Major ulcers: >1 cm in diameter—last weeks and heal with scarring.

Treatment methods (use early when ulcer worse)

Consider applying a wet, squeezed-out, black teabag directly to the ulcer regularly (the tannic acid promotes healing).

Symptomatic relief

Apply topical lignocaine gel or paint, e.g. SM-33 adult paint formula or SM-33 gel (children) every three hours. If applied before meals, eating is facilitated.

Healing

One of the following methods can be chosen.
Triamcinolone 0.1% (Kenalog in orobase) paste
    apply 8 hourly and nocte (preferred method)
            or
10% chloramphenicol in propylene glycol
    apply with cotton bud for one minute (after drying the ulcer) 6 hourly for 3–4 days
            or
Beclomethasone spray onto ulcer tds
            or
Dissolve 1 g sucralfate in 20 to 30 mL of warm water. Use this as a mouth wash.

Arm and hand pain

The various causes of the painful arm can be considered with the diagnostic model (Table 9).

Table 9 *Pain in the arm and hand: diagnostic strategy model*

Q.	*Probability diagnosis*
A.	Dysfunction of cervical spine (lower)
	Disorders of the shoulder
	Medial or lateral epicondylitis
	Overuse tendinitis of the wrist
	Carpal tunnel syndrome
	Osteoarthritis of thumb and DIP joints
Q.	*Serious disorders not to be missed*
A.	Cardiovascular
	• angina (referred)
	• myocardial infarction
	Neoplasia
	• Pancoast's tumour
	• bone tumours (rare)
	Severe infections
	• septic arthritis (shoulder/elbow)
	• osteomyelitis
	• infections of tendon sheath and fascial spaces of hand
Q.	*Pitfalls (often missed)*
A.	Entrapment neuropathies
	e.g. median nerve, ulnar nerve
	Pulled elbow—children
	Foreign body, e.g. elbow

(continues)

Table 9 *(continued)*

Rarities
Polymyalgia rheumatica (for arm pain)
Reflex sympathetic dystrophy
Thoracic outlet syndrome
Erythromelalgia (erythermalgia)

Q. *Seven masquerades checklist*
A. Depression   √
   Diabetes   possible
   Drugs   —
   Anaemia   —
   Thyroid disease   —
   Spinal dysfunction   √
   UTI   —

Q. *Is the patient trying to tell me something?*
A. Highly likely, especially with so-called RSI syndromes.

Pulled elbow

- usually 2–5 years
- child refuses to use arm

Treatment

- parental help
- support elbow with one hand
- flex elbow then
- suddenly twist forearm into full supination

Tennis elbow

Management

- rest from offending activity
- RICE and oral NSAIDs if acute
- exercises—strengthening
  e.g. dumbell exercise over table
          palm facing down for lateral epicondylitis
          palm facing up for medial epicondylitis
                    or
       towelette wringing exercise

Additional (if refractory)

- steroid/LA injection (max. 2)
- manipulation
     or
- surgery

Olecranon bursitis

For chronic recurrent traumatic bursitis with a synovial effusion:

- partial aspiration of fluid
- inject corticosteroid through same needle

Trigger finger/thumb

Consider an injection of 1 mL of LA corticosteroid into the tendon sheath adjacent to the swelling.

Raynaud's phenomenon and disease

Exclude and treat underlying causes.

Treatment (options)

- total body protection from cold
- gloves
- avoid smoking
- vasodilators, e.g. reserpine (o) 0.25–5 mg/day during cold weather
- topical glyceryl trinitrate ointment
- consider sympathectomy

Chilblains (see page 85)

Arthritis

Osteoarthritis

Optimal treatment

- *Explanation:* patient education and reassurance that arthritis is not the crippling disease perceived by most patients.
- *Rest:* during an active bout of inflammatory activity only.
- *Exercise:* a graduated exercise program is essential to maintain joint function. Aim for a good balance of relative rest with sensible exercise.
- *Heat:* recommended is a hot-water bottle, warm bath or electric blanket to soothe pain and stiffness. Advise against getting too cold.
- *Diet:* if overweight it is important to reduce weight to ideal level.
- *Physiotherapy:* referral should be made for specific purposes such as: exercises and supervision of a hydrotherapy program.
- *Occupational therapy:* refer for advice on aids in the home.

- *Simple analgesics* (regularly for pain): paracetamol (avoid codeine or dextroproproxyphene preparations and aspirin if recent history of dyspepsia or peptic ulceration).
- *NSAIDs and aspirin* are the first-line drugs for more persistent pain or where there is evidence of inflammation. The risk v benefit equation always has to be weighed carefully. As a rule, NSAIDs should be avoided if possible. If given—short courses 7–10 days.
- *Intrarticular corticosteroids:* as a rule IA corticosteroids are not recommended but occasionally can be very effective for an inflammatory episode of distressing pain, e.g. a flare-up in an osteoarthritic knee.
- Referral for surgical intervention for debilitating and intractable pain or disability. Examples include OA of hip, knee, shoulder, first CMC joint of thumb, and first MTP joint.

Rheumatoid arthritis

Investigations

- ESR usually raised according to active disease
- anaemia (normochromic and normocytic) may be present
- rheumatoid factor—positive in about 80–85%
- antinuclear antibodies—positive in 30%
- X-ray changes

Management principles

- Give patient education, support and appropriate reassurance. The diagnosis generally has distressful implications so the patient and family require careful explanation and support. It should be pointed out that the majority of patients have little or no long-term problems.

Specific advice

- Rest and splinting: this is necessary where practical for any acute flare-up of arthritis.
- Exercise: it is important to have regular exercise especially walking and swimming. Hydrotherapy in heated pools.
- Referral to physiotherapists and occupational therapists for expertise in exercise supervision, physical therapy and advice regarding coping in the home and work is important.
- Joint movement: each affected joint should be put daily through a full range of motion to keep it mobile and reduce stiffness.

Pharmaceutical agents

First line: simple analgesics, e.g. paracetamol
aspirin
NSAIDs

Second line: disease-modifying agents
          e.g. hydroxychloroquine
                gold compounds (IM or orally)
                D-penicillamine
                sulphasalazine
          immunosuppressive agents
          e.g. methotrexate
                azathioprine
                cyclophosphamide
Third line: corticosteroids

Connective tissue disorders

The three main connective tissue disorders have the common feature of arthritis or arthralgia. Other common features include vasculitis and multisystem involvement.

Systemic lupus erythematosus (SLE)

Arthritis is the commonest clinical feature of SLE (over 90%). It is a symmetrical polyarthritis involving mainly small and medium joints, especially the proximal interphalangeal and carpal joints of the hand.
    The initial presentation is similar to rheumatoid arthritis.

Investigations

- ESR—elevated in proportion to disease activity
- antinuclear antibodies—positive in at least 95%
- double-stranded DNA antibodies—> 95% specific for SLE but present in only 60%
- rheumatoid factor—positive in 50%
- LE test—inefficient and not used

Drug treatment

Mild—NSAIDs/aspirin
Moderate—low-dose antimalarials, e.g. hydroxychloroquine or chloroquine
Moderate to severe—corticosteroids; immunosuppressive drugs, e.g. azathioprine

Systemic sclerosis

It can present as a polyarthritis affecting the fingers of the hand in 25% of patients, especially in the early stages. Systemic sclerosis mainly affects the skin, presenting with Raynaud's phenomenon in over 85%.

Investigations

- ESR may be raised
- antinuclear antibodies—> 90% positive
- rheumatoid factor—positive in 30%
- antinucleolar and anticentromere ABs—specific

Treatment
- analgesics and NSAIDs for pain
- avoid vasospasm (no smoking)

Polymyositis and dermatomyositis

Arthralgia and arthritis occur in about 50% of patients and may be the presenting feature before the major feature of muscle weakness and wasting of the proximal muscles of the shoulder and pelvic girdles appear. The small joints of the hand are usually affected and it may resemble rheumatoid arthritis.

Polymyositis + associated rash = dermatomyositis.

Crystal arthritis

Arthritis, which can be acute, chronic or asymptomatic, is caused by a variety of crystal deposits in joints. The three main types of crystal arthritis are monosodium urate (gout) (see page 203), calcium pyrophosphate dihidrate (CPPD) and calcium phosphate (usually hydroxyapatite).

The spondyloarthropathies

The spondyloarthropathies are a group of disorders with common characteristics affecting the spondyles (vertebrae) of the spine. Apart from back pain this group tends to present with oligoarthropathy in younger patients.

The group of disorders

1. ankylosing spondylitis
2. Reiter's syndrome/reactive arthritis
3. inflammatory bowel disease (enteropathic arthritis)
4. psoriatic arthritis
5. juvenile chronic arthritis
6. unclassified spondyloarthritis—partial features only

Ankylosing spondylitis

This usually presents with inflammatory back pain (sacroiliac joints and spine) and stiffness in young adults and 20% present with peripheral joint involvement before the onset of back pain. It usually affects the girdle joints (hips and shoulders), knees or ankles.

Key clinical features
- insidious onset of discomfort
- age less than 40 years
- persistence for > 3 months
- associated morning stiffness
- improvement with exercise or NSAIDs

Reactive arthritis (Reiter's syndrome)

This is a form of reactive arthropathy in which non-septic arthritis and often sacroiliitis develop after an acute infection with specific venereal or dysenteric organisms.

> Reiter's syndrome = NSU + conjunctivitis ± iritis + arthritis
>
> Reactive arthritis = similar syndrome without ocular or mucocutaneous lesions

Enteropathic arthritis

Inflammatory bowel disease (ulcerative colitis, Crohn's disease and Whipple's disease) may be associated with peripheral arthritis and sacroiliitis.

Psoriatic arthritis

Like Reiter's syndrome, this can develop a condition indistinguishable from ankylosing spondylitis. It is therefore important to look beyond the skin condition of psoriasis, for about 5% will develop psoriatic arthropathy.

Management principles of spondyloarthropathus

- Identify the most active elements of the disease and treat accordingly.
- Provide patient and family education with appropriate reassurance.
- Refer for physiotherapy for exercises, postural exercises and hydrotherapy.
- Pharmacological agents:
  —NSAIDs, e.g. indomethacin 75—200 mg daily to control pain, stiffness and synovitis
  —sulphasalazine (if NSAIDs ineffective)
  —intra-articular corticosteroids for severe monoarthritis and intralesional corticosteroids for enthesopathy.

Lyme disease

Lyme disease (known as Lyme borreliosis) is caused by a spirochete, *Borrelia burgdorferi*, and transmitted by *Ixodes* ticks, in particular the deer tick.

Diagnostic serology should be considered for patients with a history of tick bites, typical rash (a doughnut-shaped red rash about 6 cm in diameter) at the bite site, heart disorders (especially arrhythmias), unusual joint arthralgia or central nervous system disease. CNS disease includes muscle weakness of the limbs, muscular pain or evidence of meningitis. In children Lyme disease can be mistaken for juvenile chronic arthritis.

The arthralgia

The typical picture is that months (even years) after the tick bite up to 60% of patients will develop joint and periarticular pain (without objective findings), specific arthritis, mainly of the large joints such as the knee, and/or chronic synovitis.

Treatment

Treatment is with penicillin, tetracycline or cephalosporins. If antibiotics are given early in the acute illness it tends to terminate abruptly.

The vasculitides

The vasculitides or vasculitis syndromes are a heterogeneous group of disorders involving inflammation and necrosis of blood vessels, the clinical effects and classification depending on the size of the vessels involved.

More common causes are the small vessel vasculitis effects associated with many important diseases such as rheumatoid arthritis, SLE, infective endocarditis, Henoch-Schoñlein purpura and hepatitis B. Skin lesions and arthritis are usually associated with these disorders.

The major vasculitides are polyarteritis nodosa, giant cell arteritis, polymyalgia rheumatica and Wegener's granulomatosis. Arthritis or limb girdle pain can be a component of the clinical presentation.

Asthma

Four big advances in the management of asthma

1. The realisation that asthma is an inflammatory disease. Therefore the appropriate first or second line treatment in moderate to severe asthma is inhaled sodium cromoglycate or corticosteroids.
2. The regular use of the mini peak flow meter.
3. The use of spacers attached to inhalers/puffers for all ages.
4. Improved and more efficient inhalers, such as Turbuhalers.

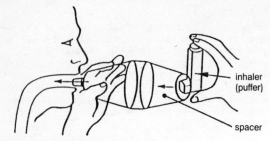

Using a spacer device. Rules: children—all puffs in at once, then inhale; adults—single puff, single breath

Definition of control of asthma

- no cough, wheeze or breathlessness most of the time
- no nocturnal waking due to asthma
- no limitation of normal activity
- no overuse of beta₂ agonist
- no severe attacks
- no side effects of medication

Pharmacological agents to treat asthma

It is useful to teach patients the concept of the 'preventer' and the 'reliever' for their asthma treatment.

'Preventer' drugs or anti-inflammatory agents

These medications are directed toward the underlying abnormalities—bronchial hyper-reactivity and associated airway inflammation.

Corticosteroids

Inhaled:	Types	beclomethasone
		budesonide
		fluticasone
	Dose range	400 μg–2000 μg (adults)
		aim to keep below
		1600 μg (if possible)

Note: Rinse mouth out with water and spit out after using inhaled steroids.

Oral: Prednisolone is used mainly for exacerbations.
It is given with the usual inhaled corticosteroids
and bronchodilators.
Dose: up to 1 mg/kg/day for 1–2 weeks

Sodium cromoglycate (SCG)

This is available as dry capsules for inhalation, metered dose aerosols or as a nebuliser solution. The availability of the metered aerosol and spacer has helped the use of SCG in the management of asthma in children.

Nedocromil sodium

A new non-steroid metered aerosol.

'Reliever' drugs or bronchodilators

The three groups of bronchodilators are:

- the β_2-adrenoceptor agonists (β-agonists)
- methylxanthines—theophylline derivatives
- anticholinergics

β_2-agonists

Oral administration of β_2-agonists is rarely required. The inhaled drugs produce measurable bronchodilatation in 1–2 minutes and peak effects by 10–20 minutes. The traditional agents such as salbutamol and terbutaline are short-acting preparations. The new longer-acting agents include salmeterol and formoterol.

Prophylactic agents

This term is reserved for those medications that are taken prior to known trigger factors, particularly exercise-induced asthma.

Exercise-induced asthma

- β_2-agonist inhaler (puffer); two puffs immediately before exercise last 1–2 hours. New longer-acting agents such as salmeterol are more effective.
- Sodium cromoglycate, two puffs.
- Combination β_2-agonist + sodium cromoglycate.

Asthma action plan (example)

Action plan

If you are distressed with severe asthma:

- Call an ambulance and say 'severe asthma attack' (best option)
  or
- Call your doctor
  or
- If you are having trouble finding medical help, get someone to drive you to the nearest hospital.

Keep using your bronchodilator inhaler continuously if you are distressed.

The acute asthma attack

Adult dosage

- continuous nebulised salbutamol with oxygen 8 L/min (if nebuliser not available: 6–10 puffs of β_2-agonist inhaler, preferably with spacer, using two loading puffs at a time following by 4–6 breaths)
- insert IV line

If slow response
- a second nebuliser using salbutamol 2 mL, ipratroprium bromide 2 mL with 4 mL N saline
- hydrocortisone 250 mg IV statim

If poor response or if in extremis
- adrenaline 1:10 000 IV (1 mL over 30 seconds) with monitor
  or
  salbutamol 200–400 mcg IV over two minutes
- chest X-ray to exclude complications
- arterial blood gases/pulse oximetry
  then
- IV infusion of salbutamol and hydrocortisone

Children

Should be referred to an intensive care unit

- continuous nebulised 0.5% salbutamol via mask
- oxygen flow 4 L/min through nebuliser
- IV infusion of:
  —salbutamol 5 mg/kg/min
  —hydrocortisone 4 mg/kg statim then six hourly

Common mistakes in children
- using assisted mechanical ventilation (it can be dangerous—main indications are physical exhaustion and cardiopulmonary arrest)
- not giving high flow oxygen
- giving excessive fluid
- giving suboptimal bronchodilator therapy

Asthma in children

Key checkpoints

- Bronchodilators, inhaled or oral, are ineffective under 12 months.
- The delivery method is a problem in children and Table 4 gives an indication of what systems can be used at various levels.
- In the very young, e.g. 1–2 years old, a spacer with a face mask can deliver the aerosol medication.

- The PEF rate should be measured in all asthmatic children older than six years.
- The Turbuhaler is usually not practical under 7–8 years.

Prophylaxis in children

Sodium cromoglycate (SCG) by inhalation is the prophylactic drug of choice in childhood chronic asthma of mild to moderate severity.

- A symptomatic response occurs in about 1–2 weeks (can take up to 4–6 weeks).
- SCG (Forte) is an alternative to low-dose inhaled corticosteroids once the asthma is stable.

If there is no clinical response to SCG, use inhaled corticosteroids, but the risks versus benefits must always be considered. Aim for a maintenance of 100–400 μg, which keeps the child symptom-free. One or two attacks only is not an indication to start corticosteroids.

Table 10 *Delivery systems for asthma in children*

| Vehicle of administration | Age in years | | | |
	Less than 2	2–4	5–6	7 to 8 and over
Inhaler alone			*	√
Inhaler + spacer		√	√	√
Inhaler + spacer + face mask/ or aerochamber	√	√		
Turbuhaler			*	√
Nebuliser/air compressor/face mask	√	√	√	√
Spincaps				√
Rotacaps				√

* possible in some individual children

B

Back pain

This section includes low (lumbosacral) back pain and thoracic back pain.

Low back pain

Low back pain (LBP) is a very common presenting problem in general practice. The major causes presenting to the author's practice are summarised in Table 11.

The most common cause of back pain presenting to the doctor is dysfunction of the spinal intervertebral joints (mechanical back pain) due to injury. This problem accounts for about 72% of cases of back pain, while lumbar spondylosis (degenerative osteoarthritis) is responsible for about 10% of painful backs presenting to the general practitioner.

The management of back pain depends on the cause.

Table 11 *Major causes of low back ± leg pain presenting in the author's general practice*

Patients	%
Vertebral dysfunction	71.8
Lumbar spondylosis	10.1
Depression	3.0
Urinary tract infection	2.2
Spondylolisthesis	2.0
Spondyloarthropathies	1.9
Musculoligamentous strains/tears	1.2
Malignant disease	0.8
Arterial occlusive disease	0.6
Other	6.4
	100.0

Table 12 *Low back pain: diagnostic strategy model*

Q.	*Probability diagnosis*
A.	Vertebral dysfunction esp. facet joint and disc
	Spondylosis (degenerative OA)

Q.	*Serious disorders not to be missed*
A.	Cardiovascular
	• ruptured aortic aneurysm
	• retroperitoneal haemorrhage (anticoagulants)
	Neoplasia
	• myeloma
	• metastases
	Severe infections
	• osteomyelitis
	• discitis
	• tuberculosis
	• pelvic abscess/PID
	Cauda equina compression

Q.	*Pitfalls (often missed)*
A.	Spondyloarthropathies
	• ankylosing spondylitis
	• Reiter's disease
	• psoriasis
	• bowel inflammation
	Sacroiliac dysfunction
	Spondylolisthesis
	Claudication
	• vascular
	• neurogenic
	Prostatitis
	Endometriosis

Q.	*Seven masquerades checklist*	
A.	Depression	√
	Diabetes	—
	Drugs	—
	Anaemia	—
	Thyroid disease	—
	Spinal dysfunction	√
	UTI	√

Q.	*Is this patient trying to tell me something?*
A.	Quite likely. Consider lifestyle, stress, work problems, malingering, conversion reaction

Note Associated buttock and leg pain included.

Summary of diagnostic guidelines for spinal pain

- Continuous pain (day and night) = neoplasia, especially malignancy or infection.
- The big primary malignancy is multiple myeloma.
- The big three metastases are from lung, breast and prostate.
- The other three metastases are from thyroid, kidney/adrenal and melanoma.

- Pain with standing/walking (relief with sitting) = spondylolisthesis.
- Pain (and stiffness) at rest, relief with activity = inflammation.
- In a young person with inflammation think of ankylosing spondylitis, Reiter's disease or reactive arthritis.
- Stiffness at rest, pain with or after activity, relief with rest = osteoarthritis.
- Pain provoked by activity, relief with rest = mechanical dysfunction.
- Pain in bed at early morning = inflammation, depression or malignancy/infection.
- Pain in periphery of limb
    = discogenic → radicular
    or vascular → claudication
    or spinal canal stenosis → claudication.
- Pain in calf (ascending) with walking = vascular claudication.
- Pain in buttock (descending) with walking = neurogenic claudication.
- One disc lesion = one nerve root (exception is L5–S1 disc).
- One nerve root = one disc (usually).
- Two or more nerve roots—consider neoplasm.
- The rule of thumb for the lumbar nerve root lesions is L3 from L2–L3 disc, L4 from L3–L4, L5 from L4–L5 and S1 from L5–S1.
- A large disc protrusion can cause bladder symptoms, either incontinence or retention.
- A retroperitoneal bleed from anticoagulation therapy can give intense nerve root symptoms and signs.

Vertebral dysfunction with non-radicular pain

Typical features
- the common cause of low back pain
- usually due to dysfunction (injury) of the pain-sensitive facet joint ± a minor disc disruption
- pain usually unilateral; can be central or bilateral

Management
Low back pain (only) without spasm
- modified home activities and relative rest for 2 days
- regular simple analgesics, e.g. paracetamol or aspirin with review as the patient mobilises
- back education program
- exercise program (when exercises do not aggravate)
- swimming (if feasible)
- spinal mobilisation or manipulation if needed after review in 4–5 days

Most of these patients can expect to be relatively pain free and able to return to work within 14 days.

Acute low back pain (only) with spasm
(indicates discogenic problem)

- strict rest lying on a firm surface for 2–3 days (keep the spine as straight as possible)
- regular simple analgesics with review as the patient mobilises
- back education program
- cold or hot compresses to the painful area
- simple mobilisation exercises as tolerated

When the acute phase settles, treat as for uncomplicated low back pain.

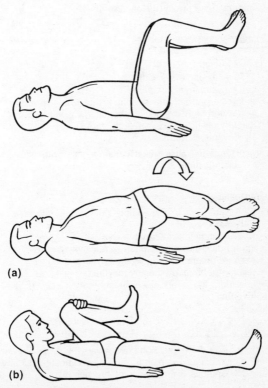

Examples of exercises for low back pain:
(a) *rotation exercise;* **(b)** *flexion exercise*

Vertebral dysfunction with radiculopathy (sciatica)

Management

Sciatica is a more complex and protracted problem to treat, but most cases will gradually settle within 12 weeks if the following approach is used:

- strict bed rest for three days (keep the spine straight—avoid sitting in soft chairs and for long periods)
- regular simple analgesics with review as the patient mobilises
- NSAIDs 7–10 days
- back education program
- exercises—straight leg raising exercises to pain tolerance
- swimming
- traction (intermittent only will suffice)
- epidural anaesthesia (if slow response)

Lumbar spondylosis

Typical profile

- > 50 years: increases with age
- dull nagging low back pain
- stiffness esp. in mornings (main feature)
- aggravated by heavy activity, bending, e.g. gardening
- relief by gentle exercise, hydrotherapy
- all movements restricted

Note: Tends to cause spinal canal stenosis with neurogenic claudication.

Management

- basic analgesics (depending on patient response and tolerance)
- NSAIDs (judicious intermittent use)
- appropriate balance between light activity and rest
- exercise program and hydrotherapy (if available)
- regular mobilisation therapy may help
- consider trials of electrotherapy such as TENS and acupuncture

Spondylolisthesis

About 5% of the population have spondylolisthesis but not all are symptomatic. The pain is caused by extreme stretching of the interspinous ligaments or of the nerve roots, or a disc lesion.

Diagnosis confirmed by lateral X-ray.

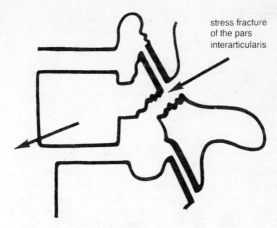

stress fracture
of the pars
interarticularis

*Spondylolisthesis: illustrating a forward shift
of one vertebra on another*

Management
- strict flexion exercise program for at least 3 months (avoid hyperextension)
- lumbar corsets help but avoid if possible
- surgery is last recourse

The spondyloarthropathies

The seronegative spondyloarthropathies are a group of disorders characterised by involvement of the sacroiliac joints with an ascending spondylitis and extraspinal manifestations such as oligoarthritis and enthesopathies (see page 43).

Typical features
- young men 15–30
- aching throbbing pain of inflammation
- low back pain radiating to buttocks
- back stiffness esp. in mornings
- absent lumbar lordosis
- positive sacroiliac stress tests

Diagnosis
confirmation:

X-ray of pelvis (sacroiliitis)
Bone scans and CT scans
ESR usually elevated
HLA-B_{27} antigen positive in over 90% of cases

Treatment

The earlier the treatment the better the outlook for the patient; the prognosis is usually good.

- advice on good back care and posture
- exercise programs to improve the range of movement
- drug therapy, especially tolerated NSAIDs, e.g. indomethacin
- sulphasalazine—a useful second-line agent if the disease progresses despite NSAIDs

---

Thoracic back pain

Thoracic (dorsal) back pain which is common in people of all ages is mainly due to dysfunction of the joints of the thoracic spine, with its unique costovertebral joints. Muscular and ligamentous strains may be common, but rarely come to light in practice because they are self-limiting and not severe.

This dysfunction can cause referred pain to various parts of the chest wall and can mimic the symptoms of various visceral diseases such as angina, biliary colic and oesophageal spasm.

Intervertebral disc prolapse is very uncommon in the thoracic spine and then occurs below T9, usually T11–T12.

Scheuermann's disorder

Typical features

- age 11–17
- males > females
- lower thoracic spine T9–T12
- thoracic pain or asymptomatic
- increasing thoracic kyphosis over 1–2 months
- cannot touch toes
- diagnosis confirmed by X-ray

Treatment

- explanation and support
- extension exercises, avoid forward flexion
- postural correction
- avoidance of sports involving lifting and bending
- consider bracing or surgery if serious deformity

Idiopathic adolescent scoliosis

The vast majority of curves, occurring equally in boys and girls, are mild and of no consequence. Eighty-five per cent of significant curves in adolescent scoliosis occur in girls. Such curves appear during the peripubertal period usually coinciding with the growth spurt. The screening test (usually in 12–14 year olds) is to note the contour of the back on forward flexion.

normal   abnormal

Screening for idiopathic adolescent scoliosis:
testing asymmetry by forward flexion

Investigation

A single erect PA spinal X-ray is sufficient; the Cobb angle is the usual measurement yardstick.

Management aims

- preserve good appearance—level shoulders and no trunk shift
- prevent increasing curve in adult life: less than 45°
- *not* to produce a straight spine on X-ray
- refer for expert opinion

Dysfunction of the thoracic spine

This is the outstanding cause of pain (often interscapular) presenting to the practitioner, is relatively easy to diagnose and usually responds dramatically to a simple spinal manipulation treatment.

Association: Chronic poor posture
Diagnosis   Examination of spine, X-ray (mainly to
confirmation: exclude disease)

Management

- continued activity if pain permits
- explanation and reassurance
- back education program
- spinal manipulation (very effective)
- spinal mobilisation (if manipulation contraindicated)
- simple analgesics as required
- exercise program especially extension exercises
- posture education

Balanitis (balanoposthitis)

Balanitis is inflammation of the foreskin which usually affects the glans penis and tissues behind the foreskin (balanoposthitis).

Causative factors
- poor hygiene
- Candida albicans infection

In men screen for
- diabetes
- Reiter's disease (especially if asymptomatic)

Treatment
- take swabs for culture
- careful washing behind foreskin

if yeasts present
—topical nystatin or miconazole or clotrimazole cream
if trichomonads present
—metronidazole or tinidazole (oral treatment)
if bacteria present
—appropriate topical antibiotic, e.g. chloramphenicol or chlortetracycline

Thickening of the foreskin with skin pallor suggests balanitis xerotica obliterans which responds to corticosteroid cream if it is mild. Circumcision is indicated for recurrent problems.

Bed sores (pressure sores)

The decubitus ulcer is typically undermined at the edges.

Management
Prevention
- Good nursing care including turning patient every two hours.
- Special care of pressure areas, including gentle handling.
- Special beds, mattresses (e.g. air-filled ripple) and sheepskin to relieve pressure areas.
- Good nutrition and hygiene.
- Control of urinary and faecal incontinence.
- Avoid the donut cushion.

Treatment of ulcer

Use above measures, plus:

• Clean base with saline solution (applied gently via a syringe) or Intra Site Gel.
• General guidelines for dressings:
  —deep ulcers: alginates, e.g. Tegagel
  —shallow ulcers: hydrocolloids, e.g. Duoderm, Cutinova Hydro
  —dry or necrotic ulcers: hydrogels, e.g. Intra Site
  —heavy exudative ulcers: foams, e.g. Lyofoam
• Give vitamin C, 500 mg bd.
• Give antibiotics for spreading cellulitis (otherwise of little use).
• Healing is usually satisfactory but, if not, surgical intervention with debridement of necrotic tissue and skin grafting may be necessary.

Belching (aerophagia)

(patient swallows air without admitting it)

• Make patient aware of excessive swallowing.
• Avoid fizzy (carbonated) soft drinks.
• Avoid chewing gum.
• Don't drink with meals.
• Don't mix proteins and starches.
• Eat slowly and chew food thoroughly before swallowing.
• Eat and chew with the mouth closed.

If persistent
   Simethicone preparation, e.g. Mylanta II, Phazyme

Bell's palsy

Prednisolone 60 mg daily for three days then taper to zero over next seven days (start within three days of onset)

• adhesive tape or patch at night over eye if corneal exposure
• consider artificial tears if eye dry
• massage and facial exercises during recovery
• about 90% spontaneous recovery

Benzodiazepine problems

Long-term use should be avoided and care should be taken with 'new patients' requesting a prescription.

Benzodiazepine withdrawal syndrome

This syndrome is usually relatively delayed in its onset and may continue for weeks or months. Withdrawal features include:

- anxiety (rebound)
- depression
- insomnia
- nausea
- loss of appetite
- tremor
- confusion

An effective management method is to withdraw the drug very slowly while providing counselling and support, including referral to a self-help group. Antidepressants can be substituted if there is evidence of depression, while beta-blockers may help the withdrawal syndrome if other measures have failed.

Bites and stings

Bites and stings from animals, spiders, marine stingers and insects in Australia are commonplace but fatal bites are uncommon.

Bite wounds

Snake bites

Most bites do not result in envenomation, which tends to occur in snake handlers or in circumstances where the snake has a clear bite of the skin.

First aid
- Keep the patient as still as possible.
- Do not wash, cut or manipulate the wound, or apply ice or use a tourniquet.
- Immediately bandage the bite site firmly (not too tight). A crepe bandage is ideal: it should extend above the bite site for as high as possible, at least 15 cm, e.g. if bitten around the ankle, the bandage should cover the leg to above the knee.
- Splint the limb to immobilise it: a firm stick or slab of wood would be ideal.
- Transport to a medical facility for definite treatment. Do not give alcoholic beverages or stimulants.
- If possible, the dead snake should be brought along.

   Note: A venom detection kit can be used to examine a swab of the bitten area or a fresh urine specimen (the best) or blood.

The bandage can be removed when the patient is safely under medical observation. Observe for symptoms and signs of envenomation.

Envenomation
Important early symptoms of snake bite envenomation include:

- nausea and vomiting (a reliable early symptom)
- abdominal pain
- excessive perspiration
- severe headache
- blurred vision
- difficult speaking or swallowing
- coagulation defects, e.g. haematuria
- lymphadenopathy—tender

Note: Do not give antivenom unless clinical signs of envenomation or biochemical signs, e.g. positive urine, or abnormal clotting profile.

Treatment of envenomation
- set up a slow IV infusion of N saline
- give IV antihistamine cover (15 minutes beforehand) and 0.3 mL adrenaline 1:1000 SC (0.1 mL for a child)
- dilute the specific antivenom (1 in 10 in N saline) and infuse slowly over 30 minutes via the tubing of the saline solution
- have adrenaline, oxygen and steroids on standby
- monitor vital signs
- provide basic life support as necessary

Note: A test dose of antivenom is not recommended.

Spider bites

The toxin of most species of spider causes only localised pain, redness and swelling, but the toxin of some, notably the deadly Sydney funnel-web spider (*Atrax robustus*), can be rapidly fatal.

First aid
- Sydney funnel-web: as for snake bites.
- Other spiders: apply an ice pack, do not bandage.

Treatment of envenomation
- Sydney funnel-web:
  —specific antivenom
  —resuscitation and other supportive measures
- Red back spider:
  —give antihistamines
  —antivenom IM (IV if severe) 15 minutes later

Human bites and clenched fist injuries

Human bites, including clenched fist injuries, often become infected by organisms such as *Staphylococcus aureus*.

Principles of treatment
- Clean and debride the wound carefully, e.g. aqueous antiseptic solution or hydrogen peroxide.
- Give prophylactic penicillin if a severe or deep bite.
- Avoid suturing if possible.
- Tetanus toxoid.
- Consider possibility of HIV, hepatitis B or C infections.

For wound infection
- Take swab.
- Procaine penicillin 1 g IM, plus amoxycillin/clavulanate 500 mg, 8-hourly for five days.

For severe penetrating injuries, e.g. joints, tendons
- IV antibiotics for seven days.

Dog bites (non-rabid)

Animal bites are also prone to infection by the same organisms as for humans, plus Pasteurella multocida.

Principles of treatment
- Clean and debride the wound with aqueous antiseptic, allowing it to soak for 10–20 minutes.
- Aim for open healing—avoid suturing if possible.
- Apply non-adherent, absorbent dressings (paraffin gauze and Melolin) to absorb the discharge from the wound.
- Tetanus prophylaxis: immunoglobulin or tetanus toxoid.
- Give prophylactic penicillin for a severe or deep bite: 1.5 million units of procaine penicillin IM statim, then orally for five days. Tetracycline or flucloxacillin are alternatives.
- Inform the patient that slow healing and scarring are likely.

Cat bites

Cat bites have the most potential for suppurative infection. The same principles apply as for management of human or dog bites, but use flucloxacillin. It is important to clean a deep and penetrating wound. Another problem is cat-scratch disease, presumably caused by a Gram-negative bacterium.

Sandfly bites

For some reason, possibly the nature of body odour, the use of oral thiamine may prevent sandfly bites.

Dose: Thiamine 100 mg orally, daily.

Mollusc bite (blue-ringed octopus, cone shell)

Mollusc venoms can be rapidly fatal because of prolonged muscular weakness leading to respiratory paralysis.

Treatment

- compression bandage to bite site (usually hand/arm)
- immobilise the limb
- arrange transport (preferably by ambulance) to a medical facility
- observe (and manage) for respiratory paralysis. Ensure adequate ABC.

Stings

Bee stings

First aid

- Scrape the sting off sideways with a fingernail or knife blade. Do not squeeze it with the fingertips.
- Apply 20% aluminium sulfate solution (Stingose) or methylated spirits.
- Apply ice to the site.
- Rest and elevate the limb that has been stung.

If anaphylaxis, treat as appropriate.

Centipede and scorpion bites/stings

The main symptom is pain, which can be very severe and prolonged.

First aid

- Apply local heat, e.g. hot water with ammonia (household bleach).
- Clean site.
- Local anaesthetic, e.g. 1–2 mL of 1% lignocaine infiltrated around the site (if still painful).
- Check tetanus immunisation status.

Other bites and stings

This includes bites from ants, wasps and some jellyfish.

First aid
- Wash the site with large quantities of cool water.
- Apply methylated spirits to the wound for about 30 seconds.
- Apply ice for several minutes.
- Use soothing anti-itch cream or 5% lignocaine cream or ointment if very painful.

Medication is not usually necessary, although for a jellyfish sting the direct application of Antistine-Privine drops onto the sting (after washing the site) is effective.

Box jellyfish or sea wasp (Chironex fleckeri)

Treatment
- The victim should be removed from the water to prevent drowning.
- Inactivate the tentacles by pouring vinegar over them for 30 seconds (do not use alcohol)—use up to 2 L of vinegar at a time.
- Check respiration and the pulse.
- Start immediate cardiopulmonary resuscitation (if necessary).
- Use compression/immobilisation for major stings.
- Give box jellyfish antivenom by IM or IV injection.
- Provide pain relief if required (ice, lignocaine and analgesics).

Stinging fish

The sharp spines of the stinging fish have venom glands which can produce severe pain if they spike or even graze the skin. The best known of these is the stonefish. The toxin is usually heat sensitive.

Envenomation
- intense pain
- localised swelling
- bluish discolouration

Treatment
- Bathe or immerse the affected part in very warm to hot water (not scalding)—this may give instant relief.
- If pain persists, give a local injection/infiltration of lignocaine 1% or even a regional block. If still persisting, try pyroxidine 50 mg intralesional injection.
- A specific antivenom is available for the sting of the stonefish.

Bladder dysfunction (in women during night)

Women with urethral syndrome constantly wake at night with the urge to micturate but produce only a small dribble of urine.

* instruct patient to perform a pelvic lift exercise by balancing on upper back, lifting her pelvis with knees flexed and holding position for 30 seconds
* squeeze pelvic floor inwards (as though holding back urine or faeces)
* repeat a few times

Blepharitis

Precautions: corneal ulceration, recurrent staphylococcal infections

Treatment

* eyelid hygiene—clean with a cotton bud dipped in 1:10 dilution of baby shampoo, once or twice daily
* artificial tears, e.g. hypromellose 1%
* tetracycline 1% or bacitracin ointment to lid margins 3–6 hourly
* control scalp seborrhoea with medicated shampoos, e.g. ketaconazole
* if chronic: short term use hydrocortisone 0.5% ointment

Body odour

Cause: poor hygiene, excessive perspiration and active skin
      bacteria
      axilla and groin main focus
Precautions: consider uraemia, vaginitis

Treatment method

* Scrub body, especially groins and axillae, with deodorant soap at least morning and night.
* Try an antibacterial surgical scrub.
* Keep clothes clean, regular laundry.
* Choose suitable clothes—natural fibres, e.g. cotton, not synthetics.
* Use an antiperspirant deodorant.
* Alternative soap—pine soap.
* Diet: avoid garlic, fish, curry, onions, asparagus.
* Reduce caffeine (coffee, tea and cola drinks), which stimulates sweat activity.
* Shave axillary hair.
* Axillary wedge resection for excessive perspiration.

Boils (recurrent)

- obtain swabs
- 3% hexachlorophane body wash daily
- mupirocin to the lesions and nares
- antibiotics (according to swabs), e.g. erythromycin 500 mg bd for 10 days (may require up to three months)

Breast lumps

Key facts and checkpoints

- The commonest lumps are those associated with benign mammary dysplasia.
- Benign mammary dysplasia is also a common cause of cysts, especially in the premenopause phase.
- Over 75% of isolated breast lumps prove to be benign but clinical identification of a malignant tumour can only definitely be made following aspiration biopsy or histological examination of the tumour.
- Breast cancer is the most common cancer in females, affecting 1 in 12–15 women.
- About 25% of all new cancers in women are breast neoplasms.
- A 'dominant' breast lump in an older woman should be regarded as malignant.

The clinical approach

Breast symptoms

- lump
- tenderness or pain
- nipple discharge
- nipple retraction
- periareolar inflammation—usually due to nipple retraction or mammary duct ectasia
- Paget's disease of nipple = underlying malignancy

Nipple discharge

This may be intermittent from one or both nipples. It can be induced by quadrant compression.

- bloodstained   — intraduct papilloma (commonest)
                     intraduct carcinoma
                     mammary dysplasia
- green-grey   — mammary dysplasia
                     mammary duct ectasia
- yellow   — mammary dysplasia (serous)
                     breast abscess (pus)

| • milky white (galactorrhoea) | — lactation cysts lactation hyperprolactinaemia drugs, e.g. chlorpromazine |

Investigations

X-ray mammography

Mammography can be used as a screening procedure and as a diagnostic procedure. It is currently the only effective screening tool for breast cancer.

Screening:

- established benefit for women over 50
- possible benefit for women in their 40s
- follow-up in those with breast cancer, as 6% develop in the opposite breast
- localisation of the lesion for fine needle aspiration

Breast ultrasound

This is mainly used to elucidate an area of breast density and is the best method of defining benign breast disease, especially with cystic changes. It is generally most useful in women less than 30 years old.

Needle aspiration techniques

- cyst aspiration
- fine needle aspiration or core needle biopsy: this is a very useful diagnostic test in solid lumps with an accuracy of 90–95% (better than mammography).

Carcinoma of the breast

Breast carcinoma is uncommon under the age of 30 but it then steadily increases to a maximum at the age of about 60 years. About one-third are premenopausal and two-thirds postmenopausal.

Clinical features

- The majority of patients with breast cancer present with a lump.
- The lump is usually painless (5% associated with pain).
- Usually the lump is hard and irregular.
- Other symptoms include breast pain, nipple discharge and nipple retraction.
- Rarely cancer can present with Paget's disease.
- Rarely it can present with bony secondaries, e.g. back pain, dyspnoea, weight loss, headache.

Management

Immediate referral to an expert surgeon on suspicion or proof of breast cancer is essential.

Benign mammary dysplasia

Synonyms: fibroadenosis, chronic mastitis, fibrocystic disease, cystic hyperplasia.

Management

- Consider mammography if diffuse lumpiness is present in patient > 40.
- Perform needle biopsy if a discrete lump is present and aspirate palpable cysts.
- Reassure patient that there is no cancer.
- Give medication to alleviate any mastalgia.
- Use analgesics as necessary.
- Surgically remove undiagnosed mass lesions.

Breast cyst

Diagnosis

- mammography
- ultrasound (X-ray of choice)
- cytology of aspirate

Lactation cysts

- These present postpartum with similar signs to perimenopausal cysts.
- They vary from 1–5 cm in diameter.
- Treat by aspiration: fluid may be clear or milky.
- Consider possibility of malignancy.

Fibroadenoma

Clinical features

- a discrete asymptomatic lump
- usually in twenties (range: second to sixth decade)
- firm, smooth and mobile (the 'breast mouse')
- usually rounded
- usually in upper outer quadrant

Management

Ultrasound and fine needle aspiration with cytology is recommended. It may be left in those in the late teens but as a rule the lump should be removed to be certain of the diagnosis.

Fat necrosis

Fat necrosis is usually the end result of a large bruise or trauma which may be subtle such as protracted breast feeding. The mass that results is often accompanied by skin or nipple retraction and thus closely resembles carcinoma.

Mammary duct ectasia

Synonyms: plasma cell mastitis, periductal mastitis.

In this benign condition a whole breast quadrant may be indurated and tender. The lump is usually located near the margin of the areola and is a firm or hard, tender, poorly defined swelling. There may be a toothpaste-like nipple discharge.

Breast pain (mastalgia)

Key facts and checkpoints

- The typical age span for mastalgia is 30–50 years.
- The peak incidence is 35–45 years.
- There are four common clinical presentations:
  1. diffuse, bilateral cyclical mastalgia (commonest)
  2. diffuse, bilateral non-cyclical mastalgia
  3. unilateral diffuse non-cyclical mastalgia
  4. localised breast pain

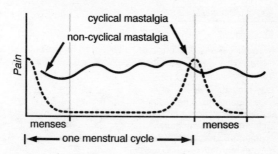

Pain patterns for cyclical and non-cyclical mastalgia

Cyclical mastalgia

The features of cyclical mastalgia are:

- the typical age is about 35
- discomfort and sometimes pain are present

- usually bilateral but one breast can dominate
- mainly premenstrual
- breasts diffusely nodular or lumpy
- variable relationship to the pill

It is rare after the menopause.

Management

After excluding a diagnosis of carcinoma and aspirating palpable cysts, various treatments are possible and can be given according to severity. (See Table 13.)

Table 13 *Management plan for cyclical mastalgia*

	Progressive stepwise therapy
Step 1	Reassurance Proper brassiere support Diet—exclude caffeine
Step 2	Add Vitamin B₁ 100 mg daily Vitamin B₆ 100 mg daily
Step 3	Substitute Evening primrose oil 4 g daily
Step 4	Add Danazol 200 mg daily

Non-cyclical mastalgia

Management

Non-cyclical mastalgia is very difficult to treat, being less responsive than cyclical mastalgia. It is worth a therapeutic trial.

First-line treatment
- exclude caffeine from diet
- weight reduction if needed
- vitamin B₁ 100 mg daily
- vitamin B₆ 100 mg daily
- evening primrose oil 4–6 g daily

Second-line treatment
- norethisterone 5 mg daily

Costochondritis (Tietze's syndrome)

Features:
- palpable swelling about 4 cm from sternal edge due to enlargement of costochondral cartilage
- aggravated by deep breathing and coughing

- self-limiting, but may take several months to subside

Treatment: infiltration with local anaesthetic and corticosteroid.

Mastitis

Clinical features:

- a lump and then soreness (at first)
- a red tender area

possibly

- fever, tiredness, muscle aches and pains

Treatment

- antibiotics: resolution without progression to an abscess will usually be prevented by antibiotics

    flucloxacillin 500 mg (o) qid for 10 days

    or

    cephalaxin 500 mg (o) qid for 10 days
- therapeutic ultrasound (2W/cm^2 for six minutes) daily for 2–3 days
- aspirin or paracetamol for pain

Instructions to patients

- Keep the affected breast well drained.
- Continue breast-feeding: do frequently and start with the sore side.
- Heat the sore breast before feeding, e.g. with hot shower or hot face washer.
- Cool the breast after feeding: use a cold face washer from the freezer.
- Empty the breast well: hand express if necessary.

Breast abscess

If tenderness and redness persist beyond 48 hours and an area of tense induration develops, then a breast abscess has formed. It requires surgical drainage under general anaesthesia (usually) or aspiration with a large bore needle under LA every second day until resolution, antibiotics, rest and complete emptying of the breast. Temporary weaning of breast-feeding from the affected side is necessary because of the surgical disruption.

Breath-holding attacks

This is a dramatic emergency. There are two types: one is related to a tantrum (description follows) and the other is a simple faint.

Clinical features

- age group—usually six months to six years (peak 2–3 years)
- precipitating event (minor emotional or physical)
- children emit a long loud cry, then hold their breath
- they become pale and then blue
- if severe, may result in unconsciousness or even a brief tonic-clonic fit
- lasts 10–60 seconds

Management

- Reassure the parents that attacks are self-limiting, not harmful and are not associated with epilepsy or mental retardation.
- Advise parents to maintain discipline and to resist spoiling the child.
- Try to avoid incidents known to frustrate the child or to precipitate a tantrum.

Bronchiolitis

- an acute viral illness due to RSV
- the commonest acute LRTI in infants
- usual age two weeks to nine months (up to 12 months)
- coryza then irritating cough
- wheezy breathing—often distressed
- tachypnoea
- hyperinflated chest

Auscultation

- widespread fine crackles (not with asthma)
- frequent expiratory wheezes

X-ray: hyperinflation of lungs with depression of diaphragm

Management

Admission to hospital is usual esp. with increasing respiratory distress reflected by difficulty in feeding.

- Minimal handling/good nursing care.
- Observation colour, pulse, respiration, oxygen saturation (pulse oximetry).
- Oxygen: to maintain PaO_2 above 90%.
- Fluids IV or by nasogastric tube if unable to feed orally.
- Antibiotics not indicated except if secondary bacterial infection.

Bronchitis

Acute bronchitis

- cough and sputum (main symptoms)
- wheeze and dyspnoea

- usually viral infection
- can complicate chronic bronchitis usually due to *H. influenzae* and *S. pneumoniae*
- scattered wheezes on auscultation
- ± fever or haemoptysis (uncommon)

Outcome

- improves spontaneously in 4–8 days in healthy patients

Treatment

- symptomatic treatment
- inhaled bronchodilators for airflow limitation
- antibiotics usually not needed in previously healthy adult or child
- use antibiotics if severe infection with fever, e.g. amoxycillin/ clavulanate tds for 5 days; use doxycycline or erythromycin if mycoplasma suspected

Chronic bronchitis

Definition: chronic productive cough for at least three successive months in two successive years

- wheeze, progressive dyspnoea
- recurrent exacerbations with acute bronchitis
- occurs mainly in smokers

Refer to COAD (page 99)

Bruising and bleeding

Many patients present with the complaint that they bruise easily but only a minority turn out to have an underlying blood disorder.

Key facts and checkpoints

- Purpura = petechiae + ecchymoses.
- Abnormal bleeding is basically the result of disorders of (1) the platelet, (2) the coagulation mechanism, or (3) the blood vessel.
- There is no substitute for a good history in the assessment of patients with bleeding disorders.
- An assessment of the personal and family histories is the first step in the identification of a bleeding disorder.
- When a patient complains of 'bruising easily' it is important to exclude thrombocytopenia due to bone marrow disease and clotting factor deficiencies such as haemophilia.
- *Differential diagnosis:* 'Palpable purpura' due to an underlying systemic vasculitis is an important differential problem.

The petechiae are raised so finger palpation is important. The cause is an underlying vasculitis affecting small vessels, e.g. polyarteritis nodosa.

- In general, bleeding secondary to platelet defects is spontaneous, associated with a petechial rash and occurs immediately after trauma or a cut wound.
- Laboratory assessment should be guided by the clinical impression.
- Bleeding caused by coagulation factor deficiency is usually traumatic and delayed, e.g. haemorrhage occurring 24 hours after a dental extraction in a haemophiliac.
- The routine screening tests for the investigation of patients with bleeding disorders can be normal despite the presence of a severe haemorrhagic state.

Investigations

The initial choice of investigations depends upon the bleeding pattern.

If coagulation defect suspected:

- prothrombin time (PT)
- activated partial thromboplastin time (APTT)

If platelet pathology suspected:

- platelet count
- skin bleeding time

The full blood examination and blood film is useful in pinpointing the aetiology. The bone marrow examination is useful to exclude the secondary causes of thrombocytopenia such as leukaemia, other marrow infiltrations and aplastic anaemia.

Vascular disorders

The features are:

- easy bruising and bleeding into skin
- ± mucous membrane bleeding
- investigations normal

Simple purpura (easy bruising syndrome)

This is a benign disorder occurring in otherwise healthy women usually in their twenties or thirties. The feature is bruising on the arms, leg and trunk with minor trauma. The patient may complain of heavy periods. Major challenges to the haemostatic mechanism such as dental extraction, childbirth and surgery have not been complicated by excessive blood loss.

Platelet disorders

The features are:

- petechiae ± ecchymoses
- bleeding from mucous membranes
- platelet counts <50 000/mm³ (50 × 10⁹/L)

Coagulation disorders

The features are:

- ecchymoses
- haemarthrosis and muscle haematomas
- usually traumatic and delayed

The inherited disorders such as haemophilia A and B are uncommon and involve deficiency of one factor only. The acquired disorders such as disseminated intravascular coagulation (DIC) occur more commonly and invariably affect several anticoagulation factors.

Henoch-Schönlein (anaphylactoid) purpura

This is a palpable purpura due to small vessel vasculitis.

Clinical features

- all ages, mainly in children
- rash mainly on buttocks and legs
- can occur on hands, arms and trunk
- arthritis: mainly ankles and knees
- abdominal pain (vasculitis of GIT)
- haematuria (reflects nephritis)

Prognosis is generally excellent. No specific therapy is available but corticosteroids may be helpful.

Bruxism (teeth grinding)

- Practise keeping teeth apart.
- Slowly munch an apple before retiring.
- Practise relaxation techniques, including meditation, before retiring (bruxism is related to stress).
- Place a hot face towel against the sides of the face before retiring to achieve relaxation.
- If this fails and bruxism is socially unacceptable during the night, use a mouthguard.

Burning feet syndrome

Anterior burning pain in forefoot—consider tarsal tunnel syndrome or peripheral neuropathy, e.g. from diabetes or vascular insufficiency.

Burns

Management depends on extent and depth (burns are classified as superficial or deep).

Small burns should be immersed in cold water immediately, e.g. tap water for 20 minutes.

Chemical burns should be liberally irrigated with water.

Refer the following burns to hospital:

- > 10% surface area, especially in a child
- all deep burns
- burns of difficult or vital areas, e.g. face, hands, perineum/genitalia, feet
- burns with potential problems, e.g. electrical, chemical, circumferential

Treatment of superficial burns

Most scalds cause partial thickness (superficial) burns. Smear the clean burnt or scalded area with silver sulfadiazide (Silvazine) cream with a sterile gloved hand or spatula (3 mm thick layer).

Exposure (open method)

- keep open without dressings (good for face, perineum or single surface burns)
- renew coating of cream every 24 hours

Dressings (closed method)

- suitable for circumferential wounds
- cover creamed area with non-adherent tulle, e.g. paraffin gauze
- dress with an absorbent bulky layer of gauze and wool
- use a plaster splint if necessary

Burns to hands

A first aid method for partial thickness burns to hands is to place the hand in a suitable plastic bag containing a liberal quantity of Silvazine. If a sterile plastic bag is unavailable a standard household bag will suffice.

Then apply a crepe bandage around the hand, leaving the fingers and thumb free so that the fingers can move freely in the bag. Consider placing the arm in a sling. Change the bag every day or second day to review the wound. Leave blisters intact.

C

Cannabis (marijuana)

The effects of smoking cannabis vary from person to person.
The effects of a small to moderate amount include:

- feeling of well-being and relaxation
- decreased inhibitions
- woozy, floating feeling
- lethargy and sleepiness
- talkativeness and laughing a lot
- red nose, gritty eyes and dry mouth
- unusual perception of sounds and colour
- nausea and dizziness
- loss of concentration
- looking 'spaced out' or drunk
- lack of co-ordination

Long-term use and addiction

The influence of 'pot' has a severe effect on the personality
and drive of the users. They lose their energy, initiative and
enterprise. They become bored, inert, apathetic and careless.
A serious effect of smoking pot is loss of memory. Some serious
problems include:

- crime
- lack of morality—scant respect for others and their property
- respiratory disease (more potent than nicotine)
- often prelude to taking hard drugs
- becoming psychotic (resembling schizophrenia): the drug
  appears to unmask an underlying psychosis
- paranoia especially with a new form called 'mad weed'

Management

The best treatment is prevention. People should either not use
it or limit it to experimentation. If it is used, people should be
prepared to 'sleep it off' and not drive.

Cardiopulmonary resuscitation (CPR)

The ABC basic life support for cardiac arrest should be followed, but ideally DABC is best (defibrillation first if a defibrillator is available).

Basic life support

The following represents a logical ABC plan for the adult patient who collapses or is found apparently unconscious.

1. Shake and shout at the patient.
2. Check breathing.
3. Check pulse (feel carotid adjacent to thyroid cartilage).
4. Call for help (if no pulse).
5. Finger sweep oropharynx (clear it).
6. Place victim on back on firm surface.
7. Thump precordium (if arrest witnessed).
8. Tilt head back (to maximum).
9. Lift chin (use airway if available).
10. Commence basic life support:
    Expired air resuscitation (EAR)—5 quick breaths
    External chest compression
    One rescuer: 15 : 2 (compressions/breaths)
                         80 beats/min
    Two rescuers: 5:1
                         60 beats/min

Advanced life support

Optimal initial support involves:

- endotracheal intubation (otherwise bag and oxygen)
- ECG monitoring
- intravenous access (large peripheral or central vein)

Optimal initial therapy involves:

- defibrillation
- oxygen
- cardioactive drugs, especially adrenaline

If an ECG recording is unavailable the best course of action is:

- Defibrillate 200 J 'paddles mode'
- Defibrillate 200 J at 10 secs (if no response)
- Defibrillate 360 J
- Adrenaline 1:10 000, 10 mL IV

'Cellulite'

The best way to overcome 'cellulite' is to keep to ideal weight. If overweight, lose it slowly and exercise to improve the muscle tone in the buttocks and thighs.

Cervical cancer and Pap smears

Facts and figures

- Carcinoma of the cervix is the most common malignancy in women world-wide;

- There are two small peaks of incidence, in the late 30s and late 60s.
- On average, cervical cancer takes at least a decade to develop from a focus of cervical intraepithelial neoplasia.
- SCC of the cervix occurs almost exclusively in women who have had coitus.
- The earlier the age of first intercourse the greater the chance of developing cervical cancer.
- Invasive cervical cancer is a disease for which definite curable premalignant lesions can be identified using a Papanicolaou's (Pap) smear as a screening test.
- The incidence of cervical cancer has been decreased significantly through the screening procedures of the Pap smear, colposcopy and colposcopically directed cervical biopsy.
- Poor Pap smear technique is a common cause of a false negative result.

Clinical presentation

Many patients with cervical cancer are asymptomatic and when early symptoms do arise they are often dismissed as of little consequence.

Symptoms, if present, may be:

- vaginal bleeding, especially postcoital bleeding
- vaginal discharge
- symptoms of advanced disease, e.g. vaginal urine or flatus, weakness

Screening recommendations

Routine Pap smears:

- Perform every two years for women with no clinical evidence of cervical pathology (some authorities recommend annual smears).
- Perform from beginning of sexual activity up to 70 years.
- Begin Pap smears at 18–20 years or 1–2 years after first sexual intercourse (whichever is later).
- Cease at 70 years in those who have had two normal Pap smears within the last five years.

Taking a Pap smear

The importance of a good specimen

The optimal Pap smear contains:

- sufficient mature and metaplastic squamous cells to indicate adequate sampling from the whole of the transformation zone
- sufficient endocervical cells to indicate that the upper limit of the transformation zone was sampled; and to provide a sample for screening of adenocarcinoma and its precursors

Optimal timing of specimens

- The best time is any time after the cessation of the period.
- Avoid smear-taking during menstruation.
- Avoid in the presence of obvious vaginal infection.
- Avoid within 24 hours of use of vaginal creams or pessaries or douching.

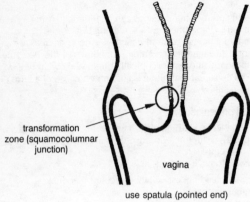

transformation
zone (squamocolumnar
junction)

vagina

use spatula (pointed end)
+
endocervical brush

The transformation zone
in menopausal women:
it is vital that Pap smears
take cells from this zone

Chest pain

Checkpoints and golden rules

- Chest pain represents myocardial infarction until proved otherwise.
- Immediate life-threatening causes of spontaneous chest pain are (1) myocardial infarction, (2) pulmonary embolism, (3) dissecting aneurysm of the aorta, and (4) tension pneumothorax.
- The main differential diagnoses of myocardial infarction include angina, dissecting aneurysm, pericarditis, oesophageal reflux and spasm and hyperventilation with anxiety.
- The history remains the most important clinical factor in the diagnosis of ischaemic heart disease. With angina a vital clue is the reproducibility of the symptom.

Table 13 *Chest pain: diagnostic strategy model*

Q.   *Probability diagnosis*
A.   Musculoskeletal (chest wall)
     Psychogenic
     Angina

Q.   *Serious disorders not to be missed*
A.   Cardiovascular
     • myocardial infarction
     • dissecting aneurysm
     • pulmonary embolism
     Neoplasia
     • carcinoma lung
     • tumours of spinal cord and meningitis
     Severe infections
     • pneumonia-pleurisy
     • mediastinitis
     • pericarditis
     Pneumothorax

Q.   *Pitfalls (often missed)*
A.   Mitral valve prolapse
     Oesophageal spasm
     Gastro-oesophageal reflux
     Herpes zoster
     Fractured rib, e.g. cough fracture
     Spinal dysfunction

     Rarities
     • Bornholm disease (pleurodynia)
     • cocaine inhalation
     • hypertrophic cardiomyopathy

Q.   *Seven masquerades checklist*
A.   Depression   √ possible
     Diabetes   —
     Drugs   —
     Anaemia   √ indirect
     Thyroid disease   —
     Spinal dysfunction √
     UTI   —

Q.   *Is the patient trying to tell me something?*
A.   Consider functional causes, especially anxiety with
     hyperventilation

Note Chest pain is myocardial ischaemia until proved otherwise.

| Site, radiation and features of chest pain syndromes |

Myocardial infarction and angina

The typical retrosternal distribution is shown in the figure below. Retrosternal pain or pain situated across the chest

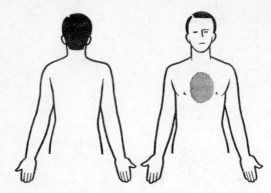

Pain of myocardial ischaemia: typical site

anteriorly should be regarded as cardiac until proved otherwise.

The wide variation of sites of pain, e.g. jaw, neck, inside of arms, epigastrium and interscapular, should always be kept in mind. Pain is referred into the left arm twenty times more commonly than into the right arm.

The quality of the pain is usually typical. The patient often uses the clenched fist sign to illustrate a sense of constriction.

Angina is described on page 29, myocardial infarction on page 260.

The main types of myocardial ischaemia are summarised in Table 14.

Table 14 *Types of myocardial ischaemia*

	Duration of pain	Precipitating factors or characteristic setting	Other features
Angina pectoris			
Stable	3–10 minutes	Physical or emotional stress	Relieved by rest and glyceryl trinitrate
Unstable	5–15 minutes	Not defined; rest or effort	Slow relief from glyceryl trinitrate
Myocardial infarction	> 15–20 minutes	Any time	May be nausea, vomiting, hypotension, arrhythmia Not relieved by glyceryl trinitrate

Dissecting aneurysm

The pain, which is usually sudden, severe and midline, has a tearing sensation and is usually situated retrosternally and between the scapulae (see figure below). It radiates to the abdomen, flank and legs. An important diagnostic feature is the inequality in the pulses, e.g. carotid, radial and femoral. Control of associated hypertension is the basis of treatment while emergency surgery may be needed.

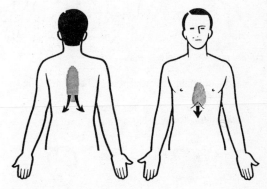

Pain of dissecting aneurysm

Pulmonary embolism

This has a dramatic onset following occlusion of the pulmonary artery or a major branch, especially if more than 50% of the cross-sectional area of the pulmonary trunk is occluded.

The diagnosis can present clinical difficulties, especially when dyspnoea is present without pain. Embolism usually presents with retrosternal chest pain (see figure below) and may be associated with syncope and breathlessness. Treatment is by urgent anticoagulation: heparin then warfarin.

Acute pericarditis

Pericarditis causes three distinct types of pain (see figure below):

1. pleuritic (the commonest) aggravated by cough and deep inspiration, sometimes brought on by swallowing;

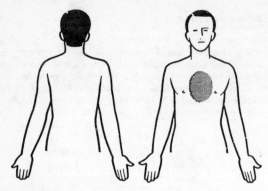

Pain of pulmonary embolism

2. steady, crushing, retrosternal pain that mimics myocardial infarction;
3. pain synchronous with the heartbeat and felt over the praecordium and left shoulder.

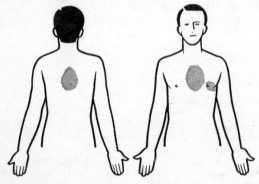

Pain of pericarditis

Spontaneous pneumothorax

The acute onset of pleuritic pain and dyspnoea in a patient with a history of asthma or emphysema is the hallmark of a pneumothorax. It often occurs in young slender males without a history of lung disorders.

Psychogenic pain

Psychogenic chest pain can occur anywhere in the chest, but often it is located in the left submammary region, usually without radiation (see figure below). It tends to be continuous and sharp or stabbing. It may mimic angina but tends to last for hours or days. It is usually aggravated by tiredness or emotional tension and may be associated with shortness of breath, fatigue and palpitations.

Typical site of psychogenic pain

Chilblains

Precautions: think Raynaud's
protect from trauma and secondary infection
do not rub or massage injured tissues
do not apply heat or ice
Physical Rx: elevate affected part
warm gradually to room temperature
Drug Rx: apply glyceryl trinitrate vasodilator
spray or ointment or patch
(use plastic gloves and wash hands for ointment)
Other Rx: rum at night
nifedipine

Child abuse

The various types of abuse are classified as:

- physical
- neglect

- emotional
- sexual
- potential

Facts and figures

- Girls are more likely to be abused than boys.
- Girls are more often assaulted by someone they know.
- Most of the adults who sexually abuse are men (> 90%)
- About 75% of offenders are known to the child.
- Abuse is the misuse of a power situation, e.g. a close relative, coupled with the child's immaturity.
- An Australian study showed that the distribution of child abuse was physical 15%, emotional 48%, sexual 9% and neglect 28%.

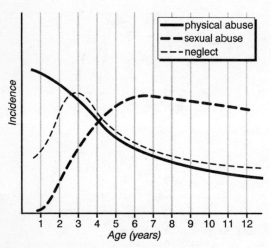

Typical relative age patterns for child abuse

Definition

Child abuse can be defined by the nature of the abusive act or by the result of the abuse. A parent, guardian or other carer can harm a child by a deliberate act or by failure to provide adequate care.

Physical abuse

Physical abuse should be suspected, especially in a child aged under three, if certain physical or behavioural indicators in either the child or the parents are present. Bruising, especially fingertip bruising, is the most common sign of the physically abused child.

Management

The family doctor should diplomatically confront the parent or parents and always act in the best interests of the child. Offer to help the family. An approach would be to say, 'I am very concerned about your child's injuries as they don't add up— these injuries are not usually caused by what I'm told has been the cause. I will therefore seek assistance—it is my legal obligation. My duty is to help you and, especially, your child.'

The stages of management are:

• recognition or disclosure of abuse
• the family separation phase
• working towards rehabilitation
• finding a new family for the child, when rehabilitation fails

Sexual abuse

Incest and sexual abuse of children within the family occur more frequently than is acknowledged.

Sexual abuse presents in three main ways:
• allegations by the child or an adult
• injuries to the genitalia or anus
• suspicious presentations, especially:
— genital infection
— recurrent urinary infection
— unexplained behavioural changes/psychological disorders

Sexual abuse can take many forms, including:

• genital fondling
• digital penetration
• penetration with various objects
• simulated sexual intercourse (anal in boys)
• full sexual penetration
• pornography
• prostitution

Management

It is important to act responsibly in the best interests of the child. It is important to realise that the child will be in *crisis*. Children are trapped into the secrecy of sexual abuse, often by a trusted adult, by powerful threats of the consequences of disclosure. When we encounter real or suspected child abuse, immediate action is necessary. The child needs an advocate to act on its behalf and our intervention actions may have to override our relationship with the family.

Some golden rules are:

- Never attempt to solve the problem alone.
- Do not attempt confrontation and counselling in isolation (unless under exceptional circumstances).
- Seek advice from experts (only a phone call away).
- Avoid telling the alleged perpetrator what the child has said.
- Refer to a child sexual assault centre where an experienced team can take the serious responsibility for the problem.

Supporting the child

- Acknowledge the child's fear and perhaps guilt.
- Assure the child it is not his or her fault.
- Tell the child you will help.
- Obtain the child's trust.
- Tell the child it has happened to other children and you have helped them.

Practice tips and guidelines

- A child's statement alleging abuse should be accepted as true until proved otherwise.
- Children rarely lie about sexual abuse.
- False allegations, however, are a sign of family disharmony and an indication that the child may need help.
- Do not insist that the child 'has got it wrong', even if you find the actions by the alleged perpetrator unbelievable.
- Do not procrastinate—move swiftly to solve the problem.
- Be supportive to the child by listening, believing, being kind and caring.

When to refer

Unless there are exceptional circumstances, referral to an appropriate child abuse centre where an expert team is available is recommended. If doubtful, relatively urgent referral to a paediatrician is an alternative.

Children: special observations

The diagnostic approach to the child is based on the ability to achieve good lines of communication with both the child and the parent.

Establishing rapport

Showing a genuine interest in the child with strategies such as:

- asking them what they like to be called

- passing a compliment about the child such as a clothing item or a toy or book they are carrying
- taking time to converse with them
- asking them if they would like to be a doctor when they grow up
- asking about their teacher or friends

To facilitate the examination:

- play games such as a flashing light, tickling or peek-a-boo, and use any type of noise, particularly animal noises

Distract attention with strategies such as:

- small animal images, e.g. koalas on stethoscopes
- a small toy duck with rattle inside to palpate abdomen
- a clockwork revolving musical toy over examination couch
- a mechanical toy, e.g. rabbit playing a drum on the desk

Recognition of serious illness in infancy

It is vital to diagnose serious life-threatening disease in children, especially in early infancy. The signs of a very sick child include:

- inactive, lying quietly, disinterested
- increased respiratory rate
- increased work of breathing
- noisy breathing —chest wall retraction
                   —wheezes, grunting, stridor
- tachycardia
- sunken eyes
- mottled, cold, pale skin
- drowsiness

Serious illnesses to consider include:
- haemophilus influenza type B (Hib) infection
  — acute epiglottitis
  — meningitis

(Now uncommon since Hib immunisation):

- meningococcal infection
  — septicaemia
  — meningitis
- other forms of meningitis
- acute myocarditis
- asthma/bronchitis
- intussusception

The child as a barometer of the family

A disturbed child is a very common indicator of family disharmony. There is a saying that 'love is to a child what sunlight is to a flower'.

The child's reaction to the family disharmony may manifest in three ways (with significant overlap):

- behavioural problems
- psychosomatic symptoms
- school difficulties

Children's behaviour and developmental disorders

Temper tantrums

The tantrum is a feature of the 'terrible twos' toddler whose protestation to frustration is a dramatic reaction of kicking, shouting, screaming, throwing, or banging of the head. Tantrums are more likely to occur if the child is tired or bored.

Management

Reassure parents that the tantrums are relatively commonplace and not harmful. Explain the reasons for the tantrums and include the concept that 'temper tantrums need an audience'.

Advice

- Ignore what is ignorable: parents should pretend to ignore the behaviour and leave the child alone without comment, including moving to a different area (but not locking the child in its room).
- Avoid what is avoidable: try to avoid the cause or causes of the tantrums, e.g. visiting the supermarket.
- Distract what is distractable: redirect the child's interest to some other object or activity.

Medication has no place in the management of temper tantrums.

Breath-holding attacks

(see page 71)

Conduct disorders

Conduct disorders affect 3–5% of children and represent the largest group of childhood psychiatric disorders.

Clinical features

- antisocial behaviour which is repetitive and persistent
- lack of guilt or remorse for offensive behaviour
- generally poor interpersonal relationships
- manipulative
- tendency to aggressive, destructive, 'criminal' behaviour
- learning problems (about 50%)
- hyperactivity (one-third)

Management

- early intervention and family assistance to help provide a warm, caring family environment
- family therapy to reduce interfamily conflict
- appropriate educational programs to facilitate self-esteem and achievement
- provision of opportunities for interesting, socially positive activities, e.g. sports, recreation, jobs, other skills
- behaviour modification programs

Sleep disorders

Management

Advice to parents:

- Resist taking the child into bed during the night unless they are happy to encourage this.
- Avoid giving attention to the child in the middle of the night—it encourages attention seeking.
- Return the child to bed promptly and spend only a brief time with it to give reassurance.
- A rigid series of rituals performed before bedtime helps the child to develop a routine. Settling to sleep may be assisted by soft music, a soft toy and a gentle night-light.

Medication has a minimal place in the management of sleep disturbances, although the judicious use of sedative/hypnotic for a short term may break the sleepless cycle. Such drugs include promethazine and trimeprazine (Vallergan).

Attention deficit hyperactivity disorder

Diagnostic criteria

A. Either 1 or 2
   1. Inattention
   2. Hyperactivity and impulsiveness

B. Onset no later than 7 years of age

C. Symptoms must be present in two or more situations, e.g. at school and at home

D. Disturbance causes clinically significant distress or impairment in social, academic or occupational functioning

Management

- Protect child's self-esteem.
- Counsel and support family.
- Involve teachers.
- Refer to appropriate consultant, e.g. child psychiatrist.
- Refer to parent support group.

Diet: exclusion diet probably ineffective but encourage good diet (consider dietitian's help).

Pharmacological: based on stimulants
- methylphenidate (Ritalin)
                  or
  dexamphetamine
- antidepressants, second line

Stuttering and stammering

Features of stuttering
- more common in boys
- usually begins under six years of age
- no evidence of neurotic or neurological disorder
- causes anxiety and social withdrawal

Management

Although most stutterers improve spontaneously, speech therapy from a caring empathic therapist may be very helpful.

Tics (habit spasm)

Most are minor, transient facial tics, nose twitching, or vocal tics such as grunts, throat clearing and staccato semi-coughs. Most of these tics resolve spontaneously (usually in less than a year) and reassurance can be given.

Tourette's disorder

Also known as Gilles de la Tourette's syndrome or multiple tic disorder, Tourette's disorder usually first appears in children between the ages of 4 and 15 years and has a prevalence of 1:10 000.

Clinical features
- more common in boys
- bizarre tics
- echolia (repetition of words)
- coprolalia (compulsive utterances of obscene words)
- familial: dominant gene with variable expression

Treatment: haloperidol or clonidine (if necessary).

Dyslexia

Dyslexia is the condition where a child who has no physical problems and an apparent normal IQ has difficulty in reading and spelling, because the child apparently confuses certain letters whose shape is similar but different in positioning, e.g. b and d, p and q.

Dyslexia usually manifests as a learning problem. The children have faulty interpretation and utilisation of the knowledge they have acquired. Their problem usually responds to special tuition.

Autism

Autism, described first by Kanner in 1943, is a pervasive development disorder commencing early in childhood; it affects at least four children in 10 000, boys four times as commonly as girls.

Many autistic children appear physically healthy and well developed although there is an association with a range of other disorders such as Tourette's disorder and epilepsy. Most have intellectual disability but about 20% function in the normal range.

Autistic children show many disturbed behaviours such as tantrums, hyperactivity and destructiveness, and impairment in communication.

The earliest signs of autism in infancy include:

- excessive crying
- no response to cuddling if crying
- failure to mould the body in anticipation of being picked up
- stiffening the body or resisting when being held
- failing to respond or overreacting to sensory stimuli
- persistent failure to imitate, such as waving goodbye

The diagnosis of autism remains difficult before the age of two years.

Assessment

If a child has delayed and deviant development and autism is suspected, a comprehensive multi-disciplinary assessment is necessary. Referral to professionals with experience of autism is essential.

Children's emergencies

Common important childhood emergencies include respiratory distress, poisoning, severe infections including severe gastroenteritis, seizures and SIDS/ALTE. Identification of the very sick infant (page 89) is fundamental to emergency care.

Meningitis or encephalitis

Clinical features

Infancy:

- fever, pallor, vomiting, ± altered conscious state
- lethargy and other signs

Children over three years:

- meningeal irritation more obvious, e.g. headache, fever, vomiting, neck stiffness
- later: delirium, altered conscious state

Management

If meningitis suspected, admit to hospital for lumbar puncture and ongoing management.

Meningococcaemia

Note: Treatment is urgent once suspected.

- take blood culture if time and facilities permit, then
- benzylpenicillin 60 mg/kg IV statim and four hourly 5–7 days
                     or (if uncertain)
  third generation cephalosporin (better option)
- admit to hospital
- supportive therapy, e.g. oxygen, IV fluids

Acute epiglottitis

Epiglottitis is characterised by fever, a soft voice, lack of a harsh cough, a preference to sit quietly (rather than lie down) and especially by a soft stridor with a sonorous expiratory component.

Management

- DO NOT EXAMINE THE THROAT.
- Escort the child to hospital—almost all require nasotracheal intubation.
- Keep the child calm—allow mother to nurse child.
- If obstruction, gently bag and mask with 100% oxygen.

Method of emergency cricothyroidotomy (last resort)

- Lay the child across your knees with neck fully extended.
- Insert a number 14 needle or angiocath through the crico-thyroid membrane.

Always try to intubate once before resorting to cricothyroidotomy.

Hospital treatment

Intubation: in theatre suck away profuse secretions and perform nasotracheal intubation

Antibiotics: chloramphenicol 75 mg/kg/day IV (max. 3 g in three divided doses) five days (only if severe penicillin hypersensitivity)
                     or (preferable)

cefotaxime 100–150 mg/kg/day IV (max. 6 g/day in three divided doses)

or

ceftriaxone 100 mg/kg to max. 2 g/day IV as single daily dose

Note: Continue therapy for five days. Early transfer to oral therapy, e.g. amoxycillin/clavulanate, is desirable.

Poisoning

Dangerous drugs for accidental poisoning include all cardiac drugs, antidepressants and anxiolytics, iron tablets, Lomotil, analgesics, alcohol and potassium.

Principles of treatment

- support vital functions A,B,C,D
- dilute the poison—with milk or water (one cup)
- remove the poison (if < 30 minutes and for Fe/K poisons)—induce emesis, e.g. ipecac 15 mL followed by water
- gastric lavage (within four hours)—except for acid and alkali
- delay absorption—activated charcoal (the preferred method) 1 g/kg oral or via fine bore nasogastric tube (best)
- administer antidote (if available) early, e.g. bicarbonate for tricyclics, N-acetyl-cysteine for paracetamol
- treat any complications, e.g. cardiac arrhythmias

Swallowed foreign objects

A golden rule

The natural passage of most objects entering the stomach can be expected, but very large coins need to be watched carefully.

Inhaled foreign bodies

Most cough the FB out naturally, so encourage coughing.
A finger sweep helps, as does back blows and the Himlich manoeuvre (take care with viscera).

Febrile convulsions

(see page 188)

Asthma

(see page 48)

Breath-holding attacks

(see page 71)

SIDS and ALTE

(see page 326)

Croup

(see page 113)

Bronchiolitis

(see page 72)

Collapse in children

The child's brain requires two vital factors: oxygen and glucose.

Initial basic management

1. Lay child on side.
2. Suck out mouth and nasopharynx.
3. Intubate or ventilate (if necessary).
4. Give oxygen 8–10 L/min by mask.
5. Pass a nasogastric tube (lubricated).
       0–3 years 12 FG
       4–10 years 14FG
6. Pay attention to circulation.
   ? give blood, SPPS, Haemaccel or N saline.
7. Take blood for appropriate investigations.
8. Consider 'blind' administration of IV glucose.

Note: Once an endotracheal tube is in place drugs used in
       paediatric CPR can be given by this route (exceptions
       are calcium preparations and sodium bicarbonate).

Endotracheal tube—for respiratory arrest
    use uncuffed
    size = $\dfrac{\text{age in years}}{4}$ + 4

       or size of child's little finger or nares

If intubation difficult
- oral airway
- bag and mask
- consider needle cricothyroidotomy
  14–16 g Jelco in caudal direction

Childhood common infectious diseases

Skin eruptions

Measles

If an acute exanthematous illness is not accompanied by a dry
cough and red eyes, it is unlikely to be measles.

Encephalitis (1 in 1500) is the complication of concern.

Rx: • no specific treatment
     • symptomatic, e.g. cough linctus
     • rest quietly
     • stay in bed until fever subsides
     • ample fluid intake

Prevention: combined vaccine at 12 months and 12 years.

Rubella

A minor illness in children but congenital rubella is still the most important cause of blindness and deafness in the neonate. It is completely preventable.

Post auricular lymphadenopathy and facial rash are features.

Rx: • symptomatic
     • rest quietly until well
     • paracetamol for fever and arthralgia

Prevention: combined vaccine at 12 months and 12 years if necessary.

Scarlet fever

Caused by the toxin of *Streptococcus pyogenes*. Treated with phenoxymethylpenicillin.

Viral exanthema (fourth disease)

Rubella-like rash, often misdiagnosed. Rash mainly confined to trunk. Child usually well or has mild symptoms.

Erythema infectiosum (fifth disease)

'Slapped face' disease is caused by a parvovirus. A maculopapular rash mainly on the limbs with bright red flushed cheeks. A mild illness but a problem in pregnancy.

Roseola infantum (exanthema subitum or sixth disease)

Viral infection of infancy—usually 6–18 months. Rash appears as high temperature subsides. Treatment is symptomatic.

Others

Mumps (epidemic parotitis)

Unilateral or bilateral inflammation of the parotid gland is usual: one parotid gland swells first and in 70% of cases the opposite side swells after one or two days. Relatively common complications include orchitis, aseptic meningitis (benign) and transient abdominal pain.

Rx: • symptomatic
     • paracetamol for fever
     • ample fluid intake and bed rest

Prevention: combined vaccine 12 months.

Pertussis (whooping cough)

Mainly occurs in infants under 2. Diagnosis is basically clinical—cough lasting 4–8 weeks with three distinct stages of the disease. Confirmed by culture.

Note: Chlamydia respiratory infection can cause a 'pseudopertussis' type of illness.

Rx: • symptomatic
        (cough mixtures are ineffective)
     • erythromycin estolate
        40–50 mg/kg/day (o) in four divided doses for 14 days, especially in catarrhal stage

Prevention: triple antigen 2 months, 4 months, 6 months, 18 months, prior to school.

Chickenpox (varicella)

Clinical features
Onset
• Children: no prodrome
• Adults: prodrome (myalgia, fever, headaches) for 2–3 days

Rash
• Centripetal distribution, including oral mucosa
• Scalp lesions can become infected
• 'Cropping' phenomenon: vesicles, papules, crusting lesions present together
• Pruritic

Treatment
Treatment is symptomatic and usually no specific therapy is required.

• reassurance that lesions do not usually scar
• rest in bed until feeling well
• give paracetamol for fever
• drink ample fluids; keep diet simple
• calamine lotion to relieve itching
• daily bathing with sodium bicarbonate (half a cup added) or Pinetarsol (preferable) in bath water

- avoid scratching
- antihistamines for itching if necessary
- acyclovir in immuno-compromised host
- some prescribe acyclovir to patients over 15 years (to avoid complications including scarring)

Chloasma

See Melasma on page 255.

Chronic obstructive airways disease

Chronic bronchitis and emphysema should be considered together as both these conditions usually coexist to some degree in each patient. An alternative, and preferable, term—chronic obstructive airway or pulmonary disease (COAD)—is used to cover chronic bronchitis and emphysema with chronic airflow limitation.

Factors in causation

- cigarette smoking
- air pollution
- airway infection
- familial factors
- alpha$_1$ antitrypsin deficiency (emphysema)

Clinical features

Symptoms

- onset in 5th or 6th decade
- excessive cough
- sputum production (chronic bronchitis)
- dyspnoea (chronic airflow limitation)
- wheeze (chronic bronchitis)
- susceptibility to colds

Investigations

Chest X-ray: can be normal (even with advanced disease) but characteristic changes occur late in disease.

Pulmonary function tests:

- peak expiratory flow rate—low with minimal response to bronchodilator
- ratio FEV_1/FVC—reduced with minimal response to bronchodilator
- gas transfer coefficient of CO is low if significant emphysema

Blood gases:

- may be normal
- Pa CO_2 ↑; PaO_2 ↓ (advanced disease)

Management

Advice to the patient

- If you smoke, you must stop: this is the key to management.
- Avoid places with polluted air and other irritants, such as smoke, paint fumes and fine dust.
- Go for walks in clean, fresh air.
- A warm dry climate is preferable to a cold damp place (if prone to infections).
- Get adequate rest.
- Avoid contact with people who have colds and flu.

Physiotherapy

Refer to a physiotherapist for chest physiotherapy, breathing exercises and an aerobic physical exercise program.

Drug therapy

Consider the use of bronchodilators, e.g. inhaled β_2 agonists and ipratropium bromide and corticosteroids, because of associated (often unsuspected) asthma. A carefully monitored trial of these drugs with a peak flow meter is recommended.

A trial of oral corticosteroids (prednisolone 30–40 mg (o) daily for two weeks) with FEV_1, measurements can also be assessed.

Antibiotics: Although not routinely used, the prompt use of antibiotics for acute episodes of infection is important. Patients who benefit should be instructed to commence antibiotics as soon as they develop an infection and notice their sputum turn yellow or green.

The antibiotics of choice are:

amoxycillin 500 mg (o) tds for five days

or

cefaclor 500 mg (o) tds for five days

or

doxycycline 100 mg (o) daily for five days

A sputum micro and culture may help to identify those patients with organisms resistant to antibiotics.

Other treatment

- Annual influenza vaccine
- Consider home oxygen therapy for advanced cases with persistent hypoxia at rest
- Consider pneumococcal vaccine

Acute exacerbation of COAD

- use nebulised salbutamol or terbutaline + ipratropium bromide, four times daily

- use corticosteroids (can be ceased when attack settles)
  start with prednisolone 50 mg (o) daily
                    or
  if oral medication not tolerated
  dexamethasone 4 mg IV, six hourly
                    or
  hydrocortisone 100 mg IV, six hourly

Cold sores

- Apply an ice cube to site for five minutes every 60 minutes (first 12 hours).
- Apply idoxuridine 0.5% preparation hourly at onset.
                    or
  povidone-iodine 10% cold sore paint: on swab stick four times a day until disappearance

Common cold (acute coryza)

This highly infectious URTI, which is often mistakenly referred to as 'the flu', produces a mild systemic upset and prominent nasal symptoms.

Typical clinical features

- malaise and tiredness
- sore, runny nose
- sneezing
- sore throat
- slight fever

Other possible symptoms:

- headache
- hoarseness
- cough

The watery nasal discharge becomes thick and purulent in about 24 hours and persists for up to a week. Secondary bacterial infection is uncommon.

Management

Advice to the patient includes:

- rest 24–48 hours if feeling weak
- aspirin or paracetamol (up to 8 tablets a day for adults)
- steam inhalations using menthol or Friar's balsam
- gargle aspirin in lemon juice for a sore throat
- vitamin C—2 g a day for 5–7 days
- increase fluid intake
- stop smoking (if applicable)
- use cough drops or syrup for a dry troublesome cough

Communication skills

Much of the art of general practice lies in the ability to communicate.

The Victorian Medical Board lists poor communication as the most important factor causing complaints from patients and relatives against doctors.

Important positive doctor behaviour

At first contact:

- Make the patient feel comfortable.
- Be 'unhurried' and relaxed.
- Focus firmly on the patient.
- Use open-ended questions where possible.
- Make appropriate reassuring gestures.

Active listening

Listening is the single most important skill.
Listening includes four essential elements:

- checking facts
- checking feelings
- encouragement
- reflection

Listen with understanding, in a relaxed attentive silence. Use reflective questions, such as:

- 'You seem very sad today.'
- 'You seem upset about your husband.'
- 'It seems you're having trouble coping.'
- 'You seem to be telling me that . . . '
- 'Your main concern seems to me to . . . '

Communicating strategies

- modify language
- avoid jargon
- clear explanations
- clear treatment instructions
- evaluate patient's understanding
- summarise and repeat
- avoid uncertainty
- avoid inappropriate reassurance
- appropriate referral (if necessary)
- ensure patient is satisfied
- obtain informed consent

Summary

- A fundamental prerequisite for effective communication is listening; this includes not only hearing the words but under-

standing the meaning in addition to being sensitive and compassionate.
- Undertake the strategies of paraphrasing and summarising during the consultation to emphasise that listening is occurring and to provide a basis for defining the problems.
- Associated with listening is the observation of the non-verbal language which may in many instances be the most significant part of the communication process.
- Good communication between doctors and patients decreases the chance of dissatisfaction with professional services, even with failed therapy, and the likelihood of litigation.

Conjunctivitis

Bacterial conjunctivitis

Features

- purulent, lids stuck in morning
- starts in one eye, spreads to other
- usually bilateral purulent discharge
- negative fluorescein staining

Swab for smear and culture with

- hyperacute or severe purulent conjunctivitis
- prolonged infection
- neonates

Management

Limit the spread by avoiding close contact with others, use of separate towels and good ocular hygiene.

Mild cases

Mild cases may resolve with saline irrigation of the eyelids and conjunctiva but may last up to 14 days if untreated. An antiseptic eye drop such as propamidine isethionate 0.1% (Brolene) 1–2 drops 6–8 hourly for 5–7 days can be used.

More severe cases

chloramphenicol 0.5% eye drops, 1 to 2 hourly for 2 days, decrease to 4 times a day for another 7 days (maximum 10 days—cases of aplastic anaemia have been reported with long-term use)
Use also chloramphenicol 1% eye ointment each night
    or preferably
polymyxin B sulphate 5000 units/mL with either chloramphenicol 0.5% or neomycin 2.5 mg/mL, 1 to 2 drops hourly, decreasing to 6 hourly as the infection improves.

Specific organisms:

> Pseudomonas and other coliforms: use topical gentamicin and tobramycin.
> *Neisseria gonorrhoea:* use appropriate systemic antibiotics.

Viral conjunctivitis

Features

- very contagious
- usually due to adenovirus
- tends to occur in epidemics (pink eye)
- 2–3 week course
- starts in one eye, spreads to other
- scant watery discharge
- may be tiny pale lymphoid follicles
- preauricular lymph node

Treatment

- Limit cross-infection by appropriate rules of hygiene and patient education.
- Treatment is symptomatic, e.g. cool compress and topical lubricants (artificial tear preparations).
- Do not pad.
- Watch for secondary bacterial infection.

Primary herpes simplex infection

- a follicular conjunctivitis
- 50% have lid or corneal ulcers (diagnostic)
- dendritic ulceration with fluorescein (in some)

Treatment of herpes simplex keratitis

- acyclovir 3% ointment, 5 times a day for 14 days or for at least 3 days after healing
- atropine 1% 1 drop, 12 hourly, for the duration of treatment will prevent reflex spasm of the pupil (specialist supervision)
- debridement by a consultant

Allergic conjunctivitis

Includes:

- vernal (hay fever) conjunctivitis, and
- contact hypersensitivity reactions

Vernal (hay fever) conjunctivitis

Treatment:

Tailor treatment to the degree of symptoms. Antihistamines (oral) may be required but symptomatic measures usually suffice.

- Use sodium cromoglycate 2% drops, 1–2 drops per eye 4 times daily.
- Artificial tear preparations may give adequate symptomatic relief.

Contact hypersensitivity

Treatment:

- Withdraw the causative agent.
- Apply normal saline compresses.
- If not responding, refer for possible corticosteroid therapy.

Chlamydial conjunctivitis

Chlamydial conjunctivitis is encountered in three common situations:

- neonatal infection (first 1–2 weeks)
- young patient with associated venereal disease
- isolated Aboriginal people with trachoma

Systemic antibiotic treatment:

> Neonates: erythromycin for 3 weeks
> Children aged 7 or less: erythromycin for 3 weeks
> Adults: doxycycline 100 mg bd for 3 weeks

Constipation

Definition

Constipation is the difficult passage of small hard stools. It has also been defined as infrequent bowel actions or a feeling of unsatisfied emptying of the bowel. However, the emphasis is on the consistency of the stool rather than on the frequency of defecation.

Colorectal cancer must be ruled out in adults.

Idiopathic (functional) constipation

The commonest type is simple constipation, which is essentially related to a faulty diet and bad habits. Avery-Jones, who defined the disorder, describes it as being due to one or more of the following causes:

- faulty diet
- neglect of the call to stool
- unfavourable living and working conditions
- lack of exercise
- travel

Management in children

(differentiate from encopresis)
Rule out Hirschsprung's disease and anal fissure in infants.

- Encourage relaxed child–parent interaction with toilet training, e.g. 'after breakfast habit' training.
- Establish an empty bowel: remove any impacted faeces with microenemas, e.g. Microlax.
- Advice for (parents of) children over 18 months:
  — drink ample fluids each day.
  — get regular exercise, e.g. walking, running, outside games or sport.
  — provide high-fibre foods, e.g. high-fibre cereals, wholegrain bread, fresh fruit with skins left on where possible, dried fruits such as sultanas, apricots or prunes, fresh vegetables.
- Use a pharmaceutical preparation as a last resort to achieve regularity:
  first line: bulk-producing agent, e.g. Normacol plus
  second line: osmotic laxative, e.g. lactulose:
        1–5 years: 5 mL bd
        6–12 years: 10 mL bd
        > 12 years: 15 mL bd

Management in adults

- similar principles as above
- patient education, including 'good habit'
- adequate exercise
- plenty of fluids, e.g. water, fruit juice
- avoid laxatives and codeine compounds
- optimal bulk diet
- foods with bulk forming properties (least to most): potato, banana, cauliflower, peas, cabbage, lettuce, apple, carrot, wheat fibre, bran
- fruits with natural laxatives include prunes, figs, rhubarb, apricots
- cereals with wheat fibre and bran

If unsuccessful:

- bulk producing agent, e.g. ispaghula (Fybogel, Agiolax), adults: 1 sachet in water bd

Avoid stimulant laxatives except for short sharp bursts.

Colorectal cancer

Symptoms

- blood in the stools
- mucus

Table 15 *Therapeutic agents to treat constipation (with examples)*

Hydrophilic bulk-forming agents
 psyllium mucilloid (Agiofibe, Metamucil)
 sterculia (Granocol, Normacol)
 ispaghula (Agiolax, Fybogel)
 methylcellulose (Cellulone)
 wheat bran

Stimulant (irritant) laxatives
 phenolphthalein (Laxettes)
 senna (Senokot)
 cascara
 castor oil
 bisacodyl (Durolax)

Osmotic laxatives
 magnesium sulphate (Epsom salts)
 magnesium hydroxide (Milk of Magnesia)
 lactulose
 mannitol

Stool-softening agents
 liquid paraffin (Agarol)
 dioctyl sodium sulphosuccinate (Coloxyl)
 glycerine suppositories
 sorbital/sodium compounds (Microlax)

- recent change in bowel habits (constipation more common than diarrhoea)
- bowel leakage when flatus passed
- unsatisfactory defecation (the mass is interpreted as faeces)
- abdominal pain (colicky) or discomfort (if obstructing)
- rectal discomfort
- symptoms of anaemia

Investigations

- faecal and occult blood (limited value)
- sigmoidoscopy, especially flexible sigmoidoscopy
- barium enema (accurate as a double contrast study) but may miss tumours
- colonoscopy: essential if suspicion on clinical grounds remains and barium enema normal (more useful if rectal bleeding)

Screening

Faecal occult blood testing is not currently recommended. Colonoscopy is recommended for those at risk and, in addition, flexible sigmoidoscopy and rectal biopsy for those with ulcerative colitis. Has a good prognosis if diagnosed early.

Management

Early surgical excision is the treatment, with the method depending on the site and extent of the carcinoma.

Contact dermatitis

Acute contact (exogenous) dermatitis can be either *irritant* or *allergic*.
Features:

- itchy, inflamed skin
- red and swollen
- papulovesicular

Irritant contact dermatitis

Caused by primary irritants, e.g. acids, alkalis, detergents, soaps.

Allergic contact dermatitis (about 80%)

Caused by allergens that provoke an allergic reaction in some individuals only—most people can handle the chemicals without undue effect. This allergic group also includes photo-contact allergens.

Common allergens

- ingredients in cosmetics, e.g. perfumes, preservatives
- topical antibiotics, e.g. neomycin
- topical anaesthetics, e.g. benzocaine
- topical antihistamines
- plants: (skin of mango cross reacts with these) rhus, grevillea, primula, poison ivy
- metal salts, e.g. nickel sulphate, chromate
- dyes
- perfumes
- rubber/latex
- resins
- coral

Management

- determine cause and remove it
- if acute with blistering, apply Burow's compresses
- oral prednisolone for severe cases
  60 mg reducing by 10 mg every 3 days
- topical corticosteroid cream
- oral antihistamines

Cough

Table 16 *Cough: diagnostic strategy model*

Q.	Probability diagnosis
A.	Upper respiratory infection
	Postnasal drip
	Acute bronchitis
	Chronic bronchitis

Q. Serious disorders not to be missed
A. Cardiovascular
  • left ventricular failure
  Neoplasia
  • carcinoma of lung
  Severe infections
  • tuberculosis
  • pneumonia
  • influenza
  • lung abscess
  • HIV infection
  Asthma
  Cystic fibrosis
  Foreign body
  Pneumothorax

Q. Pitfalls (often missed)
A. Gastro-oesophageal reflux (nocturnal)
  Smoking (children)
  Bronchiectasis
  Whooping cough
  Interstitial lung disorders
  Sarcoidosis

Q. Seven masquerades checklist
A.

Depression	—
Diabetes	—
Drugs	√
Anaemia	—
Thyroid disease	—
Spinal dysfunction	—
UTI	—

Q. Is the patient trying to tell me something?
A. Anxiety and habit (possible)

General pitfalls

- Attributing cough due to bronchial carcinoma in a smoker to 'smoker's cough'.
- Overlooking TB, especially in the elderly, by equating symptoms to old age, bronchitis or even smoking.

- Overlooking the fact that bronchial carcinoma can develop in a patient with other pulmonary conditions such as chronic bronchitis.
- Being slow to order a chest X-ray.

Cough in children

Common causes are:

- asthma
- acute URTIs
- allergic rhinitis

Disorders not to be missed are:

- asthma
- bronchiolitis
- cystic fibrosis
- inhaled foreign body
- tracheo-oesophageal fistula

Several clinicians describe the catarrhal child syndrome as the commonest cause of cough. This refers to children who develop a postnasal drip following acute respiratory infection and allergic rhinitis.

Bronchial carcinoma

Lung cancer accounts for 35% of cancer deaths in men and 21% of cancer deaths in women (rapidly rising) in the United States, with cigarette smoking being the most common cause of lung cancer in both sexes.

Clinical features

- most present between 50 and 70 years
- only 10–25% asymptomatic at time of diagnosis
- if symptomatic—usually advanced and not resectable

Local symptoms

- cough (42%)
- chest pain (22%)
- wheezing (15%)
- haemoptysis (7%)
- dyspnoea (5%)

General

- anorexia, malaise
- weight loss

Others

- hoarseness
- symptoms from metastases

Investigations
- chest X-ray
- computerised tomography
- fibreoptic bronchoscopy

Management
Refer for possible surgical resection.

Bronchiectasis

Clinical features
- chronic cough—worse on waking
- profuse purulent offensive yellow-green sputum (advanced cases)

Investigations
- chest X-ray (normal or bronchial changes)
- sputum examination—for resistant pathogens
                        —to exclude TB
- CT scan: can show bronchial wall thickening
- bronchograms: very unpleasant and used only if diagnosis in doubt or possible localised disease amenable to surgery (rare)

Management
- explanation and preventive advice
- postural drainage, e.g. lie over side of bed with head and thorax down for 10–20 minutes 3 times a day
- antibiotics according to organism—it is important to eradicate infection to halt the progress of the disease
- bronchodilators if evidence of bronchospasm

Tuberculosis

Pulmonary tuberculosis may be symptomless and detected by mass X-ray screening.

Typical clinical features

Respiratory symptoms
- cough
- sputum: initially mucoid, later purulent
- haemoptysis
- dyspnoea (especially with complications)
- pleuritic pain

General (usually insidious)
- anorexia
- fatigue
- weight loss
- fever (low grade)
- night sweats

Physical examination

- may be no respiratory signs or may be signs of fibrosis, consolidation or cavitation (amphoric breathing)
- finger clubbing

Investigations

- chest X-ray
- micro and culture sputum (for tubercle bacilli)
- ESR
- tuberculin test (misleading if previous BCG vaccination)

Management

Tuberculosis is a notifiable disease and must be reported to state (and local) health departments. Hospitalisation for the initial therapy of pulmonary TB is not necessary in most patients. Monthly follow-up is recommended including sputum smear and culture. Multiple drug therapy is initiated primarily to guard against the existence and/or emergence of resistant organisms. Standard initial therapy consists of rifampicin + isoniazid + pyrazinamide daily for at least 2 months, followed by rifampicin + isoniazid for 4 months if the organism is susceptible to these drugs. If isoniazid resistance is suspected, ethambutol or streptomycin (with care) is added.

Symptomatic treatment of cough

Symptomatic treatment of cough should be reserved for patients who have acute self-limiting causes of cough, especially an acute viral infection. The recommended mixture should be tailored to the patient's individual requirements. These mixtures should be used only in the short term, e.g.:

- cough suppressant for dry cough
- pholcodine 1 mg/mL, 15 mL (o) 3 to 4 times daily

  or
- codeine 5 mg/mL, 5 mL (o) 3 to 6 hourly

'Cracked' and dry lips

- Use a lip balm with sunscreen, e.g. Sunsense 15 lip balm.
- Women can use a creamy lipstick.
- Vaseline helps.

'Cracked' hands and fingers

Usually associated with atopic dermatitis or very dry skin.
Hand protection:

- Avoid domestic or occupational duties that involve contact with irritants and detergents.

- Wear protective work gloves: cotton-lined PVC gloves.
- Use soap substitutes, e.g. Cetaphil lotion, Dove.
- Apply 2–5% salicyclic acid and 10% liq picis carb in white soft paraffin ointment

  or

- Corticosteroid ointment: class II–III.

'Cracked' heels

- Soak feet for 30 minutes in warm water containing an oil such as Alpha-Keri or Derma Oil.
- Pat dry, then apply a cream such as Nutraplus (10% urea) or Eulactol heel balm.
- For severe cases use sorbolene cream with 20% glycerol and 30% urea (test skin sensitivity first).

Cramps (nocturnal cramps in legs)

Precautions: treat cause (if known), e.g. tetanus, drugs, sodium depletion, hypothyroidism.

Physical

- muscle stretching and relaxation exercises: stretch calf for three minutes before retiring then rest in chair with the feet out horizontally to the floor with cushion under tendoachilles (10 minutes)
- massage and heat to affected muscles
- try to keep bedclothes off feet and lower part of legs—use a doubled-up pillow at the foot of the bed
- tonic water before retiring may help

Drugs

- quinine sulphate 300 mg nocte

  or

- biperiden 2–4 mg nocte

Croup

Clinical features

- 6 months to 6 years of age, occasionally older
- loud inspiratory, increased if upset, harsh brassy cough
- viral cause—mostly Parainfluenza 1

Treatment

- get child to inhale humidified steaming air, e.g. in bathroom with hot water taps running (minor obstruction usually resolves after 30–60 minutes)
- special nebulisers can be hired
- paracetamol mixture 4–6 hourly
- no place for cough medicine

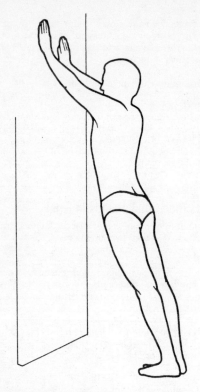

Leg-stretching exercise for cramp

- support child on pillows
- keep child calm

If significant laryngeal obstruction:

- admit to hospital (mist tents not recommended)
- adrenaline: 5 ampoules 1:1000 solution in a nebuliser run with oxygen 8L/min
- oxygen
- dexamethasone IM 0.2 mg/kg
- nurse under observation: some need intubation

Crying baby

Checklist: hunger; wet or soiled nappy; teething; colic; infection; loneliness; or seeking attention.

D

Dandruff

Dandruff (pityriasis capitis) is mainly a physiological process, the result of normal desquamation of scale from the scalp. It is most prevalent in adolescence and worse around the age of 20.

Treatment

Shampoos:
zinc pyrithione, e.g. Dan-Gard
or
selenium sulphide, e.g. Selsun
Method: massage into scalp, leave for 5 minutes, rinse thoroughly—twice weekly

Persistent dandruff with severe flaking and itching indicates seborrhoeic dermatitis or psoriasis.

Treatment

coal tar + salicyclic acid compound (Sebitar) shampoo
or
Ionil T plus shampoo
Method: as above, followed by Sebi Rinse or ketoconazole (Nizoral) shampoo

If persistent, especially itching, and Nizoral shampoo ineffective use a corticosteroid, e.g. betamethasone scalp lotion.

Deafness and hearing loss

Deafness is defined as impairment of hearing, regardless of its severity. It is a major community health problem requiring a high index of suspicion for diagnosis, especially in children. Deafness may be conductive, sensorineural (SND) or a combination of both (mixed).

- Deafness occurs at all ages but is more common in the elderly.
- The threshold of normal hearing is from 0 to 20 decibels (dB), about the loudness of a soft whisper.
- Degrees of hearing impairment
  mild = loss of 20 dB (soft spoken voice)
  moderate = loss of 40 dB (normal spoken voice)

severe = loss of 60 dB (loud spoken voice)
profound = loss of over 60 dB (shout)
- People who have worked in high noise levels (> 85 dB) are more than twice as likely to be deaf.
- There is a related incidence of tinnitus with deafness.

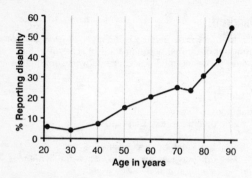

Prevalence of hearing problems with increasing age

Deafness in children

Deafness in childhood is relatively common and often goes unrecognised. A mother who believes that her child may be deaf is rarely wrong in this suspicion.

Screening

The aim of screening should be to recognise every deaf child by the age of 8 months to 1 year—before the vital time for learning speech is wasted.
Optimal screening times:

- 8 to 9 months
- school entry

No child is too young for audiological assessment. Informal office tests are inadequate to exclude hearing loss.

Otosclerosis

Features

- a progressive disease
- develops in the 20s and 30s
- family history (autosomal dominant)
- female preponderance

Table 17 *Deafness and hearing loss: diagnostic strategy model (modified)*

Q. *Probability diagnosis*
A. Impacted cerumen
   Serous otitis media
   Otitis externa
   Congenital (children)
   Presbyacusis

Q. *Serious disorders not to be missed*
A. Neoplasia
   • acoustic neuroma
   • temporal lobe tumours (bilateral)
   • otic tumours
   Severe infections
   • generalised infections, e.g. mumps
   • syphilis
   Perforated tympanic membrane
   Cholesteatoma
   Perilymphatic fistula (post-stapedectomy)

Q. *Pitfalls (often missed)*
A. Foreign body
   Temporal bone fracture
   Otosclerosis
   Barotrauma
   Noise-induced deafness

   Rarities
   Paget's disease of bone

• affects the footplate of the stapes
• conductive hearing loss
• SND may be present
• impedance audiometry shows characteristic features

Management

• stapedectomy (approximately 90% effective)

Noise-induced hearing loss

Features

• onset of tinnitus after work in excessive noise
• speech seems muffled soon after work
• temporary loss initially but becomes permanent if noise exposure continues
• high-frequency loss on audiogram

Sounds exceeding 85 dB are potentially injurious to the cochlea, especially with prolonged exposures. Common sources of injurious noise are industrial machinery, weapons and loud music.

Hearing aids

Hearing aids are most useful in conductive deafness. This is due to the relative lack of distortion, making amplification simple. In SND the dual problem of recruitment and the hearing loss for higher frequencies may make hearing aids less satisfactory.

Depression

Depressive illness, which is probably *the* greatest masquerade of general practice, is one of the commonest illnesses in medicine and is often confused with other illnesses.

Many episodes of depression are transient and should be regarded as normal but 10% of the population have significant depressive illness.

Major depression

DSM-III-R Diagnostic Criteria
for Major Depression
At least 5 of the following symptoms for
2 weeks
(criterion 1 or 2 essential)

1. Depressed mood
2. Loss of interest or pleasure
3. Significant appetite or weight loss or gain (usually poor appetite)
4. Insomnia or hypersomnia (usually early morning waking)
5. Psychomotor agitation and retardation
6. Fatigue or loss of energy
7. Feelings of worthlessness or excessive guilt
8. Impaired thinking or concentration; indecisiveness
9. Suicidal thoughts/thoughts of death

Minor depression

Minor depression is basically a condition where fluctuations of symptoms occur with some vague somatic symptoms and a transient lowering of mood that can respond to environmental influences. These patients usually respond in time to simple psychotherapy, reassurance and support.

Depression in the elderly

Depression can have bizarre features in the elderly and may be misdiagnosed as dementia or psychosis. Agitated depression is the most frequent type of depression in the aged. Features may include histrionic behaviour, delusions and disordered thinking.

Depression in children

Sadness is common in children but depression also occurs and is characterised by feelings of helplessness, worthlessness and despair. Parents and doctors both tend to be unaware of depression in children.

Major depression in children and adolescents may be diagnosed using the same criteria as for adults, namely loss of interest in usual activities and the presence of a sad or irritable mood, persisting for two weeks or more.

Management

Important considerations from the outset are:

• Is the patient a suicide risk?
• Does the patient require inpatient assessment?
• Is referral to a specialist psychiatrist indicated?

If the symptoms are major and the patient appears in poor health or is a suicide risk, referral is appropriate.

The basic treatments are:

• Psychotherapy, including education, reassurance and support. All patients require minor psychotherapy. More sophisticated techniques such as cognitive or behavioural therapy can be used for selected patients. Cognitive therapy involves teaching patients new ways of positive thinking, which have to be relevant and achievable for the patient.
• Pharmacological agents.
• Electroconvulsive treatment.

Note: Reassurance and support are needed for all depressed patients.

Useful guidelines

• mild depression: psychotherapy alone may suffice but keep medication in mind
• moderate to severe depression: psychotherapy plus antidepressants

Recommended reading for patients

Paul Hauck, *Overcoming Depression*. The Westminster Press, London, 1987.

Antidepressant medication

The initial choice of an antidepressant depends on the age and sex of the patient and the side effect profile. The following are all first line drugs.

Tricyclic antidepressants

I. amitriptyline and imipramine

- the first generation tricyclics
- the most sedating: valuable if marked anxiety and insomnia
- strongest anticholinergic side effects, e.g. constipation, blurred vision, prostatism

II. nortriptyline, desipramine, doxepin, dothiepin

- less sedating and anticholinergic activity
- nortriptyline is the least hypotensive of the tricyclics

Dosage: 50–75 mg (o) nocte, increasing every 2 to 3 days to 150 mg (o) nocte by day 7

If no response after 2 to 3 weeks, increase by 25–50 mg daily at 2 to 3 week intervals (depending on adverse effects) to 200–250 mg (o) nocte.
Trial for 6 weeks.

Tetracyclic antidepressants

Mianserin 30–60 mg (o) nocte increasing to 60–120 mg (o) nocte by day 7.

Selective serotonin reuptake inhibitors
e.g. fluoxetine, paroxetine, sertraline

Fluoxetine & paroxetine 20 mg (o) mane

This dose is usually sufficient for most patients.

If no response after 2 to 3 weeks, increase by 20 mg at 2 to 3 week intervals to 40–80 mg (o) daily in divided doses.

Sertraline, 50 mg (o) daily, starting dose: can increase up to 200 mg daily.

These new drugs have a similar efficacy profile to the tricyclics.

They should not be used with MAOIs or the tricyclics.

Moclobemide

Moclobemide 150 mg (o) bd

If no response after 2–3 weeks, increase by 50 mg daily to maximum 300 mg (o) bd.

- This is a reversible MAOI which is less toxic than the irreversible MAOIs.
- It has minimal interaction with tyramine-containing foodstuffs, so that no dietary restrictions are necessary.

Notes about antidepressants

- Tricyclics can be given once daily (usually in the evening).

- There is a delay in onset of action of 1 to 2 weeks after a therapeutic dose (equivalent to 150 mg imipramine at least) is reached.
- Each drug should have a clinical trial at an adequate dose for at least 4–6 weeks before treatment is changed.
- The SSRIs are probably now the first line drugs of choice and the tricyclics second line.
- Consider referral if there is a failed (adequate) trial.
- Full recovery may take up to 6 weeks or longer (in those who respond).
- Continue treatment at maintenance levels for at least 6 to 9 months. There is a high risk of relapse. Lifelong treatment may be necessary.
- MAOIs are often the drugs of choice for neurotic depression or atypical depression.

Electroconvulsive therapy (ECT)

ECT is safe, effective and rapidly acting. It is anticipated that the new generation treatment units will improve the management of major depression.

The usual course is 6–8 treatments over three weeks. Tricyclic antidepressants can be used in combination with ECT and after ECT to prevent relapse.

Dermatitis/eczema

The terms 'dermatitis' and 'eczema' are synonymous and denote an inflammatory epidermal rash, acute or chronic, characterised by vesicles (acute stage), redness, weeping, oozing, crusting, scaling and itch.

Atopic dermatitis (eczema)

Criteria for diagnosis
- itch
- typical morphology and distribution
- dry skin
- history of atopy
- chronic relapsing dermatitis

Distribution

The typical distribution of atopic dermatitis changes as the patient grows older. In infants the rash appears typically on the cheeks of the face, the folds of the neck and scalp. It may then spread to the limbs and groins. The change from infancy to older children is presented in the figures below.

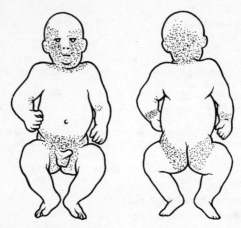

Relative distribution of atopic dermatitis in infants

Treatment

Advice to parents of affected children:

- Avoid soap. Use a bland bath oil in the bath and aqueous cream as a soap substitute.
- Older children should have short, tepid showers.
- Avoid rubbing and scratching—use gauze bandages with hand splints for infants.
- Avoid sudden changes of temperature.
- Wear light, soft, loose clothes, preferably made of cotton. Cotton clothing should be worn next to the skin.
- Avoid wool next to the skin.
- Avoid dusty conditions and sand, especially sandpits.
- Avoid contact with people with 'sores', especially herpes.

Medication

Mild atopic dermatitis

- soap substitutes, such as aqueous cream
- emollients (choose from
  — aqueous cream
  — sorbolene with 10% glycerol $\Big\}$ if not too dry
  — bath oils, e.g. Alpha-Keri
- 1% hydrocortisone (if not responding to above)

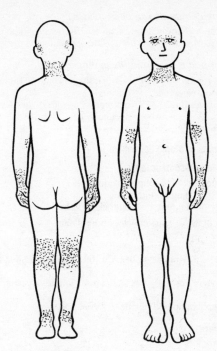

Atopic dermatitis in children

Moderate atopic dermatitis

- as for mild
- topical corticosteroids (twice daily)
  — vital for active areas
  — moderate strength, e.g. fluorinated, to trunk and limbs
  — weaker strength, e.g. 1% hydrocortisone, to face and flexures
- oral antihistamines at night for itch

Severe dermatitis

- as for mild and moderate eczema
- potent topical corticosteroids to worse areas (consider occlusive dressings)
- consider hospitalisation
- systemic corticosteroids (rarely used)

Weeping dermatitis (an acute phase)

This often has crusts due to exudate. Burow's solution diluted to 1 in 20 or 1 in 10 can be used to soak affected areas.

General points of dermatitis management

Acute weeping   →   wet dressings (saline or Burow's)
Acute, non weeping   →   creams
Dry, scaly lesions   →   ointments, with or without occlusion
Lichenified   →   pastes

Other types of atopic dermatitis

Nummular (discoid) eczema

- chronic, red, coin-shaped plaques
- crusted, scaling and itchy
- mainly on the legs, also buttocks and trunk

Treatment as for classical atopic dermatitis.

Pityriasis alba

- These are white patches on the face of children and adolescents.
- Can occur on the neck and upper limbs, occasionally on trunk.
- Full repigmentation occurs eventually.

Treatment

- reassurance
- simple emollients
- restrict use of soap and washing
- may prescribe hydrocortisone ointment (rarely necessary)

Lichen simplex chronicus

- circumscribed thick plaques of lichenification
- caused by repeated rubbing and scratching of previously normal skin
- due to chronic itch of unknown cause

Treatment

- explanation
- refrain from scratching
- fluorinated corticosteroid ointment with plastic occlusion or tar paste, e.g. liquor picis carbonis 4%, Lassar's paste to 100%

Dyshydrotic dermatitis (pompholyx)

- itching vesicles on fingers
- may be larger vesicles on palms and soles
- commonly affects sides of digits and palms

Treatment
- as for atopic dermatitis
- potent fluorinated corticosteroids topically
- oral corticosteroids may be necessary

Asteatotic dermatitis

This is the common often unrecognised very itchy dermatitis that occurs in the elderly, with a dry 'crazy paving' pattern, especially on the legs. It is a form of eczema that occurs in the elderly subjected to considerable scrubbing and bathing. Other predisposing factors include low humidity (winter, central heating) and diuretics.

Treatment
- Avoid scrubbing with soaps.
- Use aqueous cream and a soap substitute.
- Apply topical steroid diluted in white soft paraffin.

Diabetes mellitus

The classical symptoms of uncontrolled diabetes are:
- polyuria (every hour or so)
- polydypsia
- loss of weight (type 1)
- tiredness and fatigue
- characteristic breath
- propensity for infections, especially of the skin and genitals

Note: For every diagnosed diabetic there is an undiagnosed diabetic.

Diagnosis of diabetes:
Fasting plasma glucose $\geq$ 7.8 mmol/L in any person
Random plasma glucose $\geq$ 11.1 mmol/L in a symptomatic person

In symptomatic patients, a single elevated reading

In asymptomatic or mildly symptomatic patients, the diagnosis is made on two separate elevated readings including a fasting test.

Management

Both type I (IDDM) and type II (NIDDM)
- patient education, reassurance and support
- consider diabetic educator, dietitian
- dietary control vital
- exercise also very important
- referral to ophthalmologist

The importance of diet

Type I patients often require three meals and regular snacks each day.

Type II patients usually require less food intake and restriction of total intake.

Principles of dietary management

• keep to a regular nutritious diet
• achieve ideal body weight
• reduce calories (kilojoules), i.e.
>   added sugar
>   dietary fat
• increase proportions of vegetables, fresh fruit, cereal foods

Insulin dependent diabetes mellitus

Preferred insulin regimens.

1. A short-acting or neutral (regular) insulin before each meal with a long-acting insulin before the evening meal or before bed.
2. A 'split and mix' of short-acting and long-acting insulin (isophane or insulin zinc suspension), twice daily before breakfast and before the evening meal.

Maintenance insulin therapy requires an average daily insulin dose for adults of about 0.7 units ($\pm$ 0.3 units) per kg bodyweight, although it is wise to commence with a portion of this dose, e.g. 40 units a day.

Shared care with an endocrinologist is recommended.

Non insulin dependent diabetes mellitus

>   First-line treatment: * diet therapy
>   (especially if obese)   * exercise program

Most symptoms improve dramatically within 1 to 4 weeks on diet alone.

If unsatisfactory control persists after 3–6 months, consider adding one of the sulphonylurea oral agents (Table 18). Metformin can be added to a sulphonylurea or used alone, especially in the obese patient.

When oral hypoglycaemics fail (secondary failure) insulin is required.

Table 18 *Commonly prescribed oral hypoglycaemic agents*

Drug	Duration of action (hours)	Maximum effective daily dose	Notes
Sulphonylureas			Hypoglycaemia most common side effect
Tolbutamide	6–10	1 g, tds	Preferred in elderly
Gliclazide	6–12	160 mg, bd	Strong and equipotent,
Glipizide	6–12	20 mg, bd	caution in elderly
Glibenclamide	16–24	10 mg, bd	Potent—unsuitable first-line therapy in elderly
Chlorpropamide	24–72	500 mg, mane	Usually unsuitable in elderly
Biguanides			Reserved usually for obese
Metformin	6–10	1 g, tds or 850 mg bd	Side effects: GIT disturbances esp. diarrhoea Avoid in cardiac, renal and hepatic disease Vitamin B depletion

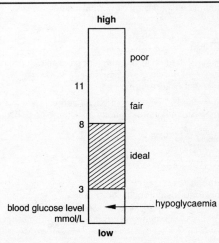

Control guidelines for diabetic management

Hypoglycaemia

Treatment of severe cases or patient unconscious

Treatment of choice

- 10–25 mL 50% Dextrose IV
  (instil rectally using the nozzle of the syringe if IV access difficult)

or

Alternative

- 1 mL glucagon IM the oral glucose

Admit to hospital if concerned (rarely necessary).

Diabetic ketoacidosis

This life-threatening emergency requires intensive management. It usually occurs during an illness (e.g. gastroenteritis) when insulin is omitted.

Management

- arrange urgent hospital admission
- give 10 units rapid-acting insulin IM (not SC)
- commence IV infusion of normal saline

Diarrhoea

Diarrhoea is defined as the frequent passage of loose or watery stools.

Essential features are:

- an increase in frequency of bowel action
- an increase in softness, fluidity or volume of stools

Probability diagnosis

Acute diarrhoea

Common causes are:

- gastroenteritis
  — bacterial • salmonella sp
  - *Campylobacter jejuni*
  - *Staphylococcus aureus* (food poisoning)

- *Clostridium perfringens*
- enteropathic *E. coli*
— viral   • rotavirus (50% of children hospital admissions)
- dietary indiscretions, e.g. binge eating
- antibiotic reactions

Chronic diarrhoea

Irritable bowel syndrome was the commonest cause of chronic diarrhoea in a UK study.

Drug reactions are also important.

Specific conditions

Pseudomembranous colitis (antibiotic-associated diarrhoea)

This colitis can be caused by the use of any antibiotic, especially clindamycin, lincomycin, ampicillin, the cephalosporins (an exception is vancomycin) and even metronidazole. It is usually due to an overgrowth of *Clostridium difficile* which produces a toxin that causes specific inflammatory lesions, sometimes with a pseudomembrane. It may occur, uncommonly, without antibiotic usage.

Features
- profuse watery diarrhoea
- abdominal cramping and tenesmus, maybe fever
- within 2 days of taking antibiotic (can start up to 4 to 6 weeks after usage)
- persists 2 weeks (up to 6) after ceasing antibiotic

Diagnosed by characteristic lesions on sigmoidoscopy and a tissue culture assay for *C. difficile* toxin.

Treatment
- cease antibiotic
- choice 1: metronidazole 400 mg (o) tds for 7–10 days
                            or
- choice 2: vancomycin 125 mg (o) qid for 10 days

Ischaemic colitis in the elderly

Due to atheromatous occlusion of mesenteric vessels.
Clinical features include:

- sharp abdominal pain in an elderly patient with bloody diarrhoea

or

- periumbilical pain and diarrhoea about 15–30 minutes after eating

---

Diarrhoea in children

The two commonest causes are infective gastroenteritis and antibiotic-induced diarrhoea.

Acute gastroenteritis

(See page   199.)

Chronic diarrhoea in children

Sugar intolerance

Synonyms: carbohydrate intolerance, lactose intolerance.

   The commonest offending sugar is lactose.

   Diarrhoea often follows acute gastroenteritis when milk is reintroduced into the diet. Stools may be watery, frothy, smell like vinegar and tend to excoriate the buttocks. They contain sugar.

Treatment

- Remove the offending sugar from the diet.
- Use milk preparations in which the lactose has been split to glucose and galactose by enzymes, or use soya protein.

Milk allergy

Not as common as lactose intolerance. Diarrhoea is related to taking a cow's milk formula and relieved when it is withdrawn.

Inflammatory bowel disorder

These disorders, which include Crohn's disease and ulcerative colitis, can occur in childhood.

Chronic enteric infection

Responsible organisms include *Salmonella sp*, *Campylobacter*, *Yersinia*, *Giardia lamblia* and *Entamoeba histolytica*. With persistent diarrhoea it is important to obtain microscopy of faeces and aerobic and anaerobic stool cultures. *Giardia lamblia* infestation is not an uncommon finding and can mimic coeliac disease.

Coeliac disease

Clinical features in childhood:

- usually presents at 9–18 months, but any age
- previously thriving infant
- anorexia, lethargy, irritability
- failure to thrive
- malabsorption: abdominal distension
- offensive frequent stools

Diagnosis: • elevated faecal fat
           • duodenal biopsy
Treatment: remove gluten from diet

Note: Coeliac disease can occur at any age.

Cystic fibrosis

Cystic fibrosis is the commonest of all inherited disorders (1 per 2500 live births). Clinical features include:

- family history
- presents in infancy
- meconium ileus in the neonate
- recurrent chest infections (cough and wheeze)
- failure to thrive
- malabsorption

Diagnosis: can be diagnosed antenatally (in utero)
            neonatal screening—immunoreactive trypsin
Treatment: pancreatic enzyme replacement for malabsorp-
            tion
            attention to respiratory problems

Acute gastroenteritis in adults

Features

- Invariably a self-limiting problem (1–3 days)
- Other meal sharers affected → food poisoning
- Consider dehydration, especially in the elderly
- Consider possibility of enteric fever

Traveller's diarrhoea

The symptoms are usually as above but very severe diarrhoea, especially if associated with blood or mucus, may be a feature of a more serious bowel infection such as amoebiasis. Most is caused by an *Escherichia coli* which produces a watery diarrhoea within 14 days of arrival in a foreign country.

It will respond to norfloxacin 400 mg (o) bd for 3 days.

Persistent traveller's diarrhoea

If there is a fever and blood or mucus in the stools, suspect amoebiasis. Giardiasis is characterised by abdominal cramps, flatulence and bubbly foul-smelling diarrhoea.

Principles of treatment

Acute diarrhoea

- maintenance of hydration
- antiemetic injection (for severe vomiting)
  prochlorperazine IM, statim
  　　　or
  metoclopramide IV, statim
- antidiarrhoeal preparations
  (avoid if possible: loperamide preferred)
  loperamide 2 mg caps (Imodium) 2 caps statim then 1 after each unformed stool (max: 8 caps/day)

Dietary advice to patient

It is vital that you starve but drink small amounts of clear fluids such as water, tea, lemonade and yeast extract (e.g. Marmite) until the diarrhoea settles. Then eat low-fat foods such as stewed apples, rice (boiled in water), soups, poultry, boiled potatoes, mashed vegetables, dry toast or bread, biscuits, most canned fruits, jam, honey, jelly, dried skim milk or condensed milk (reconstituted with water).

Avoid alcohol, coffee, strong tea, fatty foods, fried foods, spicy foods, raw vegetables, raw fruit (especially with hard skins), Chinese food, wholegrain cereals and cigarette smoking.

Antimicrobial drugs

It is advisable not to use these except where the following specific organisms are identified.

Pseudomembranous colitis See page 129.

Shigella dysentery (moderate to severe)
　　co-trimoxazole (DS) 1 tab (o) 12 hourly for 7–10 days
　　　　　　　　　　or
　　norfloxacin 400 mg (o) 12 hourly for 7–10 days

Campylobacter jejuni (if prolonged)
　　norfloxacin 400 mg (o) 12 hourly for 7 days
　　　　　　　　　or
　　erthromycin 500 mg (o) qid for 7 days (preferable)

Giardiasis
> tinidazole 2 g (o), single dose
> > or
> metronidazole 400 mg (o) tds for 7 days

Amoebiasis (intestinal)
> metronidazole 600–800 mg (o) tds for 6–10 days
>
> Specialist advice should be sought.

Special enteric infections (treatment regimes)

Typhoid/paratyphoid fever

- ciprofloxacin 500 mg (o) 12 hourly for 12 days
  If ciprofloxacin is contraindicated (e.g. in children) or not
  tolerated, then use:
- chloramphenicol 500–750 mg (o) 6 hourly for 14 days
  > or
- co-trimoxazole (DS) 1 tablet (o) 12 hourly for 14 days

Cholera

Antibiotic therapy reduces the volume and duration of
diarrhoea
> doxycycline 100 mg (o) 12 hourly for 4 days
> > or
> co-trimoxazole (DS) 1 tablet (o) 12 hourly for 4 days
> > or
> norfloxacin 400 mg (o) 12 hourly for 4 days

Inflammatory bowel disease

Inflammatory bowel disease should be considered when a
young person presents with:

- bloody diarrhoea and mucus
- colonic pain and fever
- extra-abdominal manifestations such as arthralgia, low back
  pain (spondyloarthropathy), eye problems (iridocyclitis).

Two important diseases are ulcerative colitis and Crohn's
disease which have equal sex incidence and can occur at any
age, but onset peaks between 20 and 40 years.
 Main symptom of ulcerative colitis is bloody diarrhoea and
of Crohn's disease is colicky abdominal pain.

Management principles for both diseases

- Treat under consultant supervision.
- Treatment of acute attacks depends on severity of the attack
  and the extent of the disease:
  — mild attacks: manage out of hospital
  — severe attacks: hospital, to attend to fluid and electrolyte
    balance.

- Pharmaceutical agents (the following can be considered):
    5-aminosalicylic acid derivatives (mainly UC)
    — sulfasalazine (mainstay) 1–2 g (o) 2–4 times daily
    — olsalazine; mesalazine
    corticosteroids — oral
                    — parenteral
                    — topical (rectal foam, suppositories or
                        enemas)
    immunosuppressive drugs, e.g. azathioprine
- Surgical treatment: reserve for complications.

Disturbed patients
Key facts
- Depression affects 15% of people over 65 and can mimic or complicate any other illness including delirium and dementia.
- Elderly patients with depression are at a high risk of suicide.
- Always consider the 4Ds
  - dementia
  - delirium (look for cause)
  - depression (maybe 'pseudodementia' in elderly)
  - drugs — toxicity
          — withdrawal

Dementia (chronic organic brain syndrome)

There is no cure for dementia—tender loving care is important.
    Tacrine and other drugs are being evaluated.
    Psychotropic medication is often not required.
To control psychotic symptoms or disturbed behaviour:
    haloperidol 0.5–5 mg (o) daily
To control symptoms of anxiety and agitation:
    oxazepam 15 mg (o) 1 to 4 times daily (short-term use)
Antidepressants for depression

The acutely disturbed patient

Approach to management
- React calmly.
- Try to control the disturbed patient gently.
- Ensure the safety of all staff.
- An adequate number of staff to accompany the doctor is essential—six is ideal (one for immobilisation of each limb, one for the head and one to assist with drugs).

Treatment options

- diazepam 10–20 mg (o) as single dose (if patient co-operates); repeat every 2–6 hours (up to 120 mg daily) depending on response or haloperidol 5–10 mg (o) up to 30 mg daily
- if intramuscular benzodiazepines required
  midazolam (Hypnovel) 2.5–5 mg IM as single dose
- if intravenous benzodiazepines required
  diazepam 5–20 mg IV (slow injection over minutes) as single dose

Delirium (acute organic brain syndrome)

Treatment

Principles:

- Acute delirium is a medical emergency.
- Establish normal hydration, electrolyte balance and nutrition.

Medication

Medication may not be needed but will be in the presence of anxiety, aggression or psychotic symptoms. (Doses for a fit adult.)

For anxiety and agitation:

- diazepam 5–10 mg (o) as a single dose, can repeat in 1 hour

For psychotic behaviour, add:

- haloperidol 1.5–10 mg (o) according to response

For severe symptoms, when parenteral medication required:

- haloperidol 5–10 mg (IM) as single dose

or

- droperidol 5–10 mg (IM) as single dose

For anticholinergic delirium:

- tacrine hydrochloride 15–30 mg with caution by slow IV injection (an antidote)

Schizophrenia and associated disorders

Remember explanation and support to family and patient.

Treatment of acute phase of schizophrenia

- hospitalisation usually necessary
- drug treatment for the psychosis

1. When oral medication possible and sedation desirable
   chlorpromazine 100–200 mg (o) 3 to 4 times daily

   or

   thioridazine 100–200 mg (o) 3 to 4 times daily
   (average dose about 400–600 mg daily)

2. When oral medication possible but sedation less necessary
    haloperidol 5–10 mg (o) bd
                          or
    trifluoperazine 5–10 mg (o) bd
    (average dose 20 mg daily)
3. When parenteral medication required
    haloperidol 5–10 mg IV or IM, initially, up to 20 mg in
    24 hours, depending on the response
                          add
    benztropine 1–2 mg (o) bd (to avoid dystonic reaction)
  If dystonic reaction
    benztropine 1–2 mg IV or IM
  If very agitated, use
    diazepam 10–20 mg (o) or 5–10 mg IV

Chronic phase of schizophrenia

Long-term antipsychotic medication recommended to prevent
relapse.
    Examples of oral medication regimens:
    trifluoperazine 10–30 mg (o) nocte
                          or
    haloperidol 3–20 mg (o) nocte
                          or
    thioridazine 100–400 mg (o) nocte
                          or
    risperidone 1 mg (o) bd, increasing to 2–4 mg (o) bd

Use depot preparations if compliance is a problem:
    fluphenazine decanoate 25–75 mg IM, every 2–4 weeks
                          or
    haloperidol decanoate 50–300 mg IM, every 4 weeks
                          or
    flupenthixol decanoate 20–80 mg IM, every 2–4 weeks

Bipolar disorder

Management of acute mania

Hospitalisation

• for protection of patient and family
• usually involuntary admission necessary

Drugs of choice

1. co-operative patient
    lithium carbonate 750–1000 mg (o) daily
    • this is the initial dose
    • give in 2 to 3 divided doses
    • monitor by plasma levels
    • therapeutic plasma level 0.8–1.4 mmol/L
    • required daily dosage usually 1000–2500 mg

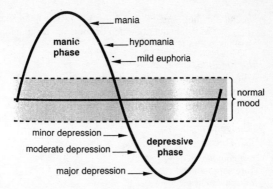

Bipolar disorder (manic depression): possible mood swings

2. unco-operative patients and manic behaviour problematic
   haloperidol 10–20 mg (o) as single dose
   • can be repeated up to 40 mg daily, depending on response
   • there is a risk of tardive dyskinesia
   If parenteral antipsychotic drug required
       haloperidol 5–10 mg IM or IV
   • repeat in 15–30 minutes if necessary
   • change to oral medication as soon as possible
   Oral diazepam will complement haloperidol.

If not responding to medication consider ECT.

Maintenance/prophylaxis
• lithium carbonate—continue for 6 months
    if not tolerated or ineffective use
• carbamazepine or sodium valproate

Diverticular disease

Diverticular disease is a problem of the colon (90% in descending colon) and is related to lack of fibre in the diet. It is usually symptomless.

Clinical features
• typical in middle aged or elderly—over 40 years
• diverticulosis—symptomless
• diverticulitis—infected diverticula and symptomatic
  constipation or alternating constipation/diarrhoea
  intermittent cramping lower abdominal pain in LIF
  tenderness in LIF

rectal bleeding—may be profuse (± faeces)
may present as acute abdomen or subacute obstruction
usually settles in 2–3 days

Investigations
- WBC and ESR—to determine inflammation
- sigmoidoscopy
- barium enema

Management
High fibre diet

Symptomatic
Fibre supplements
Antispasmodics

Diverticulitis (complicated)
Nil orally, IV fluids, analgesics
Antibiotics
(amoxy) ampicillin IV + gentamicin IV + metronidazole IV

Dizziness

The term 'dizziness' is generally used collectively to describe
all types of equilibrium disorders and, for convenience, can be
classified as shown in the figure below.

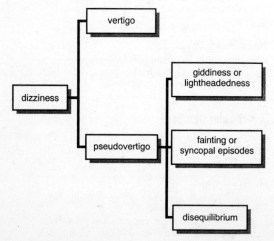

Classification of dizziness

Vertigo

Vertigo is an episodic sudden sensation of circular motion of the body or of its surroundings.

Giddiness

Giddiness is a sensation of uncertainty or ill-defined lightheadedness. It is a typical psychoneurotic symptom.

Syncopal episodes

Syncope may present as a variety of dizziness or lightheadedness in which there is a sensation of impending fainting or loss of consciousness. Common causes are cardiogenic disorders and postural hypotension, which are usually drug-induced.

Disequilibrium

Disequilibrium implies a condition in which there is a loss of balance or instability while walking, without any associated sensations of spinning.

Special causes of dizziness

Drugs

Drugs usually affect the vestibular nerve rather than the labyrinth. The causes, which are numerous, include antibiotics especially the 'mycins and tetracyclines, anticonvulsants, cardiogenic drugs and salicylates.

Cervical spine dysfunction

It is not uncommon to observe vertigo in patients with cervical spondylosis or post cervical spinal injury. It has been postulated that this may be caused by the generation of abnormal impulses from proprioceptors in the upper cervical spine. Some instances of benign positional vertigo are associated with disorders of the cervical spine.

Vestibular neuronitis and labyrinthitis

These are considered to be a viral infection of the vestibular nerve and labyrinth respectively, causing a prolonged attack of vertigo that can last for several days.

- acute vertigo with nausea and vomiting = vestibular neuronitis
- same symptoms + hearing loss ± tinnitus = acute labyrinthitis

Table 19 *Dizziness/vertigo: diagnostic strategy model (modified)*

Q.	*Probability diagnosis*
A.	Anxiety-hyperventilation (G)
	Postural hypotension (G/S)
	Simple faint—vasovagal (S)
	Ear infection—acute labyrinthitis (V)
	Vestibular neuronitis (V)
	Benign positional vertigo (V)
	Motion sickness (V)
	Post head injury (V/G)

Q.	*Serious disorders not to be missed*
A.	Neoplasia
	• acoustic neuroma
	• posterior fossa tumour
	• other brain tumours 1° or 2°
	Intracerebral infection, e.g. abscess
	Cardiovascular
	• cardiac arrhythmias
	• myocardial infarction
	• aortic stenosis
	Cerebrovascular
	• vertebrobasilar insufficiency
	• brain stem infarct
	Multiple sclerosis

Q.	*Pitfalls (often missed)*
A.	Ear wax—otosclerosis
	Arrhythmias
	Hyperventilation
	Alcohol and other drugs
	Cough or micturition syncope
	Vertiginous migraine
	Parkinson's disease
	Ménière's syndrome (overdiagnosed)

G = giddiness; S = syncope; V = vertigo

Treatment

• rest in bed, lying very still
• gaze in the direction that eases symptoms
• drugs to lessen vertigo

The following drugs can be used:
>   dimenhydrinate 50 mg (o) 4–6 hourly

>   or

>   prochlorperazine (Stemetil) 12.5 mg IM (if severe)

An alternative is diazepam (which decreases brainstem response to vestibular stimuli) 5–10 mg IM for the acute attack then 5 mg (o) tds.

Outcome

Both are self limiting disorders and usually settle over several days, e.g. 5–7 or weeks. Labyrinthitis usually lasts longer and during recovery rapid head movements may bring on transient vertigo.

Benign paroxysmal positional vertigo

This is a common type of vertigo that is induced by changing head position—particularly tilting the head backwards, changing from a recumbent to a sitting position or turning to the affected side.

Clinical features
- affects all ages especially elderly
- recurs periodically for several days
- each attack is brief, usually 10–60 seconds, and subsides rapidly
- attacks not accompanied by vomiting, tinnitus or deafness
- cause is unknown
- diagnosis confirmed by head position testing
- tests of hearing and vestibular function normal
- usually spontaneous recovery in weeks (most return to regular activity after 1 week)

Management
- appropriate explanation and reassurance
- avoidance measures: the patient quickly begins to move in a certain way and avoids attacks of vertigo
- drugs not recommended
- special exercises, e.g. Cawthorne Cooksie exercises
- cervical traction may help

Ménière's syndrome
- Commonest in 30–50 age group
- Characterised by paroxysmal attacks of:
  — vertigo
  — tinnitus
  — nausea and vomiting
  — sweating and pallor
  — deafness (progressive)
- Abrupt onset—patient may fall
- Attacks last 30 minutes to several hours
- Nystagmus observed only during an attack
- Examination
  — sensorineural deafness
  — caloric test—impaired vestibular function

— audiometry
  • sensorineural deafness
  • loudness recruitment

Note: Tends to be overdiagnosed

Treatment

Acute attack

IV diazepam 5 mg or IM prochlorperazine. Many use these drugs in combination.

Long term

• reassurance with a very careful explanation of this condition to the patient who often associates it with malignant disease
• avoid excessive intake of salt, tobacco and coffee
• alleviate anxiety by using long-term sedation
• referral for a neurological assessment
• diuretic, e.g. dyazide

Surgery may be an option for intractable cases.

Dizzy turns in elderly women

If no cause such as hypertension is found, advise them to get up slowly from sitting or lying and to wear firm elastic stockings.

Dizzy turns in girls in late teens

• common due to blood pressure fluctuations
• give advice related to stress, lack of sleep, or excessive activity
• reassure that it settles with age (rare after 25 years)

Domestic violence

Domestic violence basically means the physical, sexual or emotional abuse of one partner by the other, almost invariably abuse of a female by a male. However, the abuse can be of an elderly parent by the children or from some other member of the household to another member.

A major problem in dealing with domestic violence is that it is hidden and the victims are reluctant to divulge the cause of their injuries when visiting medical practitioners.

Possible presentations

A study by Stark defines a three-stage sequence to the battering syndrome:

Stage 1: woman presents with injuries in the central anterior regions of the body (face, head and torso).

Stage 2: multiple visits to clinics, often with vague complaints.

Stage 3: development of psychological sequelae (alcohol, drug addiction, suicide attempts, depression).

Cycle of violence

A predictable pattern that is referred to as the 'cycle of violence' has been identified in many marriages. It is controlled by the perpetrator while the victim feels confused and helpless. The cycle repeats itself with a tendency for the violence to increase in severity (see figure below).

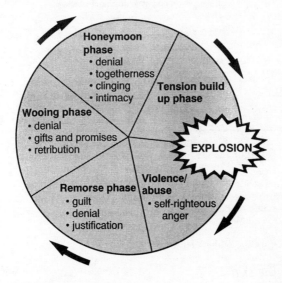

The cycle of domestic violence

Management

The key to successful management is initial recognition of the problem and establishment of empathetic caring and support for the victim and family. As with an alcohol problem, the person has to admit that he or she has a problem before effective counselling can begin. A management strategy is presented in Table 20.

Table 20 *Management strategy for domestic violence*

Treat the physical injury and
suspect domestic violence

↓

Establish the diagnosis

↓

Initiate crisis intervention
- organise admission to a refuge
- ensure informed consent for all actions
- consider notifying police

↓

Establish an empathic trusting relationship

↓

Build the victim's coping skills and self-esteem

↓

Make effective use of community resources
- support services
- women's support group
- domestic violence resource centre
- social services/police
- social workers

Dry hair

- Don't shampoo every day.
- Use a mild shampoo (labelled for 'dry or damaged hair').
- Use a conditioner.
- Snip off the split or frayed ends.
- Avoid heat, e.g. electric curlers, hair dryers.
- Wear head protection in hot wind.
- Wear a rubber cap when swimming.

Dry skin

Disorders associated with scaling and roughness of the skin include:

- atopic dermatitis—all types, e.g. pityriasis alba, nummular eczema, asteatotic dermatitis
- ageing skin
- psoriasis
- ichthyotic disorders
- keratosis pilaris

Management

- Reduce bathing and frequency and duration of showering.
- Bathe and shower in tepid water.

- Use a soap substitute, e.g. Dove, Neutrogena or Cetaphil lotion or aqueous cream.
- Rub in baby oil after patting dry.
- Avoid wool next to skin (e.g. wear cotton).
- Use emollients, e.g. Alpha-Keri lotion, Nutra D cream.
- Use moisturisers, e.g. Calmurid, Nutraplus, Aquacare HP.
- Use dilute corticosteroid ointment if resistant local patches.
- Advise a good diet and drink plenty of water.

Dyslipidaemia

Established facts

- Major risk factors for CHD include:

  ↑ LDL cholesterol + ↓ HDL cholesterol

  ratio LDLC/HDLC > 4

- Risk increases with increasing cholesterol levels (90% if > 7.8 mmol/L)
- Levels TG > 10 mmol/L increases risk of pancreatitis
- Management should be correlated with risk factors
- 10% reduction total cholesterol gives 20% ↓ in CHD after 3 years

Investigations

- Serum triglyceride
- Serum cholesterol and HDLC & LDLC if ≥ 5.5 mmol/L
- TFTs if overweight elderly female

Table 21 *Patients requiring treatment*

Patient category	Lipid level (mmol/L)
A. One or more of risk factors: • personal history CHD • peripheral vascular disease • family history (1° relative < 60 yrs) • diabetes mellitus • familial hypercholesterolaemia • smoking	total cholesterol > 6.5 with HDLC ≥ 1 or total cholesterol > 5.5 with HDLC < 1
B. If patient has: • hypertension, or • HDLC < 1 mmol/L	total cholesterol > 6.5
C. No risk factors (above) • man aged 35–75 years or • postmenopausal woman up to 75 years	total cholesterol > 7.5 or triglyceride > 4
D. Patient not in above	total cholesterol > 9 or triglyceride > 8

Appropriate treatment goals

- Total cholesterol < 5.0 mmol/L
- LDLC < 3.5 mmol/L
- HDLC > 1.0 mmol/L
- triglycerides < 2.0 mmol/L

Treat all risk factors.

Non-pharmacological measures

Dietary measures:

- Keep to ideal weight.
- Reduce fat intake esp. dairy products and meat.
- Avoid 'fast' foods and deep fried foods.
- Replace saturated fats with mono or polyunsaturated fats.
- Always trim fat off meat, remove skin from chicken.
- Avoid biscuits and cakes between meals.
- Eat fish at least twice a week.
- Ensure a high fibre diet esp. fruit and vegetables.
- Keep alcohol intake to 0–2 standard drinks/day.
- Drink more water.

Regular exercise
Cessation of smoking
Co-operation of family is essential
Exclude secondary causes, e.g. hypothyroidism, obesity, alcohol excess (especially ↑ TG), specific diuretics

Checkpoints

- diet therapy effective (TG↓, LDLC↓) within 6 to 8 weeks
- continue at least 6 months before consider drug therapy

Pharmacological measures

Use these agents in addition to diet.

Moderate LDLC elevation

Options: Choose one of the following:
1. Bile acid sequestrating resins
   e.g. cholestyramine 4 g daily in fruit juice increasing to max. tolerated dose
   Adverse effects: GIT side effects, e.g. constipation, offensive wind
2. HMG–CoA reductase inhibitors ('statins')
   e.g. simvastatin 10 mg (o) nocte
       increase to max. 40 mg/day
            or
       pravastatin 10 mg (o) nocte
           increase to max. 40 mg/day

Adverse effects: GIT side effects
             myalgia
             abnormal liver function
Monitor: Measure LFTs (ALT & CPK) and CK as
             baseline
             Repeat LFTs after 4 to 8 weeks, then every
             6 weeks for 6 months
3. Nicotinic acid 250 mg (o) with food daily
      increase to max 500 mg tds
   Adverse effects: flushing, gastric irritation, gout
   Minimise with gradual introduction, take with food and
   aspirin cover
4. Probucol 500 mg (o) bd
   Problems: slow response, care with hepatic disease

Severe LDLC elevation

Combined 'statin' and resin
e.g. cholestyramine 4–8 g (o) mane
             +
   simvastatin or pravastatin
      20 mg (o) nocte, to max. 40 mg/day

Moderate to severe (isolated) TG elevation

gemfibrozil 600 mg (o) bd

Note: slow response
      monitor LFTs
      predisposes to gall stones and myopathy

Alternatives: nicotinic acid
                  or
              n 3 fish oil concentrate 6 g (o) daily in divided
              doses
                  to max. 15 g/day

Note: Reduction in alcohol intake is essential.

Dysmenorrhoea (primary)

Management

- Provide full explanation and appropriate reassurance.
- Promote a healthy lifestyle
  — regular exercise
  — avoid smoking and excessive alcohol.
- Recommend relaxation techniques such as yoga.
- Avoid exposure to extreme cold.
- Place a hot water bottle over the painful area and curl the
  knees onto the chest.

Medication

Options include (trying in order):

- simple analgesics, e.g. aspirin or paracetamol
- prostaglandin inhibitors, e.g. mefenamic acid, 500 mg tds at first suggestion of pain (if simple analgesics ineffective). Other NSAIDs, e.g. naproxen.
- combined oral contraceptive (low-oestrogen triphasic pills preferable)
- possible: progestogen medicated IUD

Dyspepsia (indigestion)

Dyspepsia is pain or discomfort centred at the upper abdomen which is chronic or recurrent in nature.

Heartburn is a central retrosternal or epigastric burning sensation that spreads upwards to the throat.

Table 22 *Dyspepsia: diagnostic strategy model (modified)*

Q.	*Probability diagnosis*
A.	Irritable upper GIT (functional dyspepsia)
	Gastro-oesophageal reflux
	Oesophageal motility disorder (dysmotility)
Q.	*Serious disorders not to be missed*
A.	Neoplasia
	• carcinoma: stomach, pancreas
	Cardiovascular
	• ischaemic heart disease
	• congestive cardiac failure
	Pancreatitis
	Peptic ulcer
Q.	*Pitfalls (often missed)*
A.	Myocardial ischaemia
	Food allergy, e.g. lactose intolerance
	Pregnancy (early)
	Biliary motility disorder
	Other gall bladder disease
	Post vagotomy
	Duodenitis

Dyspepsia in children

Dyspepsia is an uncommon problem in children but can be caused by drugs, oesophageal disorders and gastro-oesophageal reflux in particular.

Gastro-oesophageal reflux

Prognosis

Reflux gradually improves with time and usually ceases soon after solids are introduced into the diet. Most cases clear up completely by the age of 9 or 10 months, when the baby is sitting. Severe cases tend to persist until 18 months of age.

Investigations

These are not necessary in most cases but in those with persistent problems or complications referral to a paediatrician is recommended.

Management

- Provide appropriate reassurance with parental education.
- Changes in feeding practice and positioning will control most reflux.
- Nurse infant prone at 30°.
- Place on side at 30° after meals (prop up head of cot with bricks or boards).
- Give smaller more frequent feeds.
- Thicken feeds with Carobel, infant Gaviscon or cornflour.

Dyspepsia in adults

Gastro-oesophageal reflux disease (GORD)

Features

- heartburn
- acid regurgitation, esp. lying down at night
- water brash
- diagnosis usually made on history
- investigation usually not needed
  (reserve for danger signs and non responsive treatment)
  gastroscopy is the investigation of choice

Management

Stage 1

- Patient education/appropriate reassurance
- Consider acid suppression or neutralisation
- Attend to lifestyle
  — weight reduction if overweight (this alone may abolish symptoms)
  — reduction or cessation of smoking
  — reduction or cessation of alcohol (especially with dinner)
  — avoid fatty foods, e.g. pastries
  — reduction or cessation of coffee, tea and chocolate

- — avoid coffee and alcohol late at night
- — avoid gaseous drinks
- — leave at least 3 hours between every meal and retiring
- — have main meal at mid-day with light evening meal
- — avoid spicy foods and tomato products
- Antacids
  - — best is liquid alginate/antacid mixture
    e.g., Gaviscon/Mylanta plus
      20 mL on demand or 1½–2 hours before meals and
      bedtime
- Elevation of head of bed
  - — if GORD occurs in bed, sleep with head of bed elevated
    10–20 cm on wooden blocks

Stage 2

Step 1 *Reduce acid secretion* (select from)

H_2 receptor antagonists (oral use for 8 weeks)

cimetidine 400 mg bd pc or 800 mg nocte

or

ranitidine 150 mg bd pc

or

famotidine 40 mg nocte

or

nizatadine 150 mg bd

Proton pump blocker (if no response) for 4–8 weeks

omeprozole 20–40 mg mane

or

lansoprazole 30 mg mane

(very effective for ulcerative oesophagitis and
reflux)

If step 1 not fully effective:

Step 2 *Prokinetic agents* (select from)

- — to facilitate gastric emptying
- — very useful in reflux

domperidone 10 mg tds or qid ac

or

cisapride 5–10 mg tds ac

Functional (non-ulcer) dyspepsia

There is discomfort on eating in the absence of demonstrable
organic disease and can be considered in two categories:

ulcer-like dyspepsia

or

dysmotility-like dyspepsia

Ulcer-like

Treat as for GORD.

Dysmotility-like dyspepsia

Features of dysmotility

- discomfort with early sense of fullness on eating
- nausea
- overweight
- emotional stress
- poor diet, e.g. fatty foods
- similar lifestyle to GORD

Management

Treat as for GORD (stage 1).
Include antacids.
If not responsive:

Step 1
    H_2 antagonists.

Step 2
    Prokinetic agents.

Peptic ulcer disease

Use same treatment as for GORD, i.e.:

Stage 1 General measures
         Antacids
         H_2 receptor antagonists (8 week course)

Stage 2 Proton pump blocker

Other possible agents

Mucosal-coating agents
    sucralfate 1 g tab (o) qid, 1 hour ac and nocte for 6–8
    weeks
Colloidal bismuth subcitrate (CBS)
    bismuth subcitrate (De-Nol)
        2 tabs (chewed) bd for 6–8 weeks
Prostaglandin analogue
    misoprostol 800 µg daily (divided doses)

Therapy to eradicate Helicobacter pylori

Treatment regimens (select from)—2 weeks course

1. CBS 1 tab qid
                plus
   tetracycline *or* amoxycillin
                plus
   metronidazole
2. Proton pump blocker
                plus
   amoxycillin or clarithromycin
3. As for 2 + metronidazole

Surgical treatment

Indications include:

- failed medical treatment after 1 year
- complications
  — uncontrollable bleeding
  — perforation
  — pyloric stenosis
- suspicion of malignancy in gastric ulcer
- recurrent ulcer after previous surgery

NSAIDs and peptic ulcers

1. Ulcer identified in NSAID user.
   - stop NSAID (if possible)
   - check smoking and alcohol use
   - try alternative anti-inflammatory analgesic
     e.g. paracetamol
        enteric-coated, slow-release aspirin
   - H_2 receptor antagonist (full dose)
                   or
     misoprostol 800 mg a day (used for GU)
2. Prevention of ulcers in NSAID user
   Try alternatives (as above). Prophylactic drugs are rarely justified but reasonable in those over 75 years and in those with a past history of peptic ulcer.
        misoprostol (prevents GU recurrence)
        H_2 receptor antagonist (prevents DU, not GU)

Dyspnoea

Dyspnoea is the subjective sensation of breathlessness that is excessive for any given level of physical activity.

Table 23 *Comparison of distinguishing features between dyspnoea due to heart disease and to lung disease*

Lung disease	Heart disease
History of respiratory disease	History of hypertension, cardiac ischaemia or valvular heart disease
Slow development	Rapid development
Present at rest	Mainly on exertion
Productive cough common	Cough uncommon, and then 'dry'
Aggravated by respiratory infection	Usually unaffected by respiratory infection

Table 24 *Dyspnoea: diagnostic strategy model (modified)*

Q. *Probability diagnosis*
A. Bronchial asthma
    Bronchiolitis (children)
    Left heart failure
    COAD
    Obesity
    Functional hyperventilation

Q. *Serious disorders not to be missed*
A. Cardiovascular
    e.g. acute heart failure, e.g. AMI
    • pulmonary embolism
    Neoplasia
    • bronchial carcinoma
    Severe infections
    • pneumonia
    • acute epiglottitis (children)
    Respiratory disorders
    • inhaled foreign body
    • upper airways obstruction
    • pneumothorax
    • atelectasis
    • pleural effusion
    • tuberculosis
    Neuromuscular disease
    • infective polyneuritis
    • poliomyelitis

Q. *Pitfalls (often missed)*
A. Fibrosing alveolitis
    Extrinsic allergic alveolitis
    Chemical pneumonitis
    Metabolic acidosis
    Radiotherapy
    Renal failure (uraemia)
    Multiple small pulmonary emboli

Important causes of dyspnoea

asthma (see page 45)
COAD (see page 99)
heart failure (see page 214)

Interstitial lung diseases

Interstitial lung diseases comprise a group of disorders that have the common features of inflammation and fibrosis of the interalveolar septum, representing a non-specific reaction of the lung to injury of various causes.

Causes of pulmonary infiltration include:

- sarcoidosis
- fibrosing alveolitis
- extrinsic allergic alveolitis
- lymphangitis carcinomatosis

Common clinical features:

- dyspnoea and dry cough (insidious onset)
- fine inspiratory crackles at lung base
- finger clubbing
- PFTs: restrictive ventilatory deficit
        decrease in gas transfer factor
- characteristic X-ray changes

Sarcoidosis

Clinical features:

- may be asymptomatic (one-third)
- onset usually 3rd or 4th decade (but any age)
- bilateral hilar lymphadenopathy (on CXR)
- cough
- fever, malaise, arthralgia
- erythema nodosum
- ocular lesions, e.g. anterior uveitis
- other multiple organ lesions (uncommon)
- overall mortality 2–5%

Diagnosis

Histological evidence from biopsy specimen usually transbronchial biopsy.

Supporting evidence:

- elevated serum ACE
- PFTs: restrictive pattern. Impaired gas transfusion in advanced cases.

Treatment

Sarcoidosis may resolve spontaneously (hilar lymphadenopathy without lung involvement does not require treatment).
Indications for treatment with corticosteroids:

- no spontaneous improvement after 6 months
- symptomatic pulmonary lesions
- eye, CNS and other systems involvement
- hypercalcaemia, hypercalcuria
- erythema nodosum with arthralgia
- persistent cough

Corticosteroid treatment
Prednisolone 30 mg daily for 6 weeks, then reduce to lowest
dose which maintains improvement.
Prednisolone 20–30 mg for 2 weeks for erythema nodosum of
sarcoidosis.

Fibrosing alveolitis

Cryptogenic fibrosing alveolitis (idiopathic pulmonary fibrosis)
is the most common diagnosis among patients presenting with
interstitial lung disease.

Patients usually present in the fifth to seventh decade with
the clinical features as outlined under interstitial lung diseases.
CXR abnormalities are variable but include bilateral diffuse
nodular or reticulonodular shadowing favouring the lung
bases. Open lung biopsy may be needed for diagnosis and
staging. The usual treatment is high doses of oral corticosteroids with or without cyclophosphamide.

Extrinsic allergic alveolitis

This disease is characterised by a widespread diffuse inflammatory reaction in both the small airways of the lung and
alveoli, due to the inhalation of allergens which are usually
spores of micro-organisms such as *Micropolyspora faeni* in 'far-
mer's lung' or (more commonly) avian proteins from droppings
or feathers in 'bird fancier's lung'. Management is based on
prevention, namely avoiding exposure to allergens or wearing
protective fine mesh masks. Prednisolone can be used (with
caution) to control acute symptoms. It should be pointed out
that this allergic disease is different to the infection psittacosis.

Occupational pulmonary disease

Various types of acute and chronic pulmonary diseases are
related to exposure to noxious substances such as dusts, gases
and vapours in the workplace.

Disorders due to chemical agents include:

• obstructive airways disorders, e.g. occupational asthma,
  acute bronchitis, (chronic) industrial bronchitis, byssinnosis
  (asthma-like condition due to cotton dust)
• extrinsic allergic alveolitis
• pulmonary fibrosis (pneumoconiosis) due to mineral dust
• lung cancer due to industrial agents such as asbestos, various
  hydrocarbons
• pleural diseases, usually associated with asbestosis

Practice tips

- Remember to order a chest X-ray and pulmonary function tests in all doubtful cases of dyspnoea.
- All heart diseases have dyspnoea as a common early symptom.
- Increasing dyspnoea on exertion may be the earliest symptom of incipient heart failure.
- Several drugs can produce a wide variety of respiratory disorders, particularly pulmonary fibrosis and pulmonary eosinophilia. Amiodarone and cytotoxic drugs, especially bleomycin, are the main causes.
- Dyspnoea in the presence of lung cancer may be caused by many factors such as pleural effusion, lobar collapse, upper airway obstruction and lymphangitis carcinomatosis.
- The abrupt onset of severe dyspnoea suggests pneumothorax or pulmonary embolism.
- If a patient develops a relapse of dyspnoea while on digoxin therapy, consider the real possibility of digoxin toxicity and/ or electrolyte abnormalities leading to left heart failure.
- Recurrent attacks of sudden dyspnoea, especially waking the patient at night, are suggestive of asthma or left heart failure.
- Causes of hyperventilation include drugs, asthma, thyrotoxicosis and panic attacks/anxiety.

Dysuria and frequency

Dysuria, or painful micturition, which is characterised mainly by urethral and suprapubic discomfort, indicates mucosal inflammation of the lower genitourinary tract, i.e. the urethra, bladder or prostate. It is most common in women aged 15 to 44 years.

Although urinary tract infections account for the majority of cases of dysuria in women vaginitis and post-menopausal atrophic vaginitis can cause dysuria.

Investigations

Basic investigations include:

- dipstick testing of urine
- microscopy and culture (midstream specimen of urine or suprapubic puncture), and possibly urethral swabs for sexually transmitted diseases

Further investigations depend on initial findings and referral for detailed investigation will be necessary if the primary cause cannot be found.

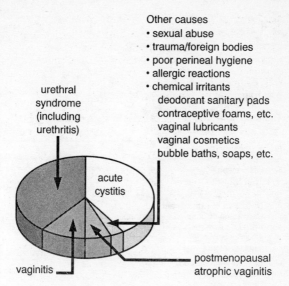

Other causes
• sexual abuse
• trauma/foreign bodies
• poor perineal hygiene
• allergic reactions
• chemical irritants
  deodorant sanitary pads
  contraceptive foams, etc.
  vaginal lubricants
  vaginal cosmetics
  bubble baths, soaps, etc.

urethral syndrome (including urethritis)

acute cystitis

postmenopausal atrophic vaginitis

vaginitis

Relative causes of dysuria in women

E

Ear pain

Table 25 *The painful ear: diagnostic strategy model (modified)*

Q.	Probability diagnosis
A.	Otitis media (viral or bacterial)
	Otitis externa
	TMJ arthralgia
Q.	Serious disorders not to be missed
A.	Neoplasia of external ear
	Carcinoma of other sites, e.g. tongue, throat
	Herpes zoster (Ramsay Hunt syndrome)
	Acute mastoiditis
	Cholesteatoma
Q.	Pitfalls (often missed)
A.	Foreign bodies in ear
	Hard ear wax
	Barotrauma
	Unerupted wisdom tooth and other dental causes
	TMJ arthralgia
	Facial neuralgias
	Post tonsillectomy
	• from the wound
	• from TMJ due to mouth gag

Otitis media in children

Features

- Two peaks of incidence: 6–12 months of age and school entry.
- Seasonal incidence coincides with URTIs.
- Bacteria cause two-thirds of cases.
- The two commonest organisms are *Streptococcus pneumoniae* and *Haemophilus influenzae*.
- Fever, irritability, otalgia and otorrhoea may be present.
- The main symptoms in older children are increasing earache and hearing loss.
- Pulling at the ears is a common sign in infants.

Treatment

- rest patient in warm room with adequate humidity
- paracetamol suspension for pain (high dosage)

- decongestants only if nasal congestion

The antibiotic of choice is amoxicillin 40 mg/kg/day (maximum 1.5 g/day) orally in three divided doses for 10 days.

If B-lactamase producing bacteria are suspected or documented or initial treatment fails, use:

cefalor 10 mg/kg/day (maximum 750 mg/day) orally in three divided doses for 10 days (cefalor is second choice irrespective of cause)

or

(if resistance to amoxicillin is suspected or proven) amoxycillin/potassium clavulanate

- most improve within 48 hours

Antibiotics not warranted for viral causes.

Follow up
- report if no improvement in 72 hours
- re-evaluate at 10 days

Complications

- Middle ear effusion: If the effusion is still present at 6–8 weeks, a second course of antibiotics should be prescribed. If the effusion persists beyond 3 months refer for an ENT opinion.
- Acute mastoiditis: pain, swelling and tenderness developing behind the ear with deterioration of the child requires immediate referral.
- Chronic otitis media.

Recurrent acute otitis media

Prevention of AOM is indicated if it occurs more often than every other month or for three or more episodes in six months.

Chemoprophylaxis (for about 4 months)
amoxicillin twice daily (first choice)
or
cefalor twice daily

Otitis media in adults

Treatment of acute episode

- analgesics to relieve pain
- adequate rest in a warm room
- nasal decongestants for nasal congestion
- antibiotics until resolution of all signs of infection
- treat associated conditions, e.g. adenoid hypertrophy
- follow-up: review and test hearing audiometrically

Antibiotic treatment
First choice:

> amoxycillin 750 mg (o) bd for 5 days
> > or
> > 500 mg (o) tds for 5 days

Alternatives:

> doxycycline 100 mg (o) bd for 5 days (daily for milder infections)
> > or
> cefaclor 250 mg (o) tds for 5 days
> > or
> (if resistance to amoxycillin is suspected or proven) amoxycillin/potassium clavulanate 500/125 mg (o) tds for 5 days (the most effective antibiotic).

Chronic otitis media

There are two types of chronic suppurative otitis media and they both present with deafness and discharge without pain. The discharge occurs through a perforation in the TM: one is safe, the other unsafe.

Table 26 *Comparison of types of discharge*

	Unsafe	*Safe*
Source	Cholesteatoma	Mucosa
Odour	Foul	Inoffensive
Amount	Usually scant, never profuse	Can be profuse
Nature	Purulent	Mucopurulent

If an attic perforation is recognised or suspected, specialist referral is essential. Cholesteatoma cannot be eradicated by medical means.

Otitis externa

Clinical features

- itching at first
- pain (mild to intense)
- fullness in ear canal
- scant discharge
- hearing loss
- pain on moving pinna

Obtain culture, especially if resistant *Psuedomonas sp.* suspected, by using small ear swab.

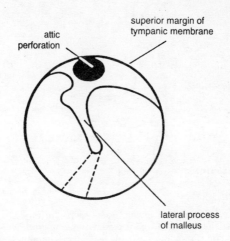

Infected ear: unsafe perforation

Infected ear: safe perforation

Management

Aural toilet
The cornerstone of treatment. Dry mopping.

Syringing
This is appropriate in some cases but the canal must be dried meticulously afterwards. For most cases it is not recommended.

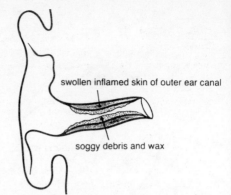

swollen inflamed skin of outer ear canal

soggy debris and wax

Otitis externa

Dressings

After cleaning and drying, insert 10–20 cm of 4 mm Nufold gauze impregnated with a steroid and antibiotic cream.

For severe otitis externa a wick is important and will reduce the oedema and pain in 12 to 24 hours. It needs replacement daily until the swelling has subsided.

Topical antimicrobials

The most effective, especially when the canal is open, is an antibacterial, antifungal and corticosteroid preparation, e.g. Kenacomb or Sofradex drops or ointment, 2 to 3 drops tds or flumethasone 0.02% with clioquinol 1% 2 to 3 drops bd.

Other measures

- Strong analgesics are essential.
- Antibiotics have little place in treatment unless a spreading cellulitis has developed.
- Prevent scratching and entry of water.

Practice tip for severe 'tropical ear'

- prednisolone (o) 15 mg statim then 10 mg 8 hourly for 6 doses
               followed by
- Merocel ear wick
- topical Kenacomb or Sofradex drops

Perichondritis

Perichondritis is infection of the cartilage of the ear characterised by severe pain of the pinna which is red, swollen and exquisitely tender.

Treatment: ciprofloxacin

Infected ear lobe

The cause is most likely a contact allergy to nickel in an earring, complicated by a *Staphylococcus aureus* infection.

Management

- Discard the ear-rings.
- Clean the site to eliminate residual traces of nickel.
- Swab the site then commence antibiotics, e.g. flucloxacillin or erythromycin.
- Instruct the patient to clean the site daily, then apply the appropriate ointment.
- Use a 'noble metal' stud to keep the tract patent.
- Advise the use of only gold, silver or platinum studs in future.

Otic barotrauma

Barotrauma affects scuba divers and aircraft travellers. The symptoms include temporary or persisting pain, deafness, vertigo, tinnitus and perhaps discharge.

Inspection of the TM may reveal (in order of seriousness): retraction; erythema; haemorrhage (due to extravasation of blood into the layers of the TM); fluid or blood in the middle ear; perforation. Perform conductive hearing loss tests with tuning fork.

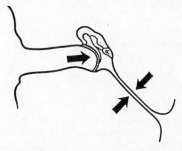

Mechanism of barotrauma, with blocking of the eustachian tube due to increased pressure at the sites indicated
COURTESY OF R. BLACK

Treatment

Most cases are mild and resolve spontaneously in a few days, so treat with analgesics and reassurance. Menthol inhalations are soothing and effective. Refer if any persistent problems.

Ectropion

- requires surgical repair (local anaesthetic)
- use a mild ointment prior to surgery

Encopresis

Definition

Involuntary passage of formed or semi-formed stools into underwear occurring repeatedly for at least one month, in children over 4 years.

Assessment

- history
- examination
- abdominal X-ray (serves as baseline)

Management

The majority are cured with the following:

- ongoing interest and support (critical)
- education and counselling
- high fibre diet
- structured toileting program, e.g. regular sitting on toilet 5–10 minutes, 3 times per day after each meal
- laxative medication, e.g. 3 day cycle: repeated 3–4 times as initial clean out
  Day 1. Microlax enema
  Day 2. Durolax rectal suppository
  Day 3. Oral bowel stimulant, e.g. Senokot (1–2 doses)
  Then lubricant or softener, e.g. paraffin oil preparation
- regular follow up with encouragement
- consider encopresis clinic if problematic

Endocarditis

Warning signs:

- unexplained fever and cardiac murmur
- febrile illness after instrumentation or minor and major surgical procedures

Main test is blood culture: at least 6 sets of samples within first hour.

Antimicrobial treatment

There are two important principles of management:

- treatment must be given intravenously for at least 2 weeks
- treatment is prolonged—usually 4 to 6 weeks

Consultation with an infectious disease physician or clinical microbiologist should be sought. Once cultures have been taken prompt empirical antimicrobial treatment should be commenced, especially in fulminating infection suspected to be endocarditis. Benzylpenicillin + gentamicin + flucloxacillin are recommended.

Prevention of endocarditis
Antibiotic prophylaxis

Low-risk patients (no prosthetic valves or previous attack of endocarditis):

- amoxycillin 3 g (50 mg/kg up to adult dose) orally, 1 hour beforehand (if not on long-term penicillin)
- (amoxy) ampicillin 1 g (50 mg/kg up to adult dose) IV just before procedure commences or IM 30 minutes before; if having a general anaesthetic, followed by 500 mg (o, IM or IV), 6 hours later.

High-risk patients (prosthetic valves or previous attacks of endocarditis), having dental procedures, oral surgery or upper respiratory tract surgery, GIT or GU surgery:

- (amoxy) ampicillin 1 g IV or IM (as above) with 500 mg (o, IM or IV), 6 hours later

plus

- gentamicin 1.5 mg/kg (2.5 mg/kg in children to maximum dose 80 mg) IV (just before) or IM (30 minutes before).

Endometriosis
Clinical features

- 10% incidence
- puberty to menopause, peak 25–35 years
- secondary dysmenorrhoea
- pre-menstrual spotting
- infertility
- dyspareunia
- non-specific pelvic pain
- menorrhagia
- acute pain with rupture of endometrioma

Diagnosis

- can be made only by direct visual inspection at laparoscopy or laparotomy
- ultrasound scan helpful

Treatment

- careful explanation—point out risk of infertility
- basic analgesics
- treatment can be surgical or medical

Medical: to induce amenorrhoea (only two-thirds respond to drugs)
- danazol (Danocrine)—current treatment of choice
- combined oestrogen-progestogen oral contraceptive: once daily continuously for about six months
- progestogens, e.g. medroxy-progesterone acetate (Depo-Provera)
- GnRH analogues

Surgical: Surgical measures depend on the patient's age, symptoms and family planning. Laser surgery and microsurgery can be performed either via laparoscopy or laparotomy.

Note: Pregnancy beneficial but endometriosis can recur.

Entropion

If unsuitable for surgery, use a strip of hypo-allergenic, non-woven surgical tape (1 cm × 3 cm) to evert lid and secure to cheek (see figure below).

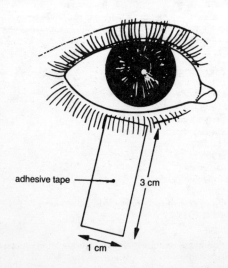

adhesive tape

3 cm

1 cm

Treatment of entropion

Enuresis (bedwetting)

Nocturnal enuresis

It is considered a problem if regular bed-wetting occurs in children 6 years and older, although many boys do not become dry until 8 years.

After the age of 5, investigations including an intravenous urogram or ultrasound are necessary to exclude urinary tract abnormalities and diabetes.

Advice for parents on managing the child

• Do not scold or punish the child.
• Praise the child often, when appropriate.
• Do not stop the child drinking after the evening meal.
• Do not wake the child at night to visit the toilet.
• Use a night-light to help the child who wakes.
• Some parents use a nappy to keep the bed dry, but try using special absorbent pads beneath the bottom sheet rather than a nappy.
• Make sure the child has a shower or bath before going to kindergarten or school.
• Reassure the child there is nothing wrong; it is a common problem that will go away.

Treatment

Many methods have been tried, but the bed-wetting alarm system is generally regarded to be the most effective. If the child has emotional problems, counselling or hypnotherapy may be desirable. Tricyclic antidepressants can be used and may be effective in some children.

The bed alarm: There are various types of alarms but recently developed body-worn alarms such as the Malem night trainer are preferred.

Epilepsy

Epilepsy is defined as a 'tendency to recurrence of seizures'. It is a symptom, not a disease. A person should not be labelled 'epileptic' until at least two attacks have occurred.

Types of epilepsy

Epileptic seizures are classified in general terms as generalised and partial (Table 27). Partial seizures are about twice as common as generalised seizures and usually due to acquired pathology.

Table 27 *Classification of epileptic seizures*

1. **Generalised seizures**
   Convulsive
      tonic clonic (previously called grand mal)
      tonic
      clonic
      atonic
   Non-convulsive
      absence (petit mal)
      atypical absence
      myoclonic

2. **Partial seizures**
   Simple partial (consciousness retained)
      with motor signs (Jacksonian)
      with somatosensory symptoms
      with psychic symptoms
   Complex partial (consciousness impaired)

3. **Secondary generalised seizures**
   Simple partial seizures evolving to tonic clonic seizures
   Complex partial seizures evolving to tonic clonic seizures
   Simple partial seizures evolving to complex partial seizures
   and then to tonic clonic seizures

Tonic-clonic seizures

Formerly called grand mal seizure, it is the classic convulsive
seizure with muscle jerking.
   Typical features (in order):

- initial rigid tonic phase (up to 60 seconds)
- convulsion (clonic phase) (seconds to minutes)
- mild coma or drowsiness (15 minutes to several hours)

Atypical tonic clonic seizures

These variants of tonic clonic seizures are more common than
realised.

- stiffen and fall = tonic
- floppy and fall = atonic
- shaking only = clonic

Diagnosis

- check short-term aggravating factors, e.g. lack of sleep, medications, drugs including alcohol
- usual tests—EEG, CT scan, basic biochemistry and
  haematology

Management

Note: Do not usually treat on one fit (chance of a further seizure is about 70%).

- profound psychosocial support
- education, counselling, advocacy
- appropriate referral

Medication

- sodium valproate (first choice)
  Adults: 500 mg bd increasing to achieve control (up to 2–3 g/day)
      Some prefer carbamazepine in young women because of risk of teratogenicity with valproate which, however, is less sedating
- carbamazepine (2nd choice)
- phenytoin (3rd choice)
- vigabatrin (used mainly as add-on for poor control)

Continue treatment until fit free for at least 2 years.

Absence seizure (previously called petit mal)

This type of generalised epilepsy typically affects children from 4 years up to puberty.

- child ceases activity and stares suddenly
- child is motionless
- no warning
- sometimes clonic (jerky) movement of eyelids, face, fingers
- may be lip-smacking or chewing (called complex absence)
- only lasts a few seconds—usually 5–10 seconds
- child then carries on as though nothing happened
- usually several per day (not just one or two)
- may lead to generalised seizures in adulthood

Diagnosis

Best evoked in the consulting room by hyperventilation.

EEG • classic 3–H_2 wave and spike
  • may be normal
  • always include hyperventilation

Medication

    sodium valproate (1st choice)
          or
    ethosuximide (2nd choice)
          or
    clonazepam or vigabatrin

Note: Beware of hepatotoxicity with sodium valproate.

Complex partial seizures

It is the commonest type of focal epilepsy and the attacks vary in time from momentary to several minutes (average 1–3 minutes).

Possible manifestations

Commonest: slight disturbance of perception and consciousness

Hallucinations • visual
• taste
• smell
• sounds

Absence attacks or vertigo
Affective feelings—fear, anxiety, anger

Dyscognitive effects, e.g. • déja vu (familiarity)
• jamais vu (unreality)

Objective signs
• lip-smacking
• swallowing/chewing/sucking
• unresponsive to commands or questions
• pacing around a room

Unreal or detached feelings and post-ictal confusion are common in complex partial seizures. There can be permanent short-term memory loss.

Diagnosis

• EEG—diagnostic in 50–60% of cases
• EEG/video telemetry helpful with frequent attacks
• CT or MRI scan—to exclude tumour when diagnosis confirmed

Medication

carbamazepine (1st choice)
200 mg daily increasing gradually by 100 mg a week to control
or
sodium valproate
or
clonazepam

New drugs: lamotrigine, gabapentin

Simple partial seizures

In simple partial seizures there is no loss of consciousness. These include focal seizures which may proceed to a generalised tonic clonic seizure or to motor seizures—Jacksonian epilepsy.

Jacksonian (motor seizure)

Typically, jerking movements begin at the angle of the mouth or in the thumb and index finger and 'march' to involve the rest of the body, e.g. thumb → hand → limb → face ± leg on one side and then on to the contralateral side. A tonic clonic or complex partial seizure may follow.

Medication

carbamazepine (1st choice)
or
phenytoin
or
sodium valproate
New drugs: lamotrigine, gabapentin

Management of status epilepticus

Focal status

* a high index of suspicion is needed to diagnose
* oral medication usually adequate
* avoid overtreatment

Generalised status

Absence attack (petit mal)
* hospitalisation
* IV diazepam

Tonic clonic (dangerous!)

* ensure adequate oxygenation: attend to airway (e.g. Guedel tube); give oxygen
* IV diazepam 5–20 mg (rate not exceeding 2 mg/min)—beware of respiratory depression and other vital parameters
* add IV phenytoin (if severe status): 1 g over 20–30 minutes (use different IV line)

Other drugs to consider instead of diazepam:

* clonazepam (next choice); phenobarbitone; thiopentone; paraldehyde, midazolam

Diazepam can be given rectally. In an adult 10 mg is diluted in 5 mL of isotonic saline and introduced via the nozzle of the syringe into the rectum.

If refractory (> 60 minutes) use full anaesthesia.

Epistaxis

Simple tamponade

* Pinch 'soft' part of nose between thumb and finger for five minutes.
* Apply ice packs to bridge of nose.

Simple cautery of Little's area (under local anaesthetic)
    use one of 3 methods: electrocautery
                                 trichloracetic acid or
                                 silver nitrate stick

Persistent anterior bleed:
    Merocel (surgical sponge) nasal tampon
'Trick of the trade' for recurrent anterior epistaxis:

- apply topical antibiotic, e.g. Aureomycin ointment, bd or tds for 10 days
- or (better option) Nasalate nose cream tds for 7–10 days
- or Rectinol ointment

Severe posterior epistaxis

Use a Foley's catheter or an Epistat catheter.

Eye: dry

Usually elderly patient complaining of a chronic gritty sensation—due to reduced tear secretion.

- artificial tear drops, e.g. polyvinyl alcohol solution or hypromellose 0.5%

Eye pain and redness

- Acute conjunctivitis accounts for over 25% of all eye complaints seen in general practice (page 103).
- Pain and visual loss suggest a serious condition such as glaucoma, uveitis (including acute iritis) or corneal ulceration.
- Beware of the unilateral red eye—think beyond bacterial or allergic conjunctivitis. It is rarely conjunctivitis and may be a corneal ulcer, keratitis, foreign body, trauma, uveitis or acute glaucoma.

The clinical approach

The five essentials of the history are:

- history of trauma (especially as indicator of IOFB)
- vision
- the degree and type of discomfort
- presence of discharge
- presence of photophobia

Table 28 *The red and tender eye: diagnostic strategy model (modified)*

Q.	*Probability diagnosis*
A.	Conjunctivitis
	• bacterial
	• adenovirus
	• allergic

Q.	*Serious disorders not to be missed*
A.	Acute glaucoma
	Uveitis
	• acute iritis
	• choroiditis
	Corneal ulcer
	Herpes simplex keratitis
	Fungal keratitis
	Herpes zoster ophthalmicus
	Penetrating injury
	Orbital cellulitis

Q.	*Pitfalls (often missed)*
A.	Scleritis/episcleritis
	Foreign body
	Trauma
	Ultraviolet light 'keratitis'

When examining the unilateral red eye keep the following diagnoses in mind:

• trauma
• foreign body including IOFB
• corneal ulcer
• iritis (uveitis)
• viral conjunctivitis (commonest type)
• acute glaucoma

Red eye in children

Of particular concern is orbital cellulitis which may present as a unilateral swollen lid and can rapidly lead to blindness if untreated. Bacterial, viral and allergic conjunctivitis are common in all children. Conjunctivitis in infants is a serious disorder because of the immaturity of tissues and defence mechanisms.

Neonatal conjunctivitis (ophthalmia neonatorum)

This is conjunctivitis in an infant less than one month old and is a notifiable disease. Chlamydial and gonococcal infections are uncommon but must be considered if a purulent discharge is found in the first few days of life. Chlamydia trachomatis usually presents one or two weeks after delivery, with moderate mucopurulent discharge.

Treatment is with oral erythromycin and local sulphacetamide or oily tetracycline eye drops.

Neisseria gonorrhoeae conjunctivitis, which usually occurs within one or two days of delivery, requires vigorous treatment with intravenous cephalosporins or penicillin and local sulphacetamide drops.

Trachoma

Trachoma is a chlamydial conjunctivitis that is prevalent in outback areas and in the Aboriginal population. Chlamydia trachomatis is transmitted by human contact and by flies, especially where hygiene is inadequate. It is the most common cause of blindness in the world. It is important to commence control of the infection in childhood as outlined above.

For adults use oily tetracycline eye drops and (if no improvement) oral doxycline or erythromycin.

Blocked nasolacrimal duct

In the majority of infants spontaneous resolution of the problem occurs by the age of six months.

Management
- local antibiotics for infective episodes
- bathing with normal saline
- frequent massage over the lacrimal sac
- referral for probing of the lacrimal passage before 6 months if the discharge is profuse and irritating or between 6 and 12 months if the problem has not self-corrected.

Orbital cellulitis

Orbital cellulitis includes two basic types—periorbital (or pre-septal) and orbital (or post-septal) cellulitis and is usually found in children.

Orbital (post-septal) cellulitis
Features
- a potentially blinding and life threatening condition
- in children blindness can develop in hours
- unilateral swollen eyelids; may be red
- an unwell patient
- tenderness over the sinuses (see figure opposite)
- restricted and painful eye movements

Periorbital (pre-septal) cellulitis
- similar presentation
- usually follows an abrasion
  but
- no pain or restriction of eye movement

Management (both types)
- immediate specialist referral
- IV cefotaxime until afebrile then amoxycillin/clavulanate for 7–10 days

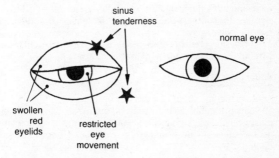

Important signs in the patient presenting with orbital (post-septal) cellulitis

---

Red eye in adults

Conjunctivitis (see page 103)

Episcleritis and scleritis

Episcleritis and scleritis present as a localised area of inflammation. Both may become inflamed but episcleritis is essentially self-limiting while scleritis (which is rare) is more serious as the eye may perforate.

History

A red and sore eye is the presenting complaint. There is usually no discharge but there may be reflex lacrimation. Scleritis is much more painful than episcleritis and tender to touch.

Management

An underlying cause such as an autoimmune condition should be identified. Refer the patient, especially for scleritis. Corticosteroids or NSAIDs may be prescribed.

Uveitis

Anterior uveitis (acute iritis or iridocyclitis) is inflammation of the iris and ciliary body and this is usually referred to as acute iritis. The pupil may become small because of adhesions and the vision is blurred.

The affected eye is red with the conjunctival injection being particularly pronounced over the area covering the inflamed ciliary body (ciliary flush). The patient should be referred to a consultant.

Management involves finding the underlying cause. Treatment includes pupil dilation with atropine drops and topical steroids to suppress inflammation. Systemic corticosteroids may be necessary.

Posterior uveitis (choroiditis) may involve the retina and vitreous and also requires referral.

Acute glaucoma

Acute glaucoma should always be considered in a patient over 50 years presenting with an acutely painful red eye. Permanent damage will result from misdiagnosis. The attack characteristically strikes in the evening when the pupil becomes semi-dilated.

Features

- patient > 50 years
- pain in one eye
- ± nausea and vomiting
- impaired vision
- haloes around lights
- fixed semi-dilated pupil
- eye feels hard

Management

Urgent ophthalmic referral is essential since emergency treatment is necessary to preserve eyesight. If immediate specialist attention is unavailable, treatment can be initiated with acetazolamide (Diamox) 500 mg IV and pilocarpine 4% drops to constrict the pupil.

Herpes zoster ophthalmicus

Herpes zoster ophthalmicus (shingles) affects the skin supplied by the ophthalmic division of the trigeminal nerve. The eye may be affected if the nasociliary branch is involved.

Immediate referral is necessary if the eye is red, vision is blurred or the cornea cannot be examined. Apart from general eye hygiene, treatment usually includes oral acyclovir 800 mg, five times daily for 10 days (provided this is commenced within three days of the rash appearing), and topical acyclovir 3% opth. ointment 4 hourly.

Flash burns (see page 179)

| Eyelid and lacrimal disorders |

There are several inflammatory disorders of the eyelid and lacrimal system that present as a 'red and tender' eye without involving the conjunctiva. Any suspicious lesion should be referred.

Stye (see page 326)

Chalazion (meibomian cyst)

May resolve spontaneously or require incision.

Blepharitis (see page 65)

Dacryocystitis

Acute dacryocystitis is infection of the lacrimal sac secondary to obstruction of the nasolacrimal duct at the junction of the lacrimal sac. The problem may vary from being mild (as in infants) to severe with abscess formation.

Management
- Local heat: steam or a hot moist compress.
- Analgesics.
- Systemic antibiotics (best guided by results of Gram stain and culture).
- Measures to establish drainage are required eventually. Recurrent attacks or symptomatic watering of the eye are indications for surgery such as dacryocystorhinostomy.

| When to refer |

- Uncertainty about the diagnosis.
- Deep central corneal and intraocular foreign bodies.
- Sudden swelling of an eyelid in a child with evidence of infection suggestive of orbital cellulitis—this is an emergency.

- Emergency referral is also necessary for hyphaemia, hypopyon, penetrating eye injury, acute glaucoma, severe chemical burn.
- Summary for urgent referral:
  — trauma (significant)
  — corneal ulcer
  — severe conjunctivitis
  — uveitis/acute iritis
  — acute glaucoma
  — orbital cellulitis
  — acute dacryocystitis
  — episcleritis/scleritis
  — herpes zoster ophthalmicus

Note: As a general rule never use corticosteroids or atropine in the eye before referral to an ophthalmologist.

Practice tips

- Avoid long-term use of any medication, especially antibiotics, e.g. chloramphenicol: course for a maximum of 10 days.
- As a general rule avoid using topical corticosteroids or combined corticosteroid/antibiotic preparations.
- Never use corticosteroids in the presence of a dendritic ulcer.
- To achieve effective results from eye ointment or drops, remove debris such as mucopurulent exudate with bacterial conjunctivitis or blepharitis by using a warm solution of saline (dissolve a teaspoon of kitchen salt in 500 mL of boiled water) to bathe away any discharge from conjunctiva, eyelashes and lids.
- Beware of the contact lens 'overwear syndrome' which is treated in a similar way to flash burns.

Eyelashes: ingrowing (trichiasis)

Perform epilation using eyebrow tweezers (available from chemists).
Regular epilation may be necessary.
Severe cases: electrolysis of hair roots.

Eyelid 'twitching' or 'jumping'

Advise that cause is usually stress or fatigue.
Reassure and counsel.
Consider prescribing clonazepam if severe.
　　Blepharospasm may be treated with botulinum toxin injection into the orbicularis oculi muscle.

Eyes: flash burns

Cause: intense ultraviolet light burns to corneas (ker-
                  atitis), e.g. arc welding, UV lamps, snow
                  reflection
Precautions: foreign bodies
                  continued use of topical anaesthetics (once
                  only)

Treatment

- topical long-acting LA drops, e.g. amethocaine, once only
- homotropine 2% eye drops, 1–2 drops statim
- broad spectrum antibiotic eye ointment, bd in lower fornix
  (48 hours)
- analgesics, e.g. codeine + paracetamol
- eye padding for 24 hours then review

The eye usually heals completely in 48 hours. If not, check for
a foreign body.

Note: Contact lens 'overwear syndrome' gives the same
         symptoms.

F

Facial pain

When a patient complains of pain in the face rather than the head the physician has to consider foremost the possibilities of dental disorders (which accounts for up to 90% of pain in and about the face), sinus disease, especially of the maxillary sinuses, temporomandibular joint dysfunction, eye disorders, lesions of the oropharynx or posterior third of the tongue, trigeminal neuralgia and chronic paroxysmal hemicrania.

The key to the diagnosis is the clinical examination because even the most sophisticated investigation may provide no additional information.

Table 29 *Pain in the face: diagnostic strategy model (modified)*

Q.	*Probability diagnosis*
A.	dental pain — caries
	— periapical abscess
	maxillary sinusitis
Q.	*Serious disorders not to be missed*
Q.	Cardiovascular
	• aneurysm of cavernous sinus
	• internal carotid aneurysm
	• ischaemia of posterior inferior cerebellar artery
	Neoplasia
	• carcinoma, e.g. — mouth, sinuses, nasopharynx
	• metastases, e.g. — orbital, base of brain
	Severe infections
	• periapical abscess → osteomyelitis
	• acute sinusitis → spreading infection
Q.	*Pitfalls*
A.	Temporomandibular joint dysfunction
	Migraine variants
	• cluster headache
	• facial migraine
	• chronic paroxysmal hemicrania
	Eye disorders—glaucoma, iritis, optic neuritis
	Chronic dental neuralgia
	Parotid gland—mumps, carcinoma, sialectesis
	Glossopharyngeal neuralgia

Cervical spinal dysfunction

The upper cervical spine can cause facial pain from lesions of C2 or C3 via the lesser occipital or greater auricular (see figure below) nerves which may give pain around the ear. It is important to remember that C2 and C3 share a common pathway with the trigeminal nerve.

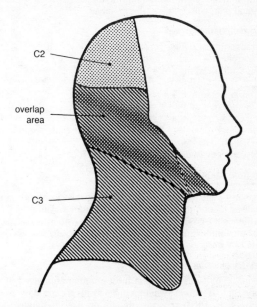

Dermatomes of C2 and C3, with the overlap area indicated

Dental disorders

Dental caries, impacted teeth, infected tooth sockets and dental roots can cause pain in the maxillary and mandibular regions. Impacted third molars (wisdom teeth) may be associated with surrounding soft tissue inflammation, causing pain which may be localised to the mandible or radiate via the auriculotemporal nerve to the ear.

Features of dental caries

- Pain is usually confined to the affected tooth but may be diffuse.
- Pain is almost always aggravated by thermal changes in the mouth:
        cold — if dental pulp vital
        hot — if dental pulp is necrotic.
- Pain may be felt in more than one tooth.
- Dental pain will not cross the midline.

Treatment of dental pain

- arrange urgent dental consultation
- pain relief
        aspirin 600 mg (o) 4 to 6 hourly
                        or
        paracetamol 0.5–1 g (o) 4 to 6 hourly
- if pain severe add
        codeine 30 mg (o) 4 to 6 hourly
- administer penicillin for associated lymphadenopathy or dental abscess formation
  e.g. procaine penicillin 1 g (IM) daily

Pain from paranasal sinuses

Infection of the paranasal sinuses may cause localised pain. Localised tenderness and pain may be apparent with frontal or maxillary sinusitis. Sphenoidal or ethmoidal sinusitis causes a constant pain behind the eye or behind the nose, often accompanied by nasal blockage.

Maxillary sinusitis

The maxillary sinus is the one most commonly infected. It is important to determine whether the sinusitis is caused by stasis following an URTI or acute rhinitis or due to dental root infection.

Clinical features of acute sinusitis

- facial pain and tenderness
- toothache
- purulent postnasal drip
- nasal discharge
- nasal obstruction
- rhinorrhoea
- cough (worse at night)
- fever
- epistaxis
- suspect bacterial cause if high fever and purulent nasal discharge

Clinical features of chronic sinusitis
- vague facial pain
- offensive postnasal drip
- nasal obstruction
- toothache
- malaise
- halitosis

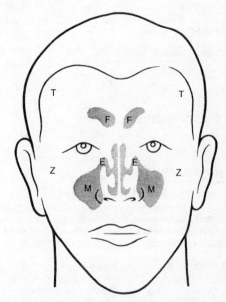

(F = frontal sinuses; E = ethmoid sinuses; M = maxillary sinuses)

*Diagnosing sinus tenderness: T (temporal)
and Z (zygoma) represent no sinus bony
tenderness, for purposes of comparison*

Management of maxillary sinusitis
- analgesics
- antibiotics (first choice)
    amoxycillin 750 mg (o) bd for 5 days
                    or
            500 mg (o) tds for 5 days
                    or

amoxycillin/potassium clavulanate tds for 5 days (if resistance to amoxycillin is suspected or proven)

or

doxycycline 100 mg (o) bd for 5 days
- nasal decongestants (ephedrine-containing nasal drops or sprays) only if congestion
- inhalations (a very important adjunct)

Invasive methods

Surgical drainage may be necessary by atrial lavage or frontal sinus trephine.

Temporomandibular joint dysfunction

This condition is due to abnormal movement of the mandible, especially during chewing. The basic cause is dental malocclusion.

Treatment of TMJ dysfunction

If organic disease such as rheumatoid arthritis and obvious dental malocclusion is excluded, a special set of instructions or exercises can alleviate the annoying problem of TMJ arthralgia in about three weeks.

Method 1 'Chewing' the piece of soft wood
- Obtain a rod of soft wood approximately 15 cm long and 1.5 cm wide. An ideal object is a large carpenter's pencil.
- Instruct the patient to position this at the back of the mouth so that the molars grasp the object with the mandible thrust forward.
- The patient then rhythmically bites on the object with a grinding movement for 2 to 3 minutes at least 3 times a day.

Method 2 The 'six by six' program

This is a specific program recommended by some dental surgeons. The six exercises should be carried out six times on each occasion, six times a day, taking about 1 to 2 minutes.

Injection into the TMJ

Indications: painful rheumatoid arthritis, osteoarthritis or TMJ dysfunction not responding to conservative measures.

Trigeminal neuralgia

Trigeminal neuralgia ('tic douloureux') is a condition of often unknown cause which typically occurs in patients over the age of 50, affecting the second and third divisions of the trigeminal nerve and on the same side of the face. Brief paroxysms of

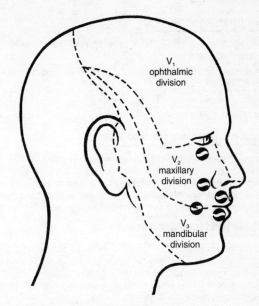

Trigeminal neuralgia: typical trigger points

pain, lasting on average 1–2 minutes often with associated trigger points, are a feature.

Treatment

Note: Precise diagnosis is essential.
- Patient education, reassurance and empathic support is very important in these patients.
- Medical therapy:
  — carbamazepine (from onset of the attack to resolution) 100 mg (o) bd initially, gradually increase the dose to avoid drowsiness by 200 mg every four days to 300–600 mg bd (maintenance); testing serum levels is unnecessary
  — alternative drugs if carbamazepine not tolerated or ineffective (but question the diagnosis if lack of response)
    phenytoin 300–500 mg daily
    clonazepam
    sodium valproate
- Surgery:
  — refer to a neurosurgeon if medication ineffective.

Glossopharyngeal neuralgia

This is a rare condition with similar clinical features of severe lancinating pains.

Sites: back of throat around tonsillar fossa and adjacent fauces deep in ear.

Triggers: swallowing, coughing, talking.

Treatment: as for trigeminal neuralgia.

Facial migraine (lower half headache)

Migraine may rarely affect the face below the level of the eyes, causing pain in the area of the cheek and upper jaw. It may spread over the nostril and lower jaw. The pain is dull and throbbing and nausea and vomiting are commonly present. The treatment is as for other varieties of migraine.

Chronic paroxysmal hemicrania

In the rare condition of chronic or episodic paroxysmal hemicrania there is a unilateral facial pain that can resemble chronic cluster headache but the duration is briefer, about 15 minutes, and it may recur many times a day even for years. It responds dramatically to indomethacin.

Herpes zoster and postherpetic neuralgia

Herpes zoster may present as hyperaesthesia or a burning sensation in any division of the fifth nerve, especially the ophthalmic division.

Atypical facial pain

This is mainly a diagnosis of exclusion whereby patients, usually middle-aged women, complain of diffuse pain in the cheek (unilateral or bilateral) without demonstrable organic disease or which does not conform to a specific nerve distribution. It is usually described as deep-seated and 'boring'.

Treatment

> dothiepin (Prothiaden) 25–150 mg nocte
> or
> other appropriate antidepressant

Fever and chills

Facts and figures

- Fever plays an important physiological role in the defence against infection.

- Normal body temperature (measured orally) is 36–37.3°C (average 36.8°C).
- Normal average values: Mouth   36.8°C
                                          Axilla   36.4°C
                                          Rectum   37.3°C
- Fever (pyrexia):   Mouth   > 37.3°C
                                          Rectum   > 37.7°C
- Fevers due to infections have an upper limit of 40.5–41.1°C (105–106°F).
- Hyperthermia (temperature above 41.1°C) and hyperpyrexia appear to have no upper limit.
- Infection remains the most important cause of acute fever.
- Symptoms associated with fever include sweats, chills, rigors and headache.
- Drugs can cause fever, e.g. allopurinol, antihistamines, barbiturates, cephalosporins, cimetidine, methyldopa, penicillins, isoniazid, quinidine, phenolphthalein (including laxatives), phenytoin, procainamide, salicylates, sulphonamides.

Fever of less than 3 days duration

- usually due to self limiting viral URTI
- watch out for an infectious disease, UTI, pneumonia or other infection
- consider routine urine examination
- most can be managed conservatively

Fever present for 4 to 14 days

If fever persists beyond 4–5 days a less common infection should be suspected since most common viral infections will have resolved by about four days, e.g. Epstein-Barr mononucleosis, PID, drug fever, zoonosis, travel acquired infection, abscess including dental abscess.

Fever in children

The fever is usually a response to a viral infection. Fever itself is not harmful until it reaches a level of 41.5°. Temperatures above 41°C are usually due to CNS infection or the result of human error, e.g.

- shutting a child in a car on a hot day
- overwrapping a febrile child.

Complications include dehydration (usually mild) and febrile convulsions.

Management

- Treatment of low-grade fevers should be discouraged.
- Treatment of high-grade fevers includes:
  — treatment of the causes of the fever (where appropriate)
  — adequate fluid intake
  — paracetamol (acetaminophen) is the preferred antipyretic since aspirin is potentially dangerous in young children. The usual dose of 10–15 mg/kg every 4–6 hours may represent undertreatment. Use 20 mg/kg as a loading dose and then 15 mg/kg maintenance.

Advice to parents

- Dress the child in light clothing (stripping off is unnecessary).
- Do not overheat with too many clothes, rugs or blankets.
- Give frequent small drinks of light fluids, especially water.
- Sponging with cool water and using fans is not effective.

Febrile convulsions

Features:

- The commonest cause is an upper respiratory infection.
- Rare under six months and over five years.
- Commonest age range 9–20 months.
- Recurrent in up to 50% of children.
- Perform lumbar puncture after first convulsion if less than two years or cause of fever not obvious.
- Epilepsy develops in about 2–3% of such children.

Management of the convulsion (if prolonged)

- Undress the child to singlet and underpants to keep cool.
- Maintain the airway and prevent injury.
- Place patient chest down with head turned to one side.
- Give diazepam by one of two routes:
  IV 0.25 mg/kg, undiluted or diluted (10 mg in 10 mL N saline)
                        or
  rectally 0.4 mg/kg (dilute with saline or in pre-prepared syringe).
- Repeat after 5 minutes if necessary but watch for respiratory depression (needs ventilation).
- Check blood glucose.
- Administer paracetamol once convulsion ceases, orally if conscious, rectally (15 mg/kg) if drowsy.

Fever of undetermined origin (FUO)

FUO, also referred to as pyrexia of unknown origin (PUO), has the following criteria:

- illness for at least 3 weeks
- fevers > 38°C (100.4°C)
- undiagnosed after 1 week of intensive study

Most cases represent unusual manifestations of common diseases and not rare or exotic diseases. Examples are shown in Table 30.

Table 30 *Common causes of FUO*

Common examples of each group selected

Infection (40%)

Bacteria, e.g.
- pyogenic abscess, e.g. liver, pelvic
- urinary infection
- biliary infection, e.g. cholangitis
- infective endocarditis
- Lyme disease
- tuberculosis
- osteomyelitis

Viral, rickettsial, chlamydia, e.g.
- Epstein-Barr mononucleosis
- cytomegalovirus
- HIV virus infection (AIDS, ARC)

Parasitic
- malaria
- toxoplasmosis

Malignancy (30%)

Reticuloendothelial
- leukaemia
- lymphomas
Solid (localised) tumours, e.g.
- kidney
- liver
- lung
Disseminated

Immunogenic (20%)

Drugs
Connective tissue diseases/vasculitides, e.g.
- rheumatic fever
- systemic lupus erythematosus
- polyarthritis nodosa
Sarcoidosis

Crohn's disease

Factitious (1–5%)

Remain unknown (5–9%)

Investigations

Basic investigations include:

- haemoglobin, red cell indices and blood film
- white cell count
- ESR
- chest X-ray and sinus films
- urine examination (analysis and culture)
- routine blood chemistry
- blood cultures

Other investigations are based on the clinical picture.

Fibromyalgia syndrome

Fibromyalgia presents an enormous management problem. It is not to be confused with so-called fibrositis or tender trigger points.

The main diagnostic features are:

1. a history of widespread pain (neck to low back)
2. pain in 11 of 18 painful points on digital palpation

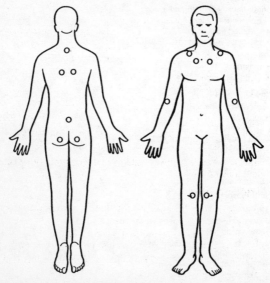

Fibromyalgia syndrome: typical tender points (the tender point map represents the 14 points recommended for use as a standard for diagnostic or therapeutic studies)

Other features

- female:male ratio 4:1
- usual age 29–37: diagnosis 44–53
- poor sleep pattern
- fatigue (similar to chronic fatigue syndrome)
- psychological disorders, e.g. anxiety, depression

Patients require considerable explanation, support and reassurance.

Treatment

- explanation and reassurance
- attention to sleep disorders, stress factors and physical factors
- rehabilitation exercise program, e.g. walking, swimming or cycling

Medication (consider as a trial)

- antidepressants (of proven value), e.g. amitriptyline, sertraline

                    or

- clonazepam (Rivotril) 0.5 mg bd

Folliculitis

A generalised acute erythematous maculopapular rash can be a manifestation of bacterial folliculitis, typically caused by *Staphylococcus aureus* and *Pseudomonas aeruginosa*.

   Pseudomonas folliculitis can cause confusion, the typical features being:

- rapidly spreading rash
- mainly on trunk, buttocks and thighs
- itchy
- small pustules surrounded by circular red-purple halo
- follows immersion in a hot spa bath or tub

Treatment is based on the sensitivity of the cultured organisms, e.g. ciprofloxacin.

Folliculitis: of groin

Folliculitis of the groin area is common in women who shave and tends to recur.

- Use tea tree lotion daily for folliculitis.
- Prior to shaving apply 'tea tree wash'.
- If persistent, use povidone-iodine or chlorhexidine (Hibiclens) solution.
- If severe, use mupirocin 2% (Bactroban) ointment.

Folliculitis: of trunk from spa baths

Due to pseudomonas or *Staphylococcus aureus*

- Rx—ciprofloxacin 500 mg (o) bd for seven days

Foot odour (smelly and sweaty feet)

Includes pitted keratolysis secondary to hyperhidrosis (common in teenagers).

Treatment

- education and reassurance
- wear cotton or woollen socks
- aluminium chloride 20% in alcohol solution (Driclor, Hidrosol) or Neat feet—apply nocte for one week, then 1–2 times weekly as necessary
- shoe liners, e.g. 'Odor eaters'; charcoal inner soles
- apply undiluted Burow's solution after a shower or bath
- the teabag treatment (if desperate)
  - prepare 600 mL of strong hot tea (from two teabags left in water for 15 minutes)
  - pour the hot tea into a basin with 2 litres of cool water
  - soak the feet in this for 20–30 minutes daily for 10 days, then as often as required

Foot pain (podalgia)

Serious disorders not to be missed

The very important serious disorders to consider include:

- vascular disease—affecting small vessels
- diabetic neuropathy
- osteoid osteoma/other tumours
- rheumatoid arthritis
- reflex sympathetic dystrophy
- foreign bodies, e.g. needles, in children

Vascular causes

The main problem is ischaemic pain that occurs only in the foot. The commonest cause is atheroma.

Symptoms:

- claudication (rare in isolation)
- sensory disturbances, especially numbness at rest or on walking
- rest pain—at night, interfering with sleep, precipitated by elevation, relieved by dependency.

Reflex sympathetic dystrophy (RSD)

RSD, which usually is a sequel of trauma, usually lasts two years and recovery to normality usually follows.

The clinical features include sudden onset in middle-aged patients, pain worse at night, stiff joints and skin warm and red. X-rays that show patchy decalcification of bone are diagnostic.

Treatment includes reassurance, analgesics, mobility in preference to rest, and physiotherapy.

Osteoid osteoma

Osteoid osteomas are benign tumours of bone that typically occur in older children and adolescents. Nocturnal pain is a prominent symptom with pain relief by aspirin being a feature.

Diagnosis is dependent on clinical suspicion and then X-ray which shows a small sclerotic lesion with a radiolucent centre. Treatment is by surgical excision.

Osteochondritis/aseptic necrosis

Three important bones to keep in mind are:

- the calcaneum—Sever's disease
- the navicular—Köhler's disease
- the head of the second metatarsal—Freiberg's disease

Sever's disease is traction osteochondritis while the other disorders are a 'crushing' osteochondritis with avascular necrosis.

Skin disorders

Two conditions commonly seen in teenagers are pitted keratolysis and juvenile plantar dermatosis.

Pitted keratolysis

This malodorous condition known as 'stinky feet' or 'sneaker's' feet is related to sweaty feet. Treatment includes keeping the feet dry and using an ointment such as Whitfield's or an imidazole or sodium fusidate to remove the responsible Corynebacterium organism.

Juvenile plantar dermatosis

'Sweaty sock dermatitis' is a painful condition of weight-bearing areas of the feet. The affected skin is red, shiny, smooth and often cracked. It is rare in adults. The treatment is to change to leather or open shoes and to cotton socks. A simple emollient cream gives excellent relief.

Arthritic conditions

Arthritis of the foot or ankle is a rather meaningless diagnosis and specificity is required. Typical sites of arthritic targets are shown in the figure below.

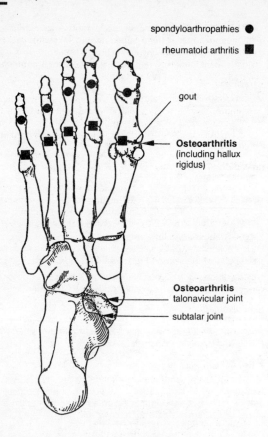

spondyloarthropathies ●

rheumatoid arthritis ■

gout

Osteoarthritis
(including hallux rigidus)

Osteoarthritis
talonavicular joint

subtalar joint

Typical sites of arthritic causes of podalgia on skeleton of right foot (plantar aspect)

Foot strain

Foot strain is probably the commonest cause of podalgia. A foot may be strained by abnormal stress, or by normal stress for which it is not prepared. In foot strain the supporting ligaments become stretched, irritated and inflamed. It is commonly encountered in athletes who are relatively unfit or who have a disorder such as flat feet. The strain may be acute or chronic.

Symptoms and signs:

- aching pain in foot or foot and calf during or after prolonged walking or standing
- initial deep tenderness felt on medial border of plantar fascia

Treatment

Acute strain is treated with rest and by reducing walking to a minimum. Try the application of cold initially and then heat. The management of chronic strain is based on an exercise program and orthotics, including arch supports, to correct any deformity.

Metatarsalgia

Metatarsalgia refers to pain and tenderness over the plantar heads of metatarsals. Causes include foot deformities (especially with depressions of the transverse arch), arthritis of the MTP joints, trauma, Morton's neuroma, Freiberg's disease and entrapment neuropathy.

Treatment involves treating any known cause, advising proper footwear and perhaps a metatarsal bar.

Stress fractures

Clinical features:

- The aches or pains may be slow in onset or sudden.
- A bone scan is the only way to confirm the suspected diagnosis.
- Basis of treatment is absolute rest for six or more weeks with strong supportive footwear.
- A walking plaster is not recommended.

Stress fractures can occur in:

- the base of 5th metatarsal (an avulsion fracture)
- neck of metatarsal (usually second)
- tarsal bones, especially the navicular

Morton's neuroma

Morton's neuroma is probably misdiagnosed more often than any other painful condition of the forefoot.

Clinical features

- usually presents in adults < 50
- four times more common in women
- bilateral in 15% of cases
- commonest between third and fourth metatarsal heads (see figure below), then 2–3

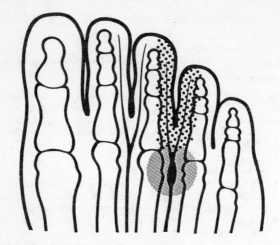

Morton's neuroma: typical site and pain distribution

- severe burning pain between third and fourth toes
- worse on weight bearing on hard surfaces (standing and walking)
- aggravated by wearing tight shoes

Treatment

Early problems are treated conservatively by wearing loose shoes with a low heel and using a sponge rubber metatarsal pad or a special orthosis. Most eventually require surgical excision, preferably with a dorsal approach.

Foot ache

- Avoid wearing high heels.
- Wear insoles to support the foot arch.
- Perform foot exercises.
- Soak the feet in a basin of warm water containing therapeutic salts (Epsom salts is suitable).
- Massage feet with baby oil followed by a special ribbed wooden foot massager.

Callus, corn and wart

The diagnosis of localised, tender lumps on the sole of the foot can be difficult.

Table 31 *Comparison of the main causes of a lump on the sole of the foot*

	Typical site	*Nature*	*Effect of paring*
Callus	where skin is normally thick: beneath heads of metatarsals, heels, inframedial side of great toe	hard, thickened skin	normal skin
Corn	where skin is normally thin: on soles, fifth toe, dorsal projections of hammer toes	white, conical mass of keratin, flattened by pressure	exposes white, avascular corn with concave surface
Wart	anywhere, mainly over metatarsal heads, base of toes and heels; has bleeding points	viral infection, with abrupt change from skin at edge	exposes bleeding points

Calluses

- Remove the cause.
- Proper footwear is essential, with cushion pads over callosities.
- Pare with a sterile sharp scalpel blade.
- Daily applications of 10% salicylic acid in soft paraffin with regular paring (if severe).

Corn

- Remove source of friction and use wide shoes.
- Use corn pads.
- Soften corn with a few daily applications of 15% salicylic acid in collodion or commercial 'corn removers' (salicylic acid), then pare.

Plantar warts

- pare wart with a 21 g scalpel blade
- apply Upton's paste to wart each night and cover (after paring)

or

- apply paste of 70% salicylic acid in raw linseed oil after paring. Occlude for one week; review; pare; apply liquid nitrogen, review

or

- apply liquid nitrogen
  repeat in one week, then as necessary

Ingrown toe nail (see page 234)

Paronychia (see page 285)

Freckles and lentigines (sun spots)

- Reassure the patient.
- Use a sunscreen.
- Otherwise, rather than use 'fade cream', use fresh lemon juice. Squeeze lemon juice (½ lemon) into a small bowl and apply the juice with a cotton ball to the spots daily. Continue for eight weeks.
- Apply tretinoin 0.05% cream daily at night, if necessary.

Frostbite

Treatment depends on severity.

Precautions: watch for secondary infection, tetanus, gangrene

Physical Rx:
- elevate affected limb
- rewarm in water just above body temperature 40°C (104°F) or use body heat, e.g. in axillae
- avoid thawing or refreezing
- surgical debridement
- don't debride early (wait until dead tissue dried)
- don't drink alcohol or smoke
- for blistering, apply warm water compresses for 15 minutes every 2 hours

Drug Rx:
- analgesics

G

Ganglion

Ganglia are firm cystic lumps associated with joints or tendon sheaths.

Management

- can be left—wait and see
- do not 'bang with a Bible'
- needle aspiration and steroid injection
  - insert 21 g needle with 5 mL syringe
  - aspirate some of contents and change syringes
  - inject 0.5 mL corticosteroid (depot)
  - can be repeated with 0.25 mL in a few weeks
  - or
- surgical excision (can be difficult)

Gastroenteritis

In children

Definition

An illness of acute onset, of less than 10 days duration associated with fever, diarrhoea and/or vomiting, where there is no other evident cause for the symptoms.

Features

Causes

- mainly rotavirus (developed countries) and adenovirus
- bacterial: *Campylobacter jejuni* and *E. coli* (two commonest), *Salmonella sp* and *Shigella sp*
- protozoal: *Giardia lamblia*, *Entamoeba histolytica*, *Cryptosporidium*
- food poisoning—staphylococcal toxin

Note: Dehydration from gastroenteritis is an important cause of death, particularly in obese infants (especially of vomiting accompanies the diarrhoea).

Exclude acute appendicitis and intussusception in the very young.

Symptoms

- anorexia, nausea, poor feeding, vomiting, fever, diarrhoea (fever and vomiting may be absent)
- fluid stools (often watery) 10–20 per day
- crying—due to pain, hunger, thirst or nausea
- bleeding—uncommon (usually bacterial)
- anal soreness

Assessment of dehydration

The simplest way is by careful clinical assessment, e.g. urine output, vomiting, level of thirst, activity, pinched skin test. The most accurate way is to weigh the child, preferably without clothes, on the same scale each time.

It is usual to classify dehydration as:

mild:	normal signs including urine
moderate:	irritable, lethargic, dry mucous membranes, decreased urine
severe:	very sick child, no urine output

Management

Management is based on the assessment and correction of fluid and electrolyte loss.

Avoid:

- drugs: antidiarrhoeals, antiemetics and antibiotics
- lemonade: osmotic load too high: can use if diluted 1 part to 4 parts water

To treat or not to treat at home:

- Treat at home—if family can cope, vomiting is not a problem and no dehydration.
- Admit to hospital—if dehydration or persisting vomiting or family cannot cope.

Advice to parents (for mild to moderate diarrhoea)

General rules

- Give small amounts of fluids often.
- Start solids after 24 hours.
- Continue breast-feeding
                    or
  start bottle feeding after 24 hours.
- Provide maintenance fluid and fluid loss.

Day 1

Give fluids, a little at a time and often (e.g. 50 mL every 15 minutes if vomiting a lot). A good method is to give 200 mL (about 1 cup) of fluid every time a watery stool is passed or a big vomit occurs.

The ideal fluid is Gastrolyte. Other suitable oral rehydration preparations are WHO recommended solutions 'Electrolade' and 'Glucolyte'.

Alternatives are:

- lemonade (not
 low-calorie)   1 part to 4 parts water
- sucrose (table
 sugar)   1 teaspoon to 120 mL water
- glucose   1 teaspoon to 120 mL water
- cordials (not
 low-calorie)   1 part to 16 parts water

Days 2 and 3

Reintroduce the baby's milk or formula diluted to half strength (i.e. mix equal quantities of milk or formula and water).

Day 4

Increase milk to normal strength and gradually reintroduce the usual diet.

Severe dehydration

Admit to hospital.
Urgent IV infusion of isotonic fluid.

> **Acute gastroenteritis in adults (see page 131)**

Genital herpes

(see page 221)

Genital warts

Treatment

Counselling and support are necessary. Not all genital warts are sexually transmitted.

For small numbers of readily accessible warts the simplest treatment is:

- podophyllin 25% solution in tinct benz co
 — apply with a cotton wool swab to each wart
 — wash off in 4 hours, then dust with talcum powder
 — repeat once weekly until warts disappear
                              or
- podophyllotoxin 0.5% paint (a more stable preparation)
 — apply bd with plastic applicator for 3 days
 — repeat in 4 days if necessary

Cryotherapy (liquid nitrogen) or laser or diathermy under general anaesthetic can be used for multiple lesions. Intralesional injection of alpha interferon is a treatment of the future.

All females (including partners of males with warts) should be referred to a specialised clinic where colposcopy is available, because of the causal link of warts to cervical cancer.

Geographical tongue

- explanation and reassurance
- no treatment if asymptomatic
- Cepacaine gargles, 10 mL tds, if tender

Gingivitis

- Use dental floss regularly (twice a day).
- Brush carefully at gumline with Sensodyne (pink) or similar toothpaste.
- Perform gum massage between thumb and index finger.
- Use Listerine mouthwash or dilute hydrogen peroxide.
- Take Vitamin C—2 g daily.

Glandular fever

Epstein-Barr mononucleosis

Epstein-Barr mononucleosis (infectious mononucleosis, glandular fever) (EBM) is a febrile illness caused by the herpes (Epstein-Barr) virus. It can mimic diseases such as HIV primary infection, streptococcal tonsillitis, cytomegalovirus, toxoplasmosis, viral hepatitis and acute lymphatic leukaemia.

It may occur at any age but usually between 10 and 35 years, commonest in 15–25 year old age group.

Diagnosis

- WCC—absolute lymphocytosis
- blood film—atypical lymphocytes
- positive Paul Bunnell test

Prognosis

EBM usually runs an uncomplicated course over 6–8 weeks. Major symptoms subside within 2 to 3 weeks. Patients should be advised to take about 4 weeks off work.

Treatment

- supportive measures (no specific treatment)
- rest (the best treatment) during the acute stage, preferably at home and indoors
- aspirin or paracetamol to relieve discomfort
- gargle soluble aspirin or 30% glucose to soothe the throat

- advise against: alcohol, fatty foods, continued activity
- corticosteroids for various complications, e.g. neurological

Post-EBM malaise

Some young adults remain debilitated and depressed for some months. Lassitude and malaise may extend up to a year or so.

Gout (monosodium urate crystal disease)

Management of acute attack

- bed rest
- keep weight of the bedclothes off the foot with a bed cradle or pillow under bedclothes
- avoid aspirin (it may exacerbate gout)
- indomethacin 100 mg (o) statim, 75 mg 2 hours later, then 50 mg (o) 8 hourly; relief can be expected in 24–48 hours, then 50–70 mg per day until total relief

Note: Any other NSAID can be used.

  add an antiemetic, e.g. metoclopramide 10 mg (o) tds
- consider corticosteroids:
    intra-articular, e.g. 1 mL of triamcinolone
    under a digital nerve block (providing sepsis excluded)
                  or
    prednisolone 40 mg/day for 3–5 days
    then taper by 5 mg over 10 days
                  or
    corticotrophin (ACTH) IM in difficult cases
- consider colchicine (only if NSAIDs not tolerated)
    0.5–1.0 mg statim then 0.5 mg every 2 hours
    until pain disappears or GIT side effects develop

Note:

- Avoid aspirin and urate pool lowering drugs (probenecid, allopurinol, sulphinpyrazone).
- Monitor renal function and electrolytes.

Long-term therapy

When acute attack subsides preventive measures include:

- weight reduction
- a normal, well-balanced diet
- avoidance of purine-rich food, e.g. organ meats (liver, brain, kidneys, sweetbread), tinned fish (sardines, anchovies, herrings) and game
- reduced intake of alcohol
- good fluid intake, e.g. water
- avoidance of drugs such as diuretics (thiazide, frusemide) and salicylates
- wearing comfortable shoes

Drug prophylaxis

Allopurinol (a xanthine oxidase inhibitor) is the drug of choice.

Dose: 100–300 mg daily

Indications:

- hyperuricaemia
- frequent acute attacks
- tophi or chronic gouty arthritis
- renal stones

Method

- Commence 4 weeks after last acute attack.
- Start with 100 mg daily and increase by 100 mg daily after each month only if necessary.
- Add colchicine 0.5 mg bd for 6 months (to avoid precipitation of gout) or indomethacin 50 mg bd.

Granuloma annularae

Granuloma annularae are a common benign group of papules arranged in an annular fashion.

- most common among children and young adults
- associated with diabetes
- usually on dorsum or sides of fingers (knuckle area), backs of hands, the elbows and knees

Management

- check urine/blood for sugar
- give reassurance (they usually subside in a year or so)
- cosmetic reasons: intradermal injection of triamcinolone (equal volume 10% with N saline). Other longacting steroids can be used.

Haematemesis and melaena

Acute severe upper gastrointestinal (GI) haemorrhage is an important medical emergency.

A sudden loss of 20% or more circulatory blood volume usually produces signs of shock such as tachycardia, hypotension, faintness and sweating.

Causes of upper GI bleeding

The major cause of bleeding is chronic peptic ulceration of the duodenum and stomach, which accounts for approximately half of all cases. The other major cause is acute gastric ulcers and erosions, which account for at least 20% of cases. Aspirin and NSAIDs are responsible for many of these bleeds. Causes are illustrated in the figure below.

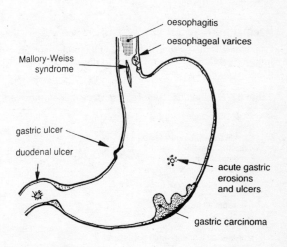

Important causes of haematemesis and melaena

Investigations

Investigations to determine the source of the bleeding should be carried out in a specialist unit. Endoscopy will detect the cause of the bleeding in at least 80% of cases.

Management

The immediate objectives are:

1. restore an effective blood volume (if necessary)
2. establish a diagnosis to allow definitive treatment

All patients with a significant bleed should be admitted to hospital and referred to a specialist unit. Urgent resuscitation is required where there has been a large bleed and there are clinical signs of shock. Such patients require an intravenous line inserted and transfusion with blood cells or fresh frozen plasma (or both) commenced as soon as possible.

In many patients bleeding is insufficient to decompensate the circulatory system and they settle spontaneously. Approximately 85% of patients stop bleeding within 48 hours.

Most patients require no specific therapy after resuscitation. In some instances surgery will be necessary to arrest bleeding but should be avoided if possible in patients with acute gastric erosion.

Haematuria

Haematuria is the presence of blood in the urine and can vary from frank bleeding (macroscopic) to the microscopic detection of red cells.

Table 32 *Haematuria: diagnostic strategy model (modified)*

Q.	*Probability diagnosis*
A.	Infection
	• cystitis/urethrotrigonitis (female)
	• urethritis (male)
	• prostatitis (male)
	Calculi-renal, ureteric, bladder
Q.	*Serious disorders not to be missed*
A.	Cardiovascular
	e.g. renal infarction
	Neoplasia
	• renal tumour
	• urothelial: bladder, renal pelvis, ureter
	• carcinoma prostate
	Severe infections
	e.g. infective endocarditis
	Renal papillary necrosis
	Other renal disease

(continues)

Table 32 *(continued)*

Q.	*Pitfalls (often missed)*
A.	Urethral prolapse/caruncle
	Pseudohaematuria, e.g. beetroot, porphyria
	Benign prostatic hyperplasia
	Trauma: blunt or penetrating
	Foreign bodies
	Bleeding disorders
	Exercise
	Radiation cystitis (massive haematuria)
	Anticoagulant therapy
	Others

All patients presenting with macroscopic haematuria or recurrent microscopic haematuria require both radiological investigation of the upper urinary system and visualisation of the lower urinary system to detect or exclude pathology.

The key radiological investigation is the intravenous urogram (pyelogram) and then ultrasound.

Haemorrhoids

(see page 33)

Halitosis

- Exclude dental disease, malignancy, pulmonary TB, nasal and sinus infection.
- Consider drugs as a cause.
- Avoid onions, garlic, peppers, spicy salami and similar meats.
- Avoid strong cheeses.
- Avoid smoking and excessive nips of alcohol.
- Brush teeth regularly during day—immediately after a meal.
- Rinse mouth out with water after meals.
- Avoid fasting for long periods during the day.
- Gargle with mouthwash, e.g. Listerine.
- Use dental floss regularly to clean the teeth.

Tip: Use an oil/water wash, e.g. equal volumes of aqueous Cepacol and olive oil, gargle a well-shaken mixture and spit out, qid.

Hangover

Preventive advice:

- Drink alcohol on a full stomach.
- Select alcoholic drinks that suit you: avoid champagne.
- Avoid fast drinking—keep it slow.

- Restrict the quantity of alcohol.
- Take two soluble aspirin before retiring.
- Drink three large glasses of water before retiring.

Treatment

- Drink ample fluids because of relative dehydration effect of alcohol.
- Take soluble aspirin, e.g. Aspro Clear (600 mg).
- Drink orange juice or tomato juice, with added sugar.
- A drink of honey in lemon juice helps.
- Coffee and tea are suitable beverages.
- Have a substantial meal but avoid fats.

Hay fever (seasonal allergic rhinitis)

- patient education
- allergen avoidance (if possible)
- non-sedating antihistamines
  — astemizole 10 mg daily, or
  — loratadine 10 mg daily, or
  — terfenadine 60 mg bd, or
  — cetirizine 10 mg daily or bd
          or
- intranasal corticosteroids (the most effective)
  — beclomethasone
  — budesonide
          or
  — flunisolide
- prednisolone 25 mg daily, reducing over 10 days if others effective

Use sodium cromoglycate (Opticrom) drops for eye irritation.
Consider immunotherapy if applicable.

Head banging or rocking in toddlers

This is common < 4 years when going to sleep, especially in 3 year olds. Reassure parents that problem settles by 4–5 years.

Headache

The commonest cause of headache presenting in general practice is respiratory infection. Common causes of chronic recurrent headache are tension and combination (mixed) headaches. Migraine is not as common as in specialist practice.

Tension headache

Tension or muscle contraction headaches are typically a symmetrical tightness. They tend to last for hours and recur each day. They are often associated with cervical dysfunction and stress or tension, although the patient may be unaware of such tension (see figure below).

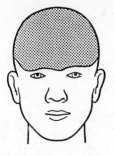 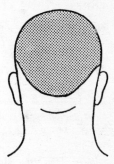

Typical distribution of pain in tension headache

Management

- Careful patient education.
- Counselling and reassurance.
- Advise stress reduction, relaxation therapy and yoga or meditation classes.
- Medication—mild analgesics such as aspirin or paracetamol. Avoid tranquillisers and antidepressants if possible but consider these drugs if symptoms warrant medication, e.g. amitriptyline 50–75 mg (o) nocte.

Migraine

Migraine, or the 'sick headache', is derived from the Greek word meaning 'pain involving half the head'. It affects at least 1 person in 10, is more common in females and peaks between 20 and 50 years. There are various types of migraine with classic migraine (headache, vomiting and aura) and common migraine (without the aura) being the best known.

Management

Patient education—explanation and reassurance about the benign nature of migraine.

Counselling and advice

- Avoid known trigger factors.
- Diet: keep a diary—consider elimination of chocolate, cheese, red wine, walnuts, tuna, vegemite, spinach and liver.
- Practise a healthy lifestyle, relaxation programs, meditation techniques and biofeedback training.

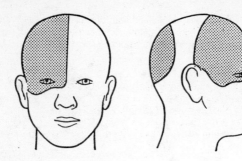

Typical distribution of pain in migraine (right side)

Treatment of the acute attack

- Commence treatment at earliest impending sign.
- Rest in a quiet, darkened, cool room.
- Cold packs on the forehead or neck.
- Avoid moving around too much.
- Do not read or watch television.
- For patients who find relief from simply 'sleeping off' an attack, consider prescribing temazepam 10 mg or diazepam 10 mg in addition to the following measures.

First signs of attack:

1st line: soluble aspirin 2–3 tablets (o)

+

metoclopramide 10 mg (o)

or

ergotamine, e.g. inhaler, 1 puff statim then every 5 minutes (max. 6/day)

2nd line: sumatriptan 50–100 mg (o) or 6 mg (SC) injection repeat in 2 hours if necessary

Established attack:

metoclopramide 10 mg (2 ml) IM or IV

Status migrainosis:

metoclopramide 10 mg IV
followed by
dihydroergotamine 0.5 mg IV slowly

Prophylaxis

(for > 2 attacks per month)

- propranolol 40 mg (o) bd increasing up to 320 mg daily if necessary

or

- pizotifen 0.5 mg (o) nocte increasing to 3 mg if necessary

Consider an antidepressant alone or in combination.
Reserve methysergide for unresponsive severe migraine.

Cluster headache

Cluster headache occurs in paroxysmal clusters of unilateral headache which typically occur nightly, usually in the small hours of the morning. A hallmark is the pronounced cyclical nature of the attacks. It occurs typically in males (6:1 ratio). Another feature is ptosis, lacrimation and rhinorrhoea on the side of the pain.

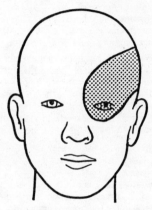

Typical distribution of pain in cluster headache

Management

Acute attack:

- avoid alcohol during cluster
- consider 100% oxygen 6–7 L/min for 15 minutes by face mask (usually good response)
- sumatriptan 6 mg SC injection
                 or
- ergotamine, e.g. medihaler or rectally

Prophylaxis (once a cluster starts); consider the following:

- ergotamine (the drug of choice: take at night during a cluster) oral or dihydroergotamine IM
- methysergide 2 mg tds
- prednisolone 50 mg/day for 3 days then reduce
- pizotifen
- indomethacin trial (helps confirm diagnosis)

Cervical dysfunction/spondylosis

Headache from neck disorders, often referred to as occipital neuralgia, is far more common than realised and is very rewarding to treat by physical therapy, including mobilisation and manipulation and exercises in particular.

Combination headache

Combined (also known as mixed) headaches are common and often diagnosed as psychogenic headache or atypical migraine. They have a combination of various degrees of:

- tension and/or depression
- cervical dysfunction
- vasospasm (migraine)
- drugs, e.g. analgesics (rebound), caffeine

The headache, which has many of the features of tension headache, tends to be constant, being present throughout every waking moment. It can last for weeks or months.

Treatment includes insight therapy, reassurance that the patient does not have a cerebral tumour, and lifestyle modification. The most effective medication is amitriptyline or other antidepressant. Consider physical treatment for a cervical component.

Temporal arteritis

Temporal arteritis (TA) is also known as giant cell arteritis or cranial arteritis. There is usually a persistent unilateral throbbing headache in the temporal region and scalp sensitivity with localised thickening, with or without loss of pulsation of the temporal artery. The mean age is 70 years: usually > 50 years.

Diagnosis is by biopsy and histological examination of the superficial temporal artery. The ESR is usually markedly elevated.

Treatment

Initial medication is prednisolone 60–100 mg orally daily. Dose reduction and progress is monitored by the clinical state and ESR levels.

Frontal sinusitis

Contrary to popular belief, sinusitis is a relatively uncommon source of headache.

Management

Principles of treatment:

- drain the sinus conservatively using steam inhalations

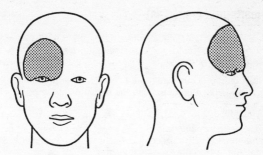

*Typical distribution of pain of frontal sinusitis
(right side)*

- antibiotics: amoxycillin or amoxycillin/clavulanate or doxycycline
- analgesics

Subarachnoid haemorrhage (SAH)

Clinical features:

- sudden onset headache (moderate to intense severity)
- occipital location
- localised at first, then generalised
- pain and stiffness of the neck follows
- vomiting and loss of consciousness often follow
- Kernig's sign positive
- about 40% die before treatment
- CT scanning is the investigation of choice

Hypertension headache

It tends to occur only in severe hypertension such as malignant hypertension or hypertensive encephalopathy. The headache is typically occipital, throbbing and worse on waking in the morning.

Benign intracranial hypertension (pseudotumour cerebri)

This is a rare but important sinister headache condition which typically occurs in young obese women. Key features are headache, visual blurring and obscurations, nausea, papilloedema. The CT and MRI scans are normal but lumbar puncture which relieves the headache reveals increased CSF pressure and normal CSF analysis.

It is sometimes linked to drugs including tetracyclines (most common), nitrofurantoin, oral contraceptive pill and vitamin A preparations.

Heartburn (dyspepsia)
(see page 149)

Heart failure

Heart failure occurs when the heart is unable to maintain sufficient cardiac output to meet the demands of the body.

Symptoms

- increasing dyspnoea
  progressing to (in order)
- fatigue, especially exertional fatigue
- paroxysmal nocturnal dyspnoea
- weight change: gain or loss

Investigations

Apart from routine investigations left ventricular function should be measured by echocardiography or nuclear gated blood pool scanning to determine the ejection fraction, which is usually very low in heart failure.

Treatment of heart failure

The treatment of heart failure includes appropriate patient education, determination and treatment of the cause, removal of any precipitating factors, general non-pharmaceutical measures and drug treatment.

Prevention of heart failure

The emphasis on prevention is very important since the onset of heart failure is generally associated with a very poor prognosis. Approximately 50% of patients with severe heart failure die within two years of diagnosis.

General non-pharmacological management

- reduction in physical activity: rest if symptoms severe; moderate activity when symptoms are absent or mild
- weight reduction, if patient obese
- salt restriction: advise no-added-salt diet (60–100 mmol/day)
- water restriction: water intake should be limited to 1.5 L/day or less in patients with advanced heart failure, especially when the serum sodium falls below 130 mmol/day
- fluid aspiration if a pleural effusion or pericardial effusion is present

Drug therapy of heart failure

Any identified underlying factor should be treated. Initial drug therapy should consist of a diuretic. Loop diuretics such as frusemide are preferred for acute episodes although other diuretics may be used for long-term maintenance therapy.

Atrial fibrillation should be treated with digoxin. Vasodilators are widely used for heart failure and ACE inhibitors are currently the most favoured vasodilator.

Note: Monitor and maintain potassium level in all patients.

Initial therapy of heart failure

1. Diuretic
   frusemide 40 mg (o) once or twice daily
   or
   chlorothiazide 500 mg (o) daily
   or
   hydrochlorothiazide 25 mg (o) daily
   or
   bumetanide 1 mg (o) daily
2. Add ACE inhibitor
   Dosage of ACE inhibitor: Commence with ¼ to ½ lowest recommended therapeutic dose and then adjust it for the individual patient by gradually increasing it to the maintenance dose (Table 33).

Table 33 *ACE inhibitors in common usage*

	Initial daily dose	Maintenance daily dose
Captopril	6.25 mg (o) nocte	25 mg (o) tds
Enalapril	2.5 mg (o) nocte	10 mg (o) bd
Lisinopril	2.5 mg (o) nocte	5–20 mg (o) nocte
Perindopril	2 mg (o) nocte	4 mg (o) nocte

ACE inhibitors

- In practice the usual initial treatment of heart failure is a diuretic plus an ACE inhibitor. This optimises response and improves diuretic safety.
- The first dose should be given at bedtime to prevent orthostatic hypotension.
- Potassium-sparing diuretics or supplements should not be given with ACE inhibitors because of the danger of hyperkalaemia.
- Renal function and potassium levels should be monitored in all patients.

Heart failure (unresponsive to first-line therapy)

frusemide 40–80 (o) bd
+
ACE inhibitor
+
digoxin (if not already taking it)
0.5–0.75 mg (o) statim
then 0.5 mg (o) 4 hours later
then 0.5 mg the following day
then individualise maintenance

If poorly controlled, consider:
metolazone 2.5–5 mg (o) statim, repeated in 2–7 days
according to diuretic response
+
heparin (only if confined to bed)

If still uncontrolled consider other vasodilators:

isosorbide dinitrate/mononitrate 80–160 mg (o) daily
and
hydralazine 200–400 mg (o) daily

Consider cardiac transplantation for appropriate patients with end-stage heart failure, e.g. patients under 50 with no other major disease.

Pitfalls in management

• The most common treatment error is excessive use of diuretics.
• Giving an excessive loading dose of ACE inhibitor.
• Failure to correct remedial causes or precipitating factors.
• Failure to measure left ventricular function.

Acute severe heart failure

(acute pulmonary oedema)

Treatment

• oxygen (mask or intranasal) 4–6 L/min
• insert IV line
• frusemide 20 mg IV, increasing to 80 mg IV as necessary
• morphine 5–10 mg IV slowly
+
metoclopramide 10 mg IV
• glyceryl trinitrate 300–600 µg sublingual

Give digoxin if rapid atrial fibrillation and patient not taking it.

Heel pain

Important causes of heel pain include:

- Achilles tendon disorders
  — tendinitis/peritendinitis
  — bursitis • postcalcaneal
           • retrocalcaneal
  — tendon tearing • partial
                 • complete
- bruised heel
- tender heel pad—usually atrophy
- 'pump bumps'
- plantar fasciitis
- calcaneal apophysitis
- peroneal tendon dislocation
- tarsal tunnel syndrome

Ultrasound examination is useful to differentiate the causes of Achilles tendon disorders.

Achilles tendon bursitis

Bursitis can occur at two sites:

- posterior and superficial—between skin and tendon
- deep (retrocalcaneal)—between calcaneus and tendon (see figure below)

Treatment

- avoid shoe pressure, e.g. wear sandals
- 1–2 cm heel raise inside the shoe
- apply local heat and ultrasound
- NSAIDs
- inject corticosteroid into bursa with a 25 g needle

Plantar fasciitis

This common condition (also known as 'policeman's heel') is characterised by pain on the plantar aspect of the heel, especially on the medial side; it usually occurs about 5 cm from the posterior end of the heel.

History

- pain:
  — under the heel
  — first steps out of bed

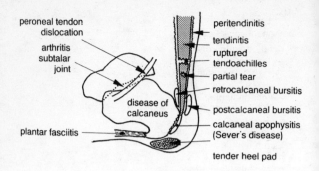

Important causes of the painful heel

- relieved after walking about
- increasing towards the end of the day
- worse after sitting
- may be bilateral—usually worse on one side
- typically over 40 years
- both sexes

Signs

- Tenderness: deep and localised.
- Heel pad may bulge or appear atrophic.
- Crepitus may be felt.
- No abnormality of gait, heel strike, or foot alignment.

Treatment

- Heals spontaneously in 12–24 months.
- Protect heel with an orthotic pad to include heel and foot arch, e.g. Rose insole or thick pad of sponge or sorbo rubber.

• Injection of local anaesthetic and depot corticosteroid into tender site helps for at least 2–3 weeks.

Achilles tendinitis/peritendinitis

Clinical features:

• history of unaccustomed running or long walk
• usually young to middle-aged males
• aching pain on using tendon
• tendon feels stiff, especially on rising
• tender thickened tendon
• palpable crepitus on movement of tendon

Treatment

• Rest: ? crutches in acute phase, plaster cast if severe
• cool with ice in acute stage, then heat
• NSAIDs
• 1–2 cm heel raise under the shoe
• ultrasound and deep friction massage
• mobilisation, then graduated stretching exercises

Avoid corticosteroid injection in acute stages and never give into tendon. Can be injected *around* the tendon if localised and tender.

Partial rupture of Achilles tendon

Clinical features:

• a sudden sharp pain at the time of injury
• sharp pain when stepping off affected leg
• a tender swelling palpable about 2.5 cm above the insertion
• may be a very tender defect about size of tip of little finger

Treatment

If palpable gap—early surgical exploration with repair.
If no gap, use conservative treatment:

- initial rest (with ice) and crutches
- 1–2 cm heel raise inside shoe
- ultrasound and deep friction massage
- graduated stretching exercises

Convalescence is usually 10–12 weeks.

Complete rupture of Achilles tendon

Clinical features:

- sudden onset of intense pain
- patient usually falls over
- feels more comfortable when acute phase passes
- development of swelling and bruising
- some difficulty walking, especially on tip toe

Diagnosis

- palpation of gap (best to test in first 2–3 hours as haematoma can fill gap)
- positive Thompson's test (calf squeeze test)

Treatment

Early surgical repair (within three weeks).

Herpes simplex

Table 34 *Herpes simplex virus: manifestations and complications*

Examples of manifestations
- Herpes labialis (synonyms: fever blisters, cold sores)
- Keratoconjunctivitis, including dendritic ulcer
- Genital infection
- Other areas of skin such as buttocks

Complications
- Eczema herpeticum
- Erythema multiforme (3–14 days postinfection), often recurrent
- Myeloradiculopathy with genital herpes
- Pneumonia
- Encephalitis

Treatment options

Herpes labialis (classical cold sores)

The objective is to limit the size and intensity of the lesions.

Topical treatment

At the first sensation of the development of a cold sore:

- apply an ice cube to the site for up to 5 minutes every 60 minutes (for first 12 hours)

  or
- saturated solution of menthol in SVR

  or
- topical applications include:
  — idoxuridine 0.5% preparations (Herplex D liquifilm, Stoxil topical, Virasolve) applied hourly, or
  — povidone-iodine 10% cold sore paint: apply on swab sticks four times a day until disappearance, or
  — 10% silver nitrate solution: apply the solution carefully with a cotton bud to the base of the lesions (deroof vesicles with a sterile needle if necessary). May be repeated, or
  —3% chromic acid.

Oral treatment

Acyclovir 200 mg five times daily or 800 mg twice daily for 7–10 days or until resolution (reserve for severe cases).

Prevention

If exposure to the sun precipitates the cold sore, use a 15+ sun protection lip balm, ointment or solastick. Zinc sulfate solution can be applied once a week for recurrences. Oral acyclovir 200–400 mg bd (6 months) can be used for severe and frequent recurrences (> six per year).

Genital herpes

Topical treatment

The proven most effective topical therapy is topical acyclovir (not the ophthalmic preparation).

Alternatives:

- 10% silver nitrate solution applied with a cotton bud to the raw base of the lesions, rotating the bud over them to provide gentle debridement. Repeat once or twice. This promotes healing and helps prevent spreading, or
- 3% chromic acid, or

- 10% povidone-iodine (Betadine) cold sore paint on swab sticks for several days.

Pain relief can be provided in some patients with topical lignocaine.

Saline baths and analgesics are advisable.

Oral treatment

Acyclovir for the first episode of primary genital herpes (preferably within 24 hours of onset).

Dosage: 200 mg five times a day for 7–10 days or until resolution of infection.

This appears to reduce the duration of the lesions from 14 days to 5–7 days. Acyclovir is not usually used for recurrent episodes, which last only 5–7 days. Very frequent recurrences (six or more attacks in 6 months) benefit from low-dose acyclovir for 6 months (200 mg two to three times per day).

Eczema herpeticum

Acyclovir 200 mg orally, 5 times daily until healed.

Herpetic whitlow

Acyclovir 200 mg orally, 5 times daily for 7 days.

Herpes simplex keratosis

Acyclovir 3% ophthalmic ointment, 5 times daily for 14 days or at least 3 days after healing
also
Atropine 1% 1 drop 12 hourly
Consider specialist referral.

Herpes zoster

Cranial nerve involvement
The trigeminal nerve: 15% of all cases.

- ophthalmic branch—50% affects nasociliary branch with lesions on tip of nose and eyes (conjunctivae and cornea)
- maxillary and mandibular—oral, palatal and pharyngeal lesions

The facial nerve: lower motor neurone facial nerve palsy with vesicles in and around external auditory meatus (notably posterior wall)—the Ramsay Hunt syndrome.

Postherpetic neuralgia
Increased incidence with age and debility, with duration greater than six months.

- it resolves within one year in 70–80% but in others it may persist for years
- eye complications of ophthalmic zoster including keratitis, uveitis and eyelid damage

Management

- Appropriate detailed explanation and reassurance. Dispel myths: namely, that it is not a dangerous disease, the patient will not go insane nor die if the rash spreads from both sides and meets in the middle.
- Explain that herpes zoster is only mildly contagious but children can acquire chickenpox after exposure to a person with the disorder.

Topical treatment

For the rash, use a drying lotion such as menthol in flexible collodion. Acyclovir ointment can be used but it tends to sting.

Oral medication

1. Analgesics, e.g. paracetamol or codeine or aspirin.
2. Acyclovir for
   - all immunocompromised,
   - over 60 years (priority) and other adults with significant pain provided rash present < 72 hours.

   Dose: 800 mg 5 times daily for 7 days.
3. Corticosteroids:
   - an alternative to acyclovir
   - if no contraindications
   - doubtful efficacy

   Dose: prednisolone

   week 1. 50 mg (o) daily,
   week 2. 25 mg (o) daily,
   week 3. 12.5 mg (o) daily.

Post-herpetic neuralgia

Some treatment options are:

1. Topical capsaicin (Capsig) cream. Apply the cream to the affected area three to four times a day.
2. TENS are often as necessary, e.g. 16 hours/day for 2 weeks, plus antidepressants.
3. Carbamazepine 100 mg bd initially increasing according to response (for lacinating pain).

Prevention

Consider giving varicella zoster immune globulin to contacts of patients who are immunosuppressed and have no history of varicella.

Hiccoughs (hiccups)

Simple brief episodes (possible options):

- valsalva manoeuvre
- rebreathing air in paper bag (as for hyperventilation)
- breath holding
- sucking ice/swallowing iced water
- catheter inserted quickly in and out of nose
- pressure on the eyeballs

Persistent (assuming exclusion of organic diseases);

- chlorpromazine orally or IV

        or

- valproic acid

Consider acupuncture, hypnosis or phrenic nerve block.

Hip pain

Hip pain in children

Children can suffer from a variety of serious disorders of the hip, e.g. congenital dislocation (CDH), Perthes' disorder, tuberculosis, septic arthritis and slipped upper femoral epiphysis (SUFE), all of which demand early recognition and management.

Congenital dislocation of the hip

Clinical features

- females : males = 6:1
- diagnosed early by Ortolani and Barlow tests (abnormal thud or clunk on abduction); test usually negative after 2 months
- ultrasound excellent (especially up to 3–4 months) and probably more sensitive than clinical examination
- X-ray usually normal

Treatment (guidelines)

- CDH must be referred to a specialist
- placed in an abduction splint or other methods if older

Perthes' disorder

A juvenile osteochondrosis leading to avascular necrosis of femoral head.

Clinical features

- males:females = 4:1
- usual age 4–8 (rarely 2–18)

- sometimes bilateral
- presents as a limp and aching
- characteristic X-ray changes

Requires urgent referral.

Transient synovitis

This common condition is also known as 'irritable hip' or observation hip and is the consequence of a self-limiting synovial inflammation.

Clinical features
- child aged 4–8
- sudden onset of hip pain and a limp
- child can usually walk (some may not)

Outcome: settles to normal within 7 days, without sequelae. Treatment is bed rest and analgesics.

Slipped upper femoral epiphysis (SUFE)

SUFE typically presents in the obese adolescent (10–15 years) with knee pain and a slight limp.
Diagnosis before major slipping is vital.
Cease weight bearing and refer urgently.

Septic arthritis

Septic arthritis of the hip should be suspected in all children with acutely painful or irritable hip problems.

Hip and buttock pain in the elderly

The following conditions are highly significant in the elderly:

- osteoarthritis of the hip
- aortoiliac arterial occlusion → vascular claudication
- spinal dysfunction with nerve root or referred pain
- degenerative spondylosis of lumbosacral spine → neurogenic claudication
- polymyalgia rheumatica
- trochanteric bursitis
- fractured neck of femur
- secondary tumours

Osteoarthritis of the hip

Osteoarthritis of the hip is the most common form of hip disease.

Clinical features

- usually after age 50, increases with age
- may be bilateral: starts in one, other follows
- at first pain worse with activity, relieved by rest then nocturnal pain and pain after resting
- stiffness, especially after rising
- stiffness, deformity and limp may dominate (pain mild)
- may present with knee pain
- abnormal gait
- first movements lost are IR and extension

Treatment

- careful explanation: patients fear OA of hip
- weight loss if overweight
- relative rest
- complete RIB for acute pain
- analgesics and NSAIDs (judicious use)
- aids and supports, e.g. walking stick
- physical therapy, including isometric exercises
- hydrotherapy is very useful
- surgery is very effective

Hirsuitism

- Exclude adrenal or ovarian pathology.
- Use bleaching, waxing or depilatory creams, or shave.
- Do not pluck hairs, especially around the lips and chin. Plucking stimulates hair growth but shaving appears to have no effect.
- Electrolysis may help.
- Drug treatment: spironolactone 100–200 mg daily; takes 6–12 months to respond.

Human immunodeficiency virus infection

About 50% of patients acquiring HIV infection develop an acute infective illness similar to glandular fever within weeks of acquiring the virus (the HIV seroconversion illness). The main features are fever, lymphadenopathy, lethargy and possibly sore throat and a generalised rash.

If these patients have a negative infectious mononucleosis test, perform an HIV antibody which may have to be repeated in four weeks or so if negative.

Patients invariably recover to enter a long period of good health for five years or more.

The level of immune depletion is best measured by the CD_4 positive T lymphocyte (helper T cell) count—the CD_4 cell count. The cut-off points for good health and severe disease appear to be 500/μL and 200/μL respectively.

Classification of HIV infection

Group I: acute illness

Group II: asymptomatic infection

Group III: persistent generalised lymphadenopathy

Group IV: A constitutional disease
B neurological disease
C secondary infectious diseases
D secondary cancers
E other conditions

Typical clinical presentation of AIDS (CDV IV)

Fever of unknown origin

Weight loss (usually severe)

Respiratory: non-productive cough, increasing dyspnoea and fever: due to opportunistic pneumonias.

Gastrointestinal
• chronic diarrhoea (many causes) with weight loss or dehydration
• oral candidiasis and oral hairy cell leukaemia

Neurological disorders, e.g. dementia, ataxia

Skin, e.g. Kaposi's sarcoma and shingles, especially multidermatomal.

Management

Patients with HIV infection require considerable psychosocial support, counselling and regular assessment from a non-judgmental caring practitioner.

The holistic approach to life is recommended (page 362)

Support groups and continuing counselling.

Medication (current guideline—CD_4^+ cells < 500)
Dose: zidovudine 250 mg (o) bd, *or*
200 mg (o) tds
Alternative drugs: didanosine, zalcitabine.

Hypertension

For adults aged 18 years and older hypertension is:
diastolic pressure > 90 mmHg
systolic pressure > 140 mmHg

Isolated systolic hypertension is that > 160 mmHg in the presence of a diastolic pressure < 90 mmHg.

Recommended basic screening tests

- Urine tests
  - urinalysis (for protein and glucose)
  - micro-urine (casts, red and white cells)
  - urine culture (only if urinalysis abnormal)
- Biochemical tests
  - potassium and sodium
  - creatinine and urea
  - uric acid
  - glucose
  - cholesterol
- ESR
- ECG

Others, e.g. renal ultrasound, only as indicated.

Management of essential hypertension

Aim to reduce the levels to $^{140}\!/_{90}$ mmHg or slightly less (ideal).
Start with non-drug therapy if diastolic BP 90–100 mmHg.

- weight reduction (if necessary)
- reduce alcohol intake to 1–2 standard drinks per day (max.)
- reduced sodium intake
- increased exercise
- reduction of particular stress
- smoking cessation
- consider drug factors, e.g. NSAIDs, steroids

Drug treatment

Monotherapy
- Start with a single drug (depends on the individual and risk factors), e.g. diuretic or β-blocker (cardioselective).
- Can use a calcium antagonist or ACE inhibitor or others as first-line.
  Need at least 4–6 weeks to test effect.
  If partly effective, increase dose to maximum or add on.
  If ineffective, substitute a different class.

Combination (for partly effective monotherapy)
      diuretic + β-blocker or ACE inhibitor
      β-blocker + dihydropyridine Ca antagonist
      ACE inhibitor + Ca antagonist
      prazosin + others

Example
Start with indapamide 2.5 mg (o) daily.
If inadequate, add
    atenolol 50–100 mg (o) daily
        or
    ramipril 2.5 mg (o) daily.

Hyperventilation

- Get patient to breathe in and out of a paper bag.
- If a paper bag is unavailable, rebreathe air from cupped hands over nose and mouth.
- Encourage them to learn to slow down breathing.
- Investigate the possibility of phobias.
- Advise cutting out caffeine and nicotine.

I

Immunisation

Immunisation is the cornerstone of preventive medicine. Basic diseases (diphtheria, tetanus, polio, whooping cough, measles, mumps, rubella) should be covered. Children should be immunised according to the NH&MRC recommendation.

All adults should receive an Adult Diphtheria & Tetanus (ADT) booster *each* 10 years.

All women of child-bearing years should have their rubella antibody status reviewed.

Table 35 *Current recommended schedule*

Age	Disease
2 months	Diphtheria, tetanus and pertussis Poliomyelitis *Haemophilus influenza* type b (Hib)
4 months	Diphtheria, tetanus and pertussis Poliomyelitis Hib
6 months	Diphtheria, tetanus and pertussis Poliomyelitis Hib
12 months	Measles, mumps and rubella
18 months	Diphtheria, tetanus and pertussis Hib
Prior to school	Diphtheria, tetanus and pertussis Poliomyelitis
10 to 16 years	Measles, mumps and rubella
Prior to leaving school (15 to 19 years)	Diphtheria and tetanus Poliomyelitis

Note: Injections should be given IM into the anterolateral thigh of children.

Other recommendations

Influenza: annually for those with chronic debilitating diseases, persons over 65, health care personnel and the immunosuppressed.

Hepatitis B: for those at risk through work or lifestyle; infants born of HBsAg positive mothers.

Q fever: those at risk, especially abattoir workers.

Tuberculosis infants at risk, e.g. Indochinese babies
(BCG vaccine): exposed to TB, health workers who are
Mantoux negative.

Impetigo

• If mild and limited: antiseptic cleansing and removal of crusts
with mupirocin (Bactroban) or chlorhexidine or povidone-
iodine.
• If extensive: flucloxacillin or erythromycin (orally).

Impotence

Impotence (erectile dysfunction) is the inability to achieve or
maintain an erection of sufficient quality for satisfactory intercourse. It doesn't refer to ejaculation, fertility or libido. Patients
often look for a cause, e.g. psychogenic, hormonal (uncommon), drug induced, vascular, diabetes.

Investigations

First-line blood tests:
• testosterone   ? androgen deficiency
• thyroxine   ? hypothyroidism
• prolactin   ? hyperprolactinaemia
• glucose

Others, e.g. nocturnal penile tumescence

Management

Treat cause.
If psychogenic, refer for sexual counselling.
If androgen deficiency:

Step-wise trial:
1. Oral: testosterone undecanoate (Andriol)
2. IM: testosterone enanthate (Primoteston Depot) or testosterone esters (Sustanon)
3. Subcutaneous implantation: testosterone implants (last 5–6
months)

Otherwise, the most effective and practical approach to
the man with impotence is to determine the response to an
intrapenile injection where prostaglandin E_1 is preferred to
papaverine.

— intracavernosal injections
— self-administered after supervised teaching
— maximum of three a week

Incontinence of urine

- Search for a cause: refer to a consultant.
- Avoid various drugs, e.g. diuretics, psychotropics, alcohol
- Weight reduction if obese.

In women:

- bladder retraining and pelvic floor exercises (mainstay of treatment)
- physiotherapist referral

Consider incontinence aids:

- absorbent pads and special pants
- condoms and catheters; urinary drainage bags
- absorbent sheeting

Infantile colic

Usually an infant 2–16 weeks old.
(see page 8)
Avoid medications if possible but consider:

simethicone preparations, e.g. Infacol wind drops

or

dicyclomine, e.g. Infacol-C syrup or Merbentyl syrup.

Infertility

Infertility is defined as the absence of conception after a period of 12 months of normal unprotected sexual intercourse.

Key facts and checkpoints

- Infertility affects 10–15% of all cohabiting couples.
- The main factors to be assessed are ovulation, tubal patency and semen analysis.
- About 30% of couples have an identifiable male factor.
- Female factors account for about 45%: tubal problems account for about 20% and ovulatory disorders about 20%.
- About 15–18% of cases have no apparent explanation.
- A significant number (25%) have combined male and female problems.
- Current specialised treatment helps 60% of subfertile couples to achieve pregnancy.

A diagnostic approach

It is important to see both partners, not just the woman.

History

A careful history should include sexual function including adequate intercourse, past history (especially STD or PID), occupational history, drug intake and menstrual history.

Physical examination

A general assessment of body habitus genitalia (including vaginal and pelvic examination), general health including diabetes mellitus, and secondary sexual characteristics should be noted in both man and woman. Urinalysis should be performed on both partners.

Note: in new testicular size

- normal size 3.5 to 5.5 cm long; 2 to 3.5 cm wide
- small testes < 3.5 cm long

Referral

The family doctor should perform the initial investigations of a couple with infertility, including temperature chart, semen analysis and hormone levels, to determine whether it is a male or female problem and then organise the appropriate referral.

Male—semen analysis:
It is advisable to obtain at least two or three samples over 2–3 months. It requires a complete ejaculation, preferably by masturbation, after at least three days sexual abstinence. Use a clean, dry wide-mouthed bottle; condoms should not be used. Semen should be kept warm and examined within one hour of collection.

Normal values: volume > 3 mL
             concentration > 20 million sperm/mL
             motility > 60% after 2 hours
             normal forms > 60%

Female—ovulation status:

- educate about temperature chart and cervical mucus diary, noting time of intercourse (take temperature with thermometer under tongue before getting out of bed in the morning)
- mid-luteal hormone assessment (21st day of cycle), i.e. serum progesterone and prolactin

Influenza

Influenza causes a relatively debilitating illness and should not be confused with the common cold. The incubation period is usually 1–3 days and the illness commences abruptly with a fever, headache, shivering and generalised muscle aching.

Typical clinical features

Initial:

- fever, shivering
- headache
- generalised muscle aching, especially limbs

Followed by:

- sore throat (not invariable)
- dry cough (can last several weeks)
- rhinorrhoea
- depression (a common sequela)

Complications

- secondary bacterial infection
- pneumonia due to *Staphylococcus aureus* (mortality up to 20%)
- encephalomyelitis (rare)

Management

Advice to the patient includes:

- Rest in bed until the fever subsides and patient feels better.
- Analgesics: aspirin is effective or codeine and aspirin (or paracetamol), especially if a dry cough.
- Fluids: maintain high fluid intake (water and fruit juice): freshly squeezed lemon juice and honey preparations help.
- Consider Vitamin C 2 g daily.

Prophylaxis

Influenza vaccination offers some protection for up to 70% of the population for about 12 months.

Ingrowing toe nails

- Correct nails properly: cut across so that the cut slopes towards the centre of the nail and do not cut towards the edges (see figure below).
- Fashion the toe nails so that the corners project beyond the skin.
- Wear good-fitting shoes (avoid tight shoes).
- Keep toe area clean and dry.

right   wrong

Correct method of cutting toe nails

Injectable contraceptives

Medroxyprogesterone acetate ('Depo-Provera') is the only injectable contraceptive available in Australia.

Dose: 150 mg by deep IM injection in first five days of the menstrual cycle. The same dose is given every 12 weeks to maintain contraception.

There are no absolute contraindications.

The main indication for this form of contraception is the desire for a highly effective method when other methods are contraindicated or disliked. Advantages are avoiding the side effects of oestrogen and overcoming compliance problems, e.g. in the mentally handicapped.

Insect stings

- Wash site with large quantities of cool water.
- Apply methylated spirits or aluminium sulfate 20% solution (Stingose) for about 30 seconds.
- Apply ice for several seconds.
- Use soothing anti-itch cream or 3–5% lignocaine ointment if very painful, e.g. Dermocaine gel.

Insomnia

- Give explanation and reassurance (treat cause if known).
- Try to recognise what helps patient to settle best, e.g. warm bath, listening to music.
- Establish a routine before going to bed.
- Avoid alcohol and drinks containing caffeine in evening.
- Try a warm drink of milk before retiring.
- Organise a comfortable quiet sleep setting.
- Sex last thing at night where appropriate is usually helpful.
- Try relaxation therapy, meditation, stress management.
- Consider hypnosis.
- If all conservative means fail, try zopiclone (Imovane) 7.5 mg (o) at night (limit to 2 weeks) or temazepam (second line).
- Consider referral to a specialist in sleep disorders.

Intertrigo

Intertrigo is skin inflammation which is caused by moisture, maceration and friction, and is strictly confined to opposing skin surfaces such as in the groin and under the breasts.

Groin rash

Common causes of a groin rash are presented in Table 36. It is important to distinguish between tinea cruris and candidiasis and the dermograms highlight the differences. Tinea cruris is described on page 335.

Table 36 *Common causes of a groin rash (intertrigo)*

Simple intertrigo

Skin disorders
• psoriasis
• seborrhoeic dermatitis
• dermatitis/eczema

Fungal
• candida
• tinea

Erythrasma

Contact dermatitis

Candida intertrigo

Candida albicans superinfects a simple intertrigo and tends to affect obese or bedridden patients, especially if incontinent.

Treatment

• Treat underlying problem, e.g. diabetes, obesity.
• Apply an imidazole preparation such as miconazole or clotrimazole (use ketoconazole if resistant).
• Use Burow's solution compresses to dry a weeping area.
• Keep area dry and skin folds apart (if possible).
• Apply zinc oxide powder, e.g. Curash.
• Use short-term hydrocortisone cream for itch or inflammation (long-term aggravates the problem).

Erythrasma

Erythrasma, a common and widespread chronic superficial skin infection, is caused by the bacterium *Corynebacterium minutissimum*. Itch is not a feature.

Clinical features

• superficial reddish-brown scaly patches
• enlarges peripherally
• mild infection but tends to chronicity if untreated
• coral pink fluorescence with Wood's light
• common sites: groin, axillae, submammary, toe webs

Treatment

- erythromycin or tetracycline (oral)
- topical imidazole

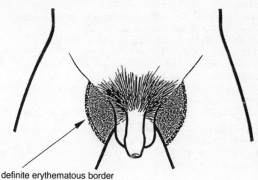

definite erythematous border

Dermogram for tinea cruris

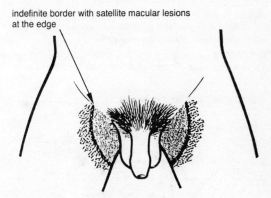

indefinite border with satellite macular lesions
at the edge

Dermogram for candidiasis of crural area

Irritable bowel syndrome

Definition: a clinical condition based on a history of at least
3 months abdominal pain and altered bowel habit without
abnormalities on radiological, endoscopic or laboratory
investigation.

Clinical features

- typically in younger women (21–40)
- any age or sex can be affected
- cramping abdominal pain (central or iliac fossa) (see figure below)
- pain usually relieved by passing flatus or by defecation
- sense of incomplete evacuation
- variable bowel habit (constipation more common)
- often precipitated by eating
- faeces sometimes like small, hard pellets or ribbon-like
- anorexia and nausea (sometimes)
- bloating, abdominal distension, ↑ borborygmi
- tiredness common
- onset and exacerbation may be associated with mental stress

IBS is a diagnosis of exclusion. FBE, ESR, stool microscopy and thorough physical examination and sigmoidoscopy is necessary. Insufflation of air at sigmoidoscopy may reproduce the abdominal pain of IBS.

Management

Basis of initial treatment is simple dietary modifications, stress management and other non-drug therapy.

- education and reassurance (including cancer absent)
- avoid dietary factors that provoke symptoms
- avoid smoking and codeine preparations

Other measures depend on whether diarrhoea or constipation dominant, e.g. short courses of loperamide for diarrhoea.

Worthwhile trial if persistent:

- dothiepin or other antidepressant

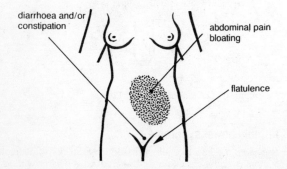

Classic symptoms of irritable bowel syndrome

J

Jaundice

- Jaundice is defined as a serum bilirubin exceed 17 μmol/L.
- Clinical jaundice manifests only when the bilirubin exceeds 50 μmol/L.
- Jaundice is difficult to detect visually below 85 μmol/L if lighting is poor.
- The most common causes of jaundice recorded in a general practice population are (in order) viral hepatitis, gallstones, carcinoma of pancreas, cirrhosis, pancreatitis and drugs.
- Always take a full travel, drug and hepatitis contact history in any patient presenting with jaundice.

Table 37 *Jaundice (adults): diagnostic strategy model (modified)*

Q.	*Probability diagnosis*
A.	Hepatitis A,B,C
	Gallstones
	Alcoholic hepatitis/cirrhosis
	Drug reactions
Q.	*Serious disorders not to be missed*
A.	Malignancy
	• pancreas
	• biliary tract
	• hepatocellular (hepatoma)
	• metastases
	Severe infections
	• septicaemia
	• ascending cholangitis
	• fulminant hepatitis
	Rarities
	• Wilson's disease
	• Reye's disease
	• acute fatty liver of pregnancy
Q.	*Pitfalls (often missed)*
A.	Gallstones
	Gilbert's disease
	Cardiac failure
	Primary biliary cirrhosis
	Chronic active hepatitis
	Haemochromatosis
	Viral infections

Investigations

The main investigations are the standard liver function tests and viral serology for the infective causes, particularly hepatitis B and C viruses.

Table 38 *Characteristic liver function tests*

Liver function tests (serological)	Hepato-cellular (viral) hepatitis	Haemolytic jaundice	Obstruction	Alcoholic liver disease
Bilirubin	↑ to ↑↑↑	↑ unconjugated	↑ to ↑↑↑	↑ to N
Alkaline phosphatase	↑ <2N	N	↑↑↑ >2N	↑
Aspartate transferase	↑↑↑ >5N	N	N or ↑	↑
Gamma glutamyl transferase	N or ↑	N	↑↑	↑↑↑
Albumin	N or ↓	N	N	N to ↓↓
Globulin	N or ↑	N	N	N to ↑

N: is within normal limits

Infective viral hepatitis

- hepatitis A,B,C common esp. B and C
- A and E—faeco-oral transmission
- B,C,D—from IV drugs and bodily fluids
- sexual transmission with B and C
- diagnosed by viral markers for A,B,C,D

Management

- patient education
- rest, fat free diet
- avoid alcohol, smoking and hepatotoxic drugs
- advice on hygiene and prevention
- interferon alpha for chronic hepatitis B and C (ideally for 12 months)

Prevention

- Hepatitis A vaccine   0,1,6 months
- Hepatitis B vaccine   0,1,6 months
- Immunoglobulin for A and B

Jet lag

Symptoms: exhaustion, disorientation, poor concentration, insomnia, anxiety, anorexia, others.

How to minimise the problem (advice to patients)

Before the flight

- Allow plenty of time for planning.
- Plan a stopover if possible.
- If possible arrange the itinerary so that you are flying into the night.
- Ensure a good sleep the night before flying.
- Ensure a relaxed trip to the airport.
- Take along earplugs if noise (75–100 decibels) is bothersome.

During the flight

- *Fluids* Avoid alcohol and coffee. Drink plenty of non-alcoholic drinks such as orange juice and mineral water.
- *Food* Eat only when hungry and even skip a meal or two.
- *Dress* Women should wear loose clothes and comfortable (not tight) shoes and take them off during flight.
- *Smoking* Reduce smoking to a minimum. Non-smokers should seek a non-smoking zone.
- *Sleep* Try to sleep on longer sections of the flight (give the movies a miss). Sedatives such as temazepam, zopiclone or antihistamines can help sleep.
- *Activity* Try to take regular walks around the aircraft and exercise at airport stops.
- *Special body care* Continually wet the face and eyes.

At the destination

Take a nap for 1–2 hours if possible.

Wander around until you are tired and go to bed at the usual time. It is good to have a full day's convalescence and avoid big decision making soon after arrival.

Jitters

(pre-occasion jitters/performance anxiety)
Propranolol 10–40 mg (o) 30–60 minutes before the event or performance.

Jock itch

see Tinea cruris, page 335

K

Keloid or hypertrophic scar

Various treatment methods
Multiple pressure injections:

- Spread film of corticosteroid solution over scar.
- Apply multiple pressure through solution with a 21 g needle held tangentially (about 20 superficial stabs per cm^2).
- Avoid bleeding.
- Repeat in 6 weeks
        or
Intralesional injection of triamcinolone
        or
Topical class III–IV corticosteroid ointment with occlusion.

Keratoacanthoma

Management

- remove by excision—perform biopsy (at least 2–3 mm margin)
- if clinically certain—curettage/diathermy
- treat as SCC (by excision) if on lip/ear

Note: Can be misdiagnosed instead of SCC.

Keratoses (solar and seborrhoeic)

Seborrhoeic keratoses

Management

- usually nil apart from reassurance
- does not undergo malignant change
- can be removed for cosmetic reasons
- light cautery to small facial lesions
- may drop off spontaneously
- if diagnosis uncertain, remove for histopathology

Decolourisation or removal:

- liquid nitrogen (regular applications, e.g. every 3 weeks)
        or
- concentrated phenol solution (with care)
    repeat in 3 weeks
        or

- trichloracetic acid: apply to surface
  and instil with multiple small needle pricks (25 g)
  Repeat twice weekly for 2 weeks.

Solar keratoses

Management

- reduced exposure to sunlight
- can disappear spontaneously
- liquid nitrogen if superficial

  or

- 5-fluorouracil 5% cream daily for 3–4 weeks
- surgical excision for suspicious and ulcerating lesions
- biopsy if doubtful

Knee pain

Key facts and checkpoints

- A ruptured anterior cruciate ligament (ACL) is the most commonly missed injury of the knee.
- A rapid onset of painful knee swelling (minutes to 1–4 hours) after injury indicates blood in the joint—*haemarthrosis:* the main causes are torn cruciate ligaments, capsular tears with collateral ligament tears, peripheral meniscal tears, fractures and dislocations.
- Swelling over 1–2 days after injury indicates synovial fluid—*traumatic synovitis.*
- Acute spontaneous inflammation of the knee may be part of a systemic condition such as rheumatoid arthritis, rheumatic fever, gout, pseudogout (chondrocalcinosis), a spondyloarthropathy (psoriasis, ankylosing spondylitis, Reiter's disease, bowel inflammation), Lyme disease and sarcoidosis.
- Consider Osgood-Schlatter disorder in the prepubertal child (especially a boy aged 10–14) presenting with knee pain.
- Disorders of the lumbosacral spine (especially L3 to S1 nerve root problems) and of the hip joint (L3 innervation) refer pain to the region of the knee joint.

Osgood-Schlatter disorder

Management

This is conservative as it is a self-limiting condition (6–18 months: average 12 months).

- If acute, use ice packs and analgesics.
- Main approach is to abstain from or modify active sports.

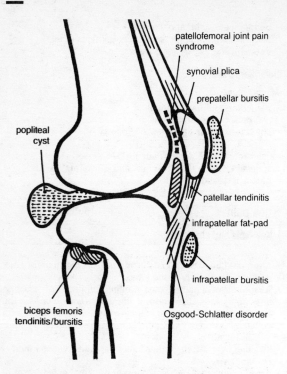

Lateral view of knee showing typical sites of various causes of knee pain

Chondrocalcinosis of knee (pseudogout)

- calcium pyrophosphate deposition
- in older people > 60
- can present with hot, red, swollen joint
- aspirate knee to search for crystals
- treat with NSAIDs or I-A steroid injection

Meniscal tears

- can occur with forced rotation on an abducted or adducted knee
- joint line pain ± locking is main symptom

Signs
- localised tenderness over joint line
- pain on hyperextension and hyperflexion of joint
- pain on rotation lower leg

Treatment
Arthroscopic meniscectomy

Anterior cruciate ligament (ACL) rupture

Sudden onset severe pain
Haemarthrosis/gross effusion

Ligament tests
— anterior draw: negative or positive
— pivot shift test: positive (only if instability)
— Lachman test: lacking an endpoint

Refer for surgery.

Medial collateral ligament rupture

Mechanism (main)
- direct valgus force to knee (lateral side knee), e.g. rugby tackle from side

Causes medial knee pain; aggravated by twisting.
Usually responds to 6 weeks in limited motion brace then knee rehabilitation.

Patellofemoral pain syndrome

Most common overuse injury of knee.

- pain behind patella or deep in knee
- pain aggravated during activities that require flexion of knee under loading, e.g. climbing stairs

Treatment
- Correct any underlying biomechanical abnormalities by use of orthotics and correct footwear.
- Give reassurance and supportive therapy.
- Employ quadriceps exercises.

Patellar tendinitis ('jumper's knee')

Gradual onset of anterior pain.
Pain localised to below knee.
Pain eased by rest, returns with activity.

Management

Early conservative treatment including rest from the offending stresses is effective. Avoid impact activity. Chronic cases invariably require surgery.

Localised tendinitis or bursitis

e.g. prepatellar bursitis, infrapatellar bursitis, biceps femoris tendinitis, anserinus tendinitis/bursitis
Generally (apart from patellar tendinitis), the treatment is an injection of local anaesthetic and long-acting corticosteroids into and deep to the localised area of tenderness. In addition it is important to restrict the offending activity with relative rest and refer for physiotherapy for stretching exercises. Attention to biomechanical factors and footwear is important.

Osteoarthritis

Management

- relative rest
- weight loss
- analgesics and/or judicious use of NSAIDs
- walking aids and other supports
- physiotherapy, e.g. hydrotherapy, quadriceps exercises, mobilisation and stretching techniques
- intra-articular injections of corticosteroids are generally not recommended but a single injection for severe pain can be very effective
- surgery: indicated for severe pain and stiffness; usually excellent results

Laryngitis

- Avoid talking.
- Drink ample fluids.
- Avoid cigarettes.
- Use steam inhalations (5 minutes bd).

Leg pain

Table 39 *Pain in the leg: diagnostic strategy model (modified)*

Q.	*Probability diagnosis*
A.	Cramps
	Nerve root 'sciatica'
	Muscular injury, e.g. hamstring
	Osteoarthritis (hip, knee)
	Overuse injury, e.g. Achilles tendinitis
Q.	*Serious disorders not to be missed*
A.	Vascular
	• Arterial occlusion (embolism/thrombosis)
	• Thrombosis popliteal aneurysm
	• Deep venous thrombosis
	Neoplasia
	• Primary, e.g. myeloma
	• Metastases, e.g. breast to femur
	Infection
	• Osteomyelitis
	• Septic arthritis
	• Erysipelas
	• Lymphangitis
	• Gas gangrene
Q.	*Pitfalls (often missed)*
A.	Osteoarthritis hip
	Osgood-Schlatter's disease
	Spinal canal stenosis
	Herpes zoster (early)
	Nerve entrapment
	'Hip pocket nerve'

Spinal causes of leg pain

Problems originating from the spine are an important, yet at times complex, cause of pain in the leg.

Important causes are:

- nerve root (radicular) pain from direct pressure, esp. sciatica (L4–S3) (page 54)
- referred pain from:
  — disc pressure on tissues in front of the spinal cord
  — apophyseal joints
  — sacroiliac joints
- spinal canal stenosis causing claudication

Vascular causes of leg pain

Occlusive arterial disease

Acute lower limb ischaemia

Sudden occlusion whether by embolism or thrombosis is a dramatic event which requires immediate diagnosis and management to save the limb.

Signs and symptoms—the 6 Ps

- pain
- pallor
- paraesthesia or numbness
- pulselessness
- paralysis
- 'perishing' cold

Management of acute ischaemia

Golden rules Occlusion is usually reversible if treated within 4 hours, i.e. limb salvage. It is often irreversible if treated after 6 hours, i.e. limb amputation.

Treatment

- intravenous heparin (immediately) 5000 U
- emergency embolectomy (ideally within 4 hours)

or

- arterial bypass if acute thrombosis in chronically diseased artery
- amputation (early) if irreversible ischaemic changes

Chronic lower limb ischaemia

Chronic ischaemia caused by gradual arterial occlusion can manifest as intermittent claudication or rest pain in the foot.

Treatment

- General measures (if applicable): control obesity, diabetes, hypertension, hyperlipidaemia, cardiac failure.
- Achieve ideal weight.
- Absolutely no smoking.
- Exercise: daily graduated exercise to the level of pain. About 50% will improve with walking so advise as much walking as possible.
- Try to keep legs warm and dry.
- Maintain optimal foot care (podiatry).
- Drug therapy: aspirin 150 mg daily.

Note: Vasodilators and sympathectomy are of little value. About one-third progress, while the rest regress or don't change.

When to refer to a vascular surgeon

- 'unstable' claudication of recent onset; deteriorating
- severe claudication—unable to maintain lifestyle
- rest pain
- 'tissue loss' in feet, e.g. heel cracks, ulcers on or between toes, dry gangrenous patches, infection

Venous disorders

Varicose veins

Varicose veins and pain

They may be painless even if large and tortuous. Pain is a feature where there are incompetent perforating veins running from the posterior tibial vein to the surface through the soleus muscle.

Severe cases lead to the lower leg venous hypertension syndrome characterised by pain worse after standing, cramps in the leg at night, irritation and pigmentation of the skin, swelling of the ankles and loss of skin features such as hair.

Management of varicose veins

Prevention:

- Maintain ideal weight.
- High-fibre diet.
- Rest and wear supportive stockings if at risk (pregnancy, a standing occupation).

Treatment:

- Keep off legs as much as possible.
- Sit with legs on a footstool.

- Use supportive stockings or tights (apply in morning before standing out of bed).
- Avoid scratching itching skin over veins.

Compression sclerotherapy:

- Use a small volume of sclerosant, e.g. 5% ethanolamine oleate; STD.
- Ideal for smaller isolated veins.

Surgical ligation and stripping:

- The best treatment when a clear association exists between symptoms and obvious varicose veins, i.e. long saphenous vein incompetence.
- Remove obvious varicosities and ligate perforators.

Superficial thrombophlebitis

Treatment

The objective is to prevent propagation of the thrombus by uniform pressure over the vein.

- Cover whole tender cord with a thin foam pad.
- Apply a firm elastic bandage (preferable to crepe) from foot to thigh (well above cord).
- Leave pad and bandage on for 7–10 days.
- Bed rest with leg elevated is recommended.
- Prescribe an NSAID, e.g. indomethacin, for 10 days.

Note:
- No anticoagulants are required.
- If the problem is above the knee, ligation of the vein at the saphenofemoral junction may be necessary.

Deep venous thrombosis (DVT)

DVT may be asymptomatic but usually causes tenderness in the calf. One or more of the following features may be present.

Clinical features

- ache or tightness in calf
- acute diffuse leg swelling
- pitting oedema
- tender 'doughy' consistency to palpation
- increased warmth
- pain on extension of foot (Homan's sign)

Investigations

- duplex ultrasound
        and/or
- radionuclide scan
- contrast venography if these two accurate tests are negative

Management

Prevention (cases at risk):

- elastic or graded compression stockings
- physiotherapy
- pneumatic compression
- electrical calf muscle stimulation during surgery
- heparin 5000 U (SC) bd or tds

Treatment

- collect blood for APTT, INR and platelet count
- bed rest with leg elevated
- one-way-stretch elastic bandages (both legs to above knees)
- IV heparin—5000 U statim then continuous monitored infusion (at least 10 days); aim for APTT 1.5 to 2 normal
- oral anticoagulant (warfarin) for 3 months (monitor with INR)
- mobilisation with resolution of pain, tenderness and swelling

Surgery is necessary in extensive and embolising cases.

Cellulitis and erysipelas of legs

- rest in bed
- elevate limb (in and out of bed)
- aspirin for pain and fever

Streptococcus pyogenes (the common cause)

severe
    benzylpenicillin 1.2 g IV 4 hourly
less severe
    procaine penicillin 1 g IM 12 hourly
             or
    phenoxymethyl penicillin 500 mg (o) 6 hourly
if penicillin sensitive
    cephalothin IV or cephalexin 500 mg (o) 6 hourly
             or
    erythromycin 500 mg (o) 12 hourly

Staphylococcus aureus

severe, may be life-threatening
    flucloxacillin 2 g IV 6 hourly
less severe
    flucloxacillin 500 mg (o) 6 hourly
             or
    cephalexin 500 mg (o) 6 hourly
             or
    erythromycin 500 mg (o) 12 hourly

Nocturnal cramps (see page 113)

Lice infestation

Treatment methods.

Head lice

Pyrethrins/piperonyl butoxide (Lyban) foam or shampoo.

Method:
- Massage well into wet hair.
- Leave at least 10 minutes (preferably overnight).
- Wash off thoroughly (avoid eye contact).
- Comb with a fine toothed comb.
- Repeat after 7 days.

Note:
- The hair does not have to be cut short.
- Treat all household child contacts.
- Wash clothing and bedclothes after treatment (normal machine wash).

Eyelash involvement:
- Apply petrolatum bd for 8 days, then pluck off remaining nits.

Pubic lice

Maldison 0.5% lotion

Method:
- Apply to pubic hair.
- Leave 12 hours (preferably overnight).
- Wash off thoroughly.
- Wash underwear and bedclothes after treatment.
- Repeat after 7 days.
- Treat sexual partners.

Alternative treatment:
Lindane 1% lotion
- Use as above.
- Avoid lindane during pregnancy and lactation.

Lichen planus

Lichen planus is a disorder of unknown aetiology characterised by pruritic violaceous flat-tipped papules, mainly on the wrists and legs.

Clinical features

- young and middle-aged adults
- small, shiny, lichenified plaques
- symmetrical and flat-tipped
- violaceous
- flexor surfaces: wrists, forearms, ankles
- can affect oral mucosa—white streaks or papules or ulcers
- can affect nails and scalp

Management

- explanation and reassurance
- usually resolves over months, leaving discoloured marks without scarring
- recurrence rare
- asymptomatic lesions require no treatment
- if symptomatic, e.g. itching
  topical fluorinated steroids under plastic occlusion
  intralesional corticosteroids for hypertrophic lesions

Melanoma

The early diagnosis of melanoma is vital to outcome. Thickness of a melanoma when it is removed is the major factor determining prognosis: it is vital to detect melanomas when they are in the thin stage and look like an unusual freckle. An irregular border or margin is characteristic of the tumour.

Clinical features

- typical age range 30–50 years (average 40)
- can occur anywhere on the body
      more common — lower limb in women
                  — upper back in men
- often asymptomatic
- can bleed or itch

Change

The sign of major importance is a recent change in a 'freckle' or mole

- change in size: at edge or thickening
- change in shape
- change in colour: brown, blue, black, red, white, including combinations
- change in surface
- change in the border
- bleeding or ulceration
- other symptoms, e.g. itching
- development of satellite nodules
- lymph node involvement

Table 40 *Features and associations of melanoma subtypes*

Melanoma subtype	Frequency %	Location	Average age
Superficial spreading	70	Trunk (back), limbs (legs)	Middle-aged
Nodular	20	Trunk, limbs	Middle-aged
Lentigo maligna	7.5	Head, neck	Elderly
Acral lentiginous	2.5	Palms, soles mucosae	Not known

Reproduced with permission of J. Kelly

Management

Early diagnosis and referral vital.
Surgical excision with a narrow but significant margin is *the* treatment, e.g. 10 mm for early (1 mm thick) lesion. There is no place for punch biopsy.

Melasma (chloasma)

2% hydroquinone in sorbolene cream

Menière's syndrome (see 141)

Menopause syndrome

The menopause is the cessation of the menses for longer than 12 months. Some women experience adverse effects.

Symptoms

Vasomotor, e.g.

- hot flushes (80%)
- night sweats (70%)
- palpitations (30%)

Psychogenic, e.g.

- irritability
- depression
- anxiety/tension

Urogenital (60%), e.g.

- atrophic vaginitis
- vaginal dryness (45%)
- dyspareunia

Musculoskeletal, e.g.

- non-specific muscular aches

Skin and other tissue changes, e.g.

- dry skin

Other, e.g.

- unusual tiredness
- headache

Investigations

Apart from a Papanicolaou smear, the following tests should be considered:

- urinalysis
- full blood count, lipids including HDL
- liver function tests

- mammography (all women, preferably after three months on HRT)
- diagnostic hysteroscopy and endometrial biopsy if undiagnosed vaginal bleeding
- bone density study (if risk factors)

If diagnosis in doubt, e.g. perimenopause; younger patient < 45 years; hysterectomy:

- serum FSH
- serum oestradiol } Diagnostic

Hormone replacement therapy

HRT has to be tailored to the individual patient and depends on several factors including the presence of a uterus, individual preferences and tolerance. Aim for 5 years treatment then review. (Consider risks.)

Table 41 *A summarised regimen for HRT*

Oestrogen
Oral medication
- conjugated oestrogen (Premarin) 0.625 mg
          or
- piperazine oestrone (Ogen) 1.25 mg
          or
- oestradiol valerate (Progynova) 2 mg
  Dosage
  - half tablet for 7 days initially, then one tablet daily continuous
Transdermal patches
- oestradiol (Estraderm) 4 mg patch

Progestogen
- medroxyprogesterone (Provera) 10 mg
          or
- norethisterone (Primolut N) 5 mg
  one tablet for first 12 days of month
To induce amenorrhoea
Give progestogen continuously daily, instead of cyclically
- medroxyprogesterone 2.5 mg
          or
- norethisterone 1.25 mg

Uterus present
Oestrogen and progestogen

No uterus (hysterectomy)
Oestrogen only

Perimenopausal regimen
Combined oestrogen and progesterone sequential therapy, e.g. Trisequens, Menoprem

Coming—the future
Combination patch
- oestrogen plus progestogen (first half of cycle)
- oestrogen only (second half of cycle)

Menorrhagia

Abnormal uterine bleeding is a common problem. Menstrual blood loss is normally less than 80 mL. Menorrhagia is a menstrual loss of more than 120 mL per menstruation (some say > 80 mL).

Features of menorrhagia:
- heavy bleeding—possibly with clots
- if dysmenorrhoea suspect endometriosis or PID
- the most common cause is dysfunctional uterine bleeding
- the most common organic causes are fibroids, endometriosis, endometrial polyps and PID, but neoplasia and ectopic pregnancy must be excluded.

Various drugs can be implicated. e.g. hormone therapy, anticoagulants, cannabis, various steroids, some antihypertensives, heavy smoking.

Dysfunctional uterine bleeding (DUB)

DUB is a diagnosis of exclusion so careful investigations are required to exclude pathology.

Symptoms

- heavy bleeding: saturated pads, frequent changing, 'accidents', 'flooding', 'clots'
- prolonged bleeding
  — menstruation > 8 days
          or
  — heavy bleeding > 4 days
- frequent bleeding—periods occur more than once every 21 days

General treatment rules

< 40 years: medical treatment
> 40 years: hysteroscopy and direct endometrial sample

Drug therapy regimens (see Tables 42 and 43)

Table 42 *Regimens used in management of menorrhagia*

NSAIDs (prostaglandin inhibitors)
Mefenamic acid 500 mg tds (first sign menses to end of menses)
                              or
Naproxen 500 mg statim then 250 mg tds

Combined oestrogen-progesterone OC
This is an important first-line therapy.
    e.g. 50 µg oestrogen + 1 mg norethisterone, e.g. Norinyl,
      OrthoNovum

(continues)

Table 42 *(continued)*

Progestogens (especially for anovulatory patients)
   Norethisterone 5–15 mg/day for 14 days
         or
   Medroxyprogesterone acetate 10–30 mg/day
Give progestogens from day 5–25 (ovulatory patients)

Danazol
Approved for short-term treatment (6 months or less) of severe menorrhagia—dosage 200 mg daily

Others
LHRL analogues
Progestogen releasing ICUDs

Table 43 *Typical treatment options for acute and chronic heavy bleeding*

Acute heavy bleeding
• curettage/hysteroscopy
• IV oestrogen (Premarin 20 mg)
     or
oral high-dose progestogens
e.g. norethisterone 5–10 mg 2 hourly for 4 doses
  then 5 mg bd or tds for 14 days

Chronic bleeding
• for anovulatory women
 — cyclical oral progestogens for 14 days
• for ovulatory women
 — cyclical prostaglandin inhibitor
     or
 oral contraceptive
 — oral progestogens (21 days/month)
 — danazol or antifibrinolytic agent

Migraine attack (see page 209)

Milker's nodules

In humans 2–5 papules appear on the hands about one week after handling cows' udders or calves' mouths.
  Self-limiting and remit in 5–6 weeks.
  Can give intralesional injection of corticosteroid.

Molluscum contagiosum

Can be spread by scratching and use of steroids.

Treatment options
- liquid nitrogen (a few seconds)
- pricking the lesion with a pointed stick soaked in 1% or 3% phenol
- application of 15% podophyllin in friar's balsam (compound benzoin tincture)
- application of 30% trichloracetic acid
- destruction by electrocautery or diathermy
- ether soap and friction method
- lifting open the tip with a sterile needle inserted from the side (parallel to the skin) and applying 10% povidone iodine (Betadine) solution (parents can be shown this method and continue to use it at home for multiple tumours)
- paint with clear nail polish/acetone

'Monkey muscle' tear

This is a torn medial head of gastrocnemius.

- RICE treatment for 72 hours
- compress with firm elastic bandage (toes to below knee)
- crutches if necessary
- raised heel on shoe
- physiotherapist referral
- active exercises after 48 hours

Morning sickness (see page 272)

Morning-after pill

(must be used within 72 hours)

- use high oestrogen pill:
    50 μg EO + 250 μg LNG (Nordiol) × 2 pills (or equiv alent dose in other pills)
- repeat in 12 hours
- add an antiemetic, e.g. metoclopramide 10 mg (o)

Mouth problems
Angular fissures
- Check dentures and hygiene.
- Apply dimethicone cream for protection.
- If persistent and/or for suspected candida, use antifungal cream.

Bad taste

- Look for cause, e.g. teeth, gums, depression.
- Consider Ascoxal tablets, 1–2 tabs dissolved in 25 mL warm water as mouthwash for two rinses up to five times daily.

Mouth ulcers

(as for aphthous ulcers)

Multiple sclerosis

Multiple sclerosis (MS) is the most common cause of progressive neurological disability in the 20–50 year age group. Early diagnosis is difficult.

Clinical features

- transient motor and sensory disturbances
- upper motor neurone signs
- common initial symptoms include:
  — visual disturbances of optic neuritis
  — diplopia (brain stem lesion)
  — weakness in one or both legs, paraparesis or hemiparesis
  — sensory impairment in the lower limbs and trunk
  — vertigo (brain stem lesion)
- subsequent remissions and exacerbations

Lesions separated in time and place.
MRI the best investigation: sensitivity 90%.

Management

Education and support.
Referral to a neurologist.
No specific drug for MS.
Corticosteroids reduce severity of acute attack.
Beta interferon and copolymer-1 may reduce number of attacks (under evaluation).

Myocardial infarction

Clinical guidelines

- variable pain; may be mistaken for indigestion
- similar to angina but more oppressive
- so severe, patient may fear imminent death—'angor animi'
- about 20% have no pain
- 'silent infarcts' in diabetics, hypertensives and elderly
- 60% of those who die do so before reaching hospital, within two hours of the onset of symptoms
- hospital mortality is 8–10%

Physical signs

These may be:

- no abnormal signs
- pale/grey, clammy, dyspnoeic
- restless and apprehensive
- variable BP ↑ with pain
                    ↓ heart pump failure
- variable pulse: watch for bradyarrhythmias
- mild cardiac failure: 3rd or 4th heart sound, basal crackles

Investigations

1. *The ECG* is valuable with characteristic changes in a full thickness infarction. The features are shown in the figure below.

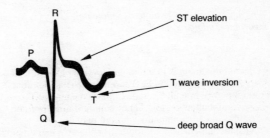

*Typical ECG features of myocardial
infarction, illustrating a Q wave, ST elevation
and T wave inversion*

2. *Cardiac enzymes* The typical enzyme patterns are presented in the figure below. As a rule large infarcts tend to produce high serum enzyme levels. The elevated enzymes can help time the infarct.
3. *Technetium pyrophosphate scanning*
   Scans for 'hot spots'.
4. *Echocardiography* is used to assist diagnosis when other tests are not diagnostic.
   Note: The clinical diagnosis may be the most reliable and the ECG and enzymes may be negative.

Management of myocardial infarction

General principles:

- Aim for immediate attendance if suspected.
- Call a mobile coronary care unit, especially if severe.

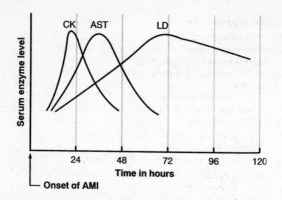

Typical cardiac enzyme patterns following myocardial infarction

- Optimal treatment is in a modern coronary care unit (if possible) with continuous ECG monitoring (first 48 hours), a peripheral IV line and intranasal oxygen.
- Pay careful attention to relief of pain and apprehension.
- Establish a caring empathy with the patient.
- Consider all patients for thrombolytic therapy, e.g. streptokinase (the sooner the better).
- Give aspirin as early as possible (if no contraindications).
- Prescribe a beta-blocker drug early (if no contraindications and appropriate)
- Prevent possible sudden death in early stages from ventricular fibrillation by monitoring and availability of a defibrillator.

First-line management, e.g. outside hospital
- oxygen 4–6 L/minute
- secure an IV line
- glyceryl trinitrate spray or 300–600 mcg (½–1 tab) SL (every 5 minutes if necessary—max. 3 doses)
- aspirin 150–300 mg

Add if necessary:

- morphine 5 mg IV statim bolus: 1 mg/min slowly until pain relief (up to 15 mg)
  ± metoclopramide 10 mg IV (as antiemetic)
  (If feasible it is preferable to give IV morphine 1 mg/min until relief of pain: this titration is easier in hospital.)

Hospital management

- As for first-line management.
- Take blood for cardiac enzymes, urea and electrolytes.
- Consider streptokinase (check rules)
  — 1 500 000 units IV infusion over 30–45 minutes
  — (aim for 30 minutes and if problems such as hypotension (BP < 80 mmHg) occur slow down the infusion)
  — do not use 3 days to 12 months after prior use; instead use alteplase (rt-PA).

  Note: Streptokinase and rt-PA are of similar efficiency but rt-PA is much more expensive.

- Full heparinisation for 24–36 hours (with rt-PA, not streptokinase), especially for large anterior transmural infarction with risk of embolisation, supplemented by warfarin.
- Beta-blocker (if no contraindications) as soon as possible in those not given thrombolytic therapy.
- Treat complications as necessary.
- Consider glyceryl trinitrate IV infusion if pain recurs.
- Consider early introduction of ACE inhibitors.

N

Nappy rash

The main factor is dampness due to urine and faeces. The commonest type is *irritant dermatitis* but consider also:

- seborrhoeic dermatitis
- *candida albicans* (tends to superinfect seborrhoea)
- atopic dermatitis
- psoriasis

Irritant dermatitis

- Keep the area dry.
- Change wet or soiled napkins often—disposable ones are good.
- Wash gently and pat dry (do not rub).
- Avoid excessive bathing and soap.
- Avoid powders and plastic pants.
- Use emollients to keep skin lubricated
    e.g. zinc oxide and castor oil cream
                    or
         nappy rash cream formula
            sol. al. acetate   16%
            wool fat   33%
            boric acid   1%
            zinc cream   add 100
            sig: apply each change

If: atopic dermatitis: 1% hydrocortisone
    seborrhoeic dermatitis: 1% hydrocortisone and ketoconazole ointment
    Candida albicans: topical nystatin at each nappy change
    widespread nappy rash: 1% hydrocortisone with nystatin or clotrimazole cream (qid after changes)

Narcotic dependence

Typical profile of a narcotic-dependent person

- Male or female: 16–30 years.
- Family history: often severely disrupted, e.g. parental problems, early death, separation, divorce, alcohol or drug abuse, sexual abuse, mental illness, lack of affection.

• Personal history: low threshold for toleration, unpleasant emotions, poor academic record, failure to fulfil aims, poor self-esteem.

Many of the severe problems are due to withdrawal of the drug.

Withdrawal effects

These develop within 12 hours of ceasing regular usage. Maximum withdrawal symptoms usually between 36–72 hours.

• anxiety and panic
• irritability
• chills and shivering
• excessive sweating
• 'gooseflesh' (cold turkey)
• loss of appetite, nausea (possibly vomiting)
• lacrimation/rhinorrhoea
• tiredness/insomnia
• muscle aches and cramps
• abdominal colic

Management

Management is complex because it includes not only the medical management of physical dependence and withdrawal but also of the individual complex social and emotional factors. The issue of HIV prevention also has to be addressed. Patients should be referred to a treatment clinic and then a shared care approach can be used. The treatments include 'cold turkey' with pharmacological support, acupuncture, megadoses of vitamin C, methadone substitution and drug-free community education programs.

Methadone maintenance programs which include counselling techniques are widely used for heroin dependence.

Neck pain

Cervical dysfunction

Cause

Minor injury causing dysfunction including stiffness in facet joints.

Features

• deep ache in neck
• pain may radiate to head or suprascapular area
• variable restriction of neck movement
• X-rays usually normal

Table 44 *Neck pain: diagnostic strategy model (modified)*

Q.	*Probability diagnosis*
A.	Vertebral dysfunction
	Traumatic 'strain' or 'sprain'
	Cervical spondylosis
Q.	*Serious disorders not to be missed*
A.	Cardiovascular
	• angina
	• subarachnoid haemorrhage
	Neoplasia
	Severe infections
	• osteomyelitis
	• meningitis
	Vertebral fractures or dislocation
Q.	*Pitfalls (often missed)*
A.	Disc prolapse
	Myelopathy
	Cervical lymphadenitis
	Fibromyalgia syndrome
	Thyroiditis
	Outlet compression syndrome, e.g. cervical rib
	Polymyalgia rheumatica
	Ankylosing spondylitis
	Rheumatoid arthritis

Management

- education with advice such as good posture
- neck exercise program (crucial)
- referral to appropriate therapist for cervical mobilisation. Consider manipulation for stubborn 'locked' neck.

Cervical spondylosis

Cause

degenerative disease in older persons

Features

dull, aching neck pain with stiffness

Management

- referral for physiotherapy, including warm hydrotherapy
- regular mild analgesics, e.g. paracetamol
- NSAIDs: a trial for three weeks then review
- gentle mobilising exercises as early as possible
- passive mobilising techniques
- outline general rules to live by

Acute torticollis

Torticollis (acute wry neck) means a lateral deformity of the neck and is usually a transient self-limiting acutely painful disorder with associated muscle spasm of variable intensity. Most likely due to acute dysfunction of mid-cervical facet joints.

Management
- gentle mobilisation
- muscle energy therapy (very effective)

Whiplash syndrome

Treatment
- Provide appropriate reassurance and patient education.
- Compare the problem with a sprained ankle which is a similar injury.
- Inform that an emotional reaction of anger, frustration and temporary depression is common (lasts about 2 weeks).
- X-ray.
- Rest.
- Cervical collar (limit to 2 days).
- Analgesics, e.g. paracetamol (avoid narcotics).
- NSAIDs for 2 weeks.
- Tranquillisers, mild—up to 2 weeks.
- Physiotherapy referral.
- Neck exercises (as early as possible).
- Heat and massage; 'spray and stretch'.
- Passive mobilisation (not manipulation).

Needlesticks and sharps injuries

Management
- Squeeze out and wash under running tap water with soap and/or dilute sodium hypochlorite solution, e.g. Milton.
- Encourage bleeding.
- Obtain information about and blood from the sharps victim and the source person (source of body fluid). ? Hepatitis B or HIV + ve.

It takes up to three months to seroconvert with HIV.

Known hepatitis B carrier source person

If injured person immune—no further action.
If non-vaccinated and non-immune
    — give hyperimmune hepatitis B gammaglobulin (within 48 hours)
    — commence course of hepatitis B vaccination.

Known HIV-positive source person

Refer to consultant about relative merits of drug prophylaxis and serological monitoring.

Options

   zidovudine (AZT) prophylaxis within 72 hours
       300 mg qid for 6 weeks
              or
   serological monitoring 0,4,6,12,24 and 52 weeks

Unknown risk source person

Take source person's blood (if consent is given) and sharps victim blood for hepatitis B (HBsAg and anti-HBs) and (if high risk for HIV) HIV status tests. Commence hepatitis B vaccination if not vaccinated.

Note: Informed consent for testing and disclosure of test results for involved person should be obtained.

Nightmares

Give a 4 week trial of phenytoin.

Nose

Offensive smell from

Ensure no foreign body present.

- mupirocin 2% nasal ointment
       instil 2 or 3 times a day
              or
- Kenacomb ointment
       instil 2 or 3 times a day

Stuffy, running

- blow nose hard into disposable paper tissue or handkerchief until clear
- nasal decongestant for 2–3 days only
- steam inhalations with Friar's balsam or menthol preparations—use 1 teaspoon to 500 mL boiled water in old container (see figure below)

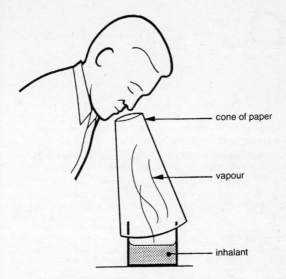

Steam inhalation

Obesity

The outstanding cause of weight gain in exogenous obesity is excessive calorie intake coupled with lack of exercise.
Useful measuring instruments include:

- body mass index (BMI): 'healthy' range is between 20 and 25 (BMI = weight (kg) ÷ height (M^2).
- waist:hip circumference ratio (W/H ratio): healthy range < 0.9
- single skinfold thickness (> 25 mm suggests increased body fat)

Table 45 *Classification of obesity*

BMI	Grading	Suggested therapy
< 18	very underweight	diet and counselling
18–20	underweight	diet and counselling
20–25	0. healthy weight	
25–30	I. overweight	more exercise diet
30–40	II. obesity	combined program: • behaviour modification • diet • exercise
> 40	III. morbid obesity	combined program plus medical therapy

Management principles

1. reduction in energy intake
2. change in diet composition
3. increased physical activity
4. behavioural therapy

Rules

- need a close supportive relationship
- promote realistic goals—lose weight slowly
- allow normal foods with reduced quantity and frequency e.g. eat one-third less than usual
- supportive counselling (never judgmental)

- provide a list of 'tips' for coping
- advise keep a food, exercise and behaviour diary
- strict follow-up, e.g. fortnightly then monthly until goal weight achieved, then 3 monthly reviews

Obsessive compulsive disorder

- refer for group therapy
- clomipramine (Anafranil)
        50–75 mg (o) nocte, increasing every 2 to 3 days to
        100–250 mg orally (o) nocte
                    or
- selective serotonin reuptake inhibitor antidepressant

Obstetric care

Basic antenatal care

Antenatal care presents preventive medicine opportunities *par excellence* and is the ideal time to develop an optimal therapeutic relationship with the expectant mother.

The initial visit

- careful history, physical examination
- establish date of confinement
- investigations (Table 46)

Visits during pregnancy

- initial in first trimester: 8–10 weeks
- up to 28 weeks: every 4–6 weeks
- up to 36 weeks: every 2 weeks
- 36 weeks—delivery: weekly

For each visit record:

- weight gain
- blood pressure
- urinalysis (protein and sugar)
- uterine size/fundal height
- foetal heart (usually audible with stethoscope at 25 weeks and definitely by 28 weeks)
- foetal movements (if present)
- presentation and position of foetus (third trimester)
- presence of any oedema

Table 46 *Standard antenatal investigations*

Essential

First visit
- full blood examination
- blood grouping and rhesus typing
- rubella antibodies
- cervical smear (if previous > 12 months)
- midstream urine: microscopy and culture
- HBs Ag (hepatitis surface antigen)
- syphilis screen
- haemoglobin electrophoresis (if indicated)

   Consider
- HIV antibodies

Subsequent visits
- ultrasound 18–20 weeks (if doubt about foetal maturity)
- midstream urine (M&C), 28 weeks (if high risk)
- haemoglobin 30 weeks
- Rh antibodies (negative mother), 28 weeks and 36 weeks
- glucose screening 28–30 weeks

   Consider
- cervical swab (group B haemolytic streptococcus) 32 weeks
- test fetoplacental function (32–38 weeks)

For prenatal diagnosis of genetic abnormalities:
- amniocentesis (14–16 weeks)
- chorionic villus sampling (9–11 weeks)
- alpha-fetoprotein
- triple test

Management of specific issues

Pregnancy sickness
- invariably disappears by end of first trimester
- explanation and reassurance
- simple measures
  — small frequent meals
  — fizzy soft drinks
  — avoid stimuli such as cooking smells
  — avoid oral iron
  — be careful cleaning teeth

Medication (for severe cases):
- pyridoxine 50–100 mg bd

   If still ineffective add:
- metoclopramide 10 mg tds

Cramps
- place pillow at foot of bed to dorsiflex feet
- tonic water before retiring

Varicose veins
Wear supportive pantyhose (not elastic bandages).
Keep to ideal weight.

Mineral supplements in pregnancy
Iron and folic acid are not routinely recommended for pregnant women who are healthy, following an optimal diet and have a normal blood test. Those at risk, e.g. with poor nutrition, will require supplementation.

Pregnancy-induced hypertension
Commonly used medications:

- Beta-blockers, e.g. labetalol, oxprenolol and atenolol (used under close supervision and after 20 weeks gestation)
- Methyldopa: good for sustained BP control

Diuretics and ACE inhibitors contraindicated.

Acute cystitis
Treatment
- cephalexin 250 mg (o) 6 hourly for 10–14 days
    or
- amoxycillin/potassium clavulanate (250/125 mg) (o) 8 hourly

---

Postnatal care

Oral contraception

- The mini pill (progestogen only)
    — norethisterone 350 micrograms/day
        or
    — levonorgestrel 30 micrograms/day taken every night
- Transfer to combined OC when breastfeeding completed.

Engorged breasts

Regular feeding and demand feeding is the best treatment.

Advice to mother
- Feed your baby on demand from day 1 until the baby has had enough.
- Finish the first breast completely; maybe use one side per feed rather than some from each breast. Offer the second breast if the baby appears hungry.

- Soften the breasts before feeds or express with a warm washer or shower, which will help to get the milk flowing.
- Avoid giving the baby other fluids.
- Express a little milk before putting the baby to your breast (a must if the baby has trouble latching on) and express a little after feeding from the other side if it is too uncomfortable.
- Massage any breast lumps gently towards the nipple while feeding.
- Apply cold packs after feeding or cool washed cabbage leaves (left in the refrigerator/between feeds.)
- Use a good, comfortable brassiere.
- Remove your bra completely before feeding.
- Take paracetamol regularly for severe discomfort.

Lactation suppression

- Avoid nipple stimulation.
- Refrain from expressing milk.
- Use well-fitting brassiere.
- Use cold packs and analgesics.

Engorgement settles over 2–3 weeks.

Hormonal suppression

- bromocriptine (Parlodel) 2.5 mg (o) bd for 10–14 days
- avoid oestrogens

Nipples: cracked

- Get baby to latch onto breast fully and properly.
- Do not feed from the affected breast—rest the nipple for 1–2 feeds.
- Express the milk from that breast by hand.
- Start feeding gradually with short feeds.
- Take paracetamol 1 g just before feeding to relieve the pain.
- Avoid drying agents such as spirits, creams and ointments.

Nipples: sore

- Use a relaxed feeding technique.
- Try to use the 'chest to chest, chin on breast' feeding position.
- Start feeding from the less painful side first if one nipple is very sore.
- Express some milk first to soften and 'lubricate' the nipple.
- Never pull the baby off the nipple: gently break the suction with your finger.
- Apply covered ice to the nipple to relieve pain.
- Keep the nipples dry (exposure to air or to hair dryer).
- Do not wear a bra at night.
- If wearing a bra by day, try Cannon breast shields.

Postnatal depressive disorders

1. Postnatal blues

- occurs in 80% women
- days 3 to 10 (lasts 4–14 days)
- feeling flat or depressed
- emotional—tearfulness
- mood swings, mainly flat

Treatment

- support and reassurance
- help from relatives and friends

2. Postnatal adjustment disorder

- occurs in first 6 months
- similar symptoms to 'blues'
- anxiety with handling baby
- psychosomatic complaints
- fearful of criticism

Treatment

- support and reassurance
- cognitive therapy
- parentcraft support
- settles with time

3. Postnatal depression

- occurs in 10–30% women
- in first 6–12 months (usually first 6)
- anxiety and agitation common
- marked mood swings
- poor memory and concentration
- typical depressive features

Treatment

- support, reassurance, counselling
- group psychotherapy
- couple therapy
- postnatal depression support group
- hospitalisation may be necessary
- medication, e.g. amitriptyline, dothiepin, sertraline

Note: Beware of puerperal psychosis with onset usually within first 2 weeks.

Postpartum hypothyroidism

Postpartum hypothyroidism (postpartum thyroiditis) may be misdiagnosed as postpartum depression and should always be considered in the tired, apparently depressed woman in the first six months after delivery.

Oily hair

- Shampoo daily with a 'shampoo for oily hair'.
- Massage the scalp during the shampoo process.
- Leave the shampoo on for at least five minutes.
- Avoid hair conditioners.
- Avoid overbrushing.
- Attend to lifestyle factors: relaxation and balanced diet are important.

Oral contraception

Combined oral contraception

Combined oral contraceptives (COC) usually contain a low-dose oestrogen and a moderate dose of progestogen.

A suitable first choice is a pill containing 20–35 μg of oestrogen: either the triphasic or monophasic pill.

- triphasic pills   Triphasil, Triquilar, Trimulet 28
- monophasic pills   Nordette, Microgynon 30, Brevinor, Marvelon, Minulet 28

The high-dose monophasic (50 μg EO) should be reserved for the following situations:

- breakthrough bleeding on low dose COCs
- control of menorrhagia
- concomitant use of enzyme-inducing drugs
- low-dose pill failure

Acne

For women with acne (not on COC), commence with a less androgenic progestogen, e.g. Diane 35 ED, Marvelon.

Important advice for the patient

- No break from the pill is necessary.
- Drugs that interact with the pill include vitamin C, antibiotics, griseofulvin, rifampicin and anticonvulsants (except sodium valproate). Warfarin and oral hypoglycaemics requirements may change for those starting the pill.
- Diarrhoea and vomiting may reduce the effectiveness of the pill.
- Yearly return visits are recommended.

The seven-day rule for the missed or late pill (more than 12 hours late):

- Take the forgotten pill as soon as possible, even if it means taking two pills in one day. Take the next pill at the usual time and finish the course.

- If you forget to take it for more than 12 hours after the usual time there is an increased risk of pregnancy so use another contraceptive method (such as condoms) for seven days.
- If these seven days run beyond the last hormone pill in your packet then miss out on the inactive pills (or seven-day gap) and proceed directly to the first hormone pill in your next packet. You may miss a period. (At least seven hormone tablets should be taken.)

Progestogen-only contraceptive pill (POP)

The POP is perhaps an underutilised method of contraception, although it is not as efficacious as the COC.

The two common formulations are:

levonorgestrel 30 μg/day
and
norethisterone 350 μ/day

Postcoital contraception

Available methods (*Note:* must be used within 72 hours)

- Use high-oestrogen-containing COC, e.g. 50 μg EO + 250 μg LNG (Nordiol)—two pills initially then repeated 12 hours later.

    Nausea is a common side effect and it is common to prescribe an antiemetic. Failure rate 2.6%.
- Danazol 200 mg tablets, e.g. two initially and repeated 12 hours later.

    Reduced incidence of nausea—failure rate 4.6%.

Orf

Orf is due to a pox virus and presents as a single papule or group of papules on the hands of sheep-handlers after handling lambs with contagious pustular dermatitis.

- Spontaneously remits in 3–4 weeks.
- For rapid resolution inject triamcinolone or other LA steroid, diluted 50:50 in N saline.

Osteoporosis

Osteoporosis refers to the increased bone fragility that accompanies ageing and many illnesses.

It literally means porous bone and is actually reduced bone mass per unit volume.

Densitometry can predict an increased risk of osteoporosis.

Treatment

Medication of value in decreasing further loss

The following medication may be valuable in preventing further bone loss, possibly reversing the osteoporosis process and preventing further fractures.

- HRT

or

- calcitriol (a vitamin D metabolite)—avoid calcium supplements during therapy—continuous

or

- etidronate disodium (a biphosphonate)—intermittent
  Anabolic agents such as nandrolone deconate may reduce further loss but the side effects are problematic.

Recommendations for prevention

- HRT within two years of the onset of menopause
- Adequate dietary intake of calcium
      800–1000 mg per day—premenopause
      1500 mg per day—postmenopausal

Note: 500 mL calcium enriched milk contains 1000 mg calcium.

- Exercise, e.g. brisk walk for 30 minutes 4 times a week.
- Lifestyle factors: stop smoking and limit alcohol and caffeine intake.

Otitis externa

(see page 160)

Otitis media

(see pages 158)

P

Paget's disease

Features

- 95% asymptomatic
- symptoms may include joint pain and stiffness, e.g. hips, knees; bone pain (usually spine); deformity; headache; deafness
- bone pain is typically deep and aching: may be worse at night
- signs may include deformity, enlarged skull 'hats don't fit any more', bowing of tibia

Diagnosis

- raised serum alkaline phosphatase (often very high > 1000 U/L)
  Note: calcium and phosphate normal
- plain X-ray: dense expanded bone—best seen in skull and pelvis. *Note:* can mimic prostatic secondaries so every male Pagetic patient should have PR & PSA
- bone isotopic scans: useful in locating specific areas

Treatment

The two major goals are relief of pain and prevention of long-term complication, e.g. deafness, deformities.

Localised and asymptomatic disease requires no treatment. Basic treatment for active Paget's disease is synthetic calcitonin (usually salmon calcitonin) e.g. 50 units SC injection daily or 100 units 3 times weekly (initially) then according to response; consider rest after 9–12 months if improvement.

Three groups of drugs currently available:

- the calcitonins (salmon, porcine, human)
- the biphosphonates, i.e. etidronate, pamidronate
- various antineoplastic agents, e.g. mithramycin

Palliative care

The fundamental principles of palliative care are:

- good communication, including information giving
- management planning
- symptom control

- emotional, social and spiritual support
- medical counselling and education
- patient involvement in decision making
- support for carers

Symptom control

Common symptoms

- boredom (the commonest symptom)
- loneliness/isolation
- fear
- pain
  — physical
  — emotional
  — spiritual
  — social
- anorexia
- nausea and vomiting
- constipation

Pain control

Step 1: Mild pain

Start with basic non-opioid analgesics:

> aspirin 600–900 mg (o) 4 hourly (preferred)
>
> or
>
> paracetamol 1 g (o) 4 hourly

Step 2: Moderate pain

Use low dose or weak opioids or in combination with non-opioid analgesics:

> codeine up to 60 mg (o) 4 hourly
>
> or
>
> morphine 5 to 10 mg (o) 4 hourly
>
> or
>
> oxycodone up to 10 mg (o) 4 hourly
>
> or
>
> 30 mg, rectally, 8 hourly

Step 3: Severe pain

Larger doses of opioids should be used and morphine is the drug of choice:

> morphine 10 mg (o) 4 hourly
>
> or
>
morphine SR tablets (MS Contin) (o) 12 hourly

Note:

- The proper dosage is that which is sufficient to alleviate pain.
- Give usual morphine 10 mg with first dose of morphine SR and then as necessary for 'rescue dosing'.

Guidelines for morphine

- If analgesia is inadequate, the next dose should be increased by 50% until pain control is achieved.
- Give it regularly, usually 4 hourly, before the return of the pain.
- Many patients find a mixture easier to swallow than tablets, e.g. 10 mg/10 mL solution.
- Give laxatives prophylactically. (See below)
- Order antiemetics.
- Reassure the patient and family about the safety and efficacy of morphine.
- If parenteral morphine needed, give subcutaneously.

Anorexia

> metoclopramide 10 mg tds
> > or
> corticosteroids, e.g. dexamethasone 2–8 mg tds
> high-energy drink supplements

Constipation

If opioids need to be maintained, the laxatives need to be peristaltic stimulants, not bulk-forming agents. Aim for firm faeces with bowels open about every third day.

> e.g. senna (Senokot) 2 daily or bd
> > bisacodyl (Durolax) 5–10 mg bd

Rectal suppositories, microenemas or enemas may be required, e.g. Microlax.

Death rattles

Hyoscine 0.4–0.8 mg, 4–8 hourly, can be used to dry secretions and stop the 'death rattle'.

Dyspnoea

Consider cause:

- tap a pleural effusion
- corticosteroids for lung metastases
- morphine
- oxygen

Nausea and vomiting

If due to morphine:

> haloperidol 1.5–5 mg daily
> > can be reduced after 10 days
> > > or
> prochlorperazine (Stemetil)
> > 5–10 mg (o) qid
> > > or
> > 25 mg rectally bd

Cerebral metastases

Common symptoms are headache and nausea. Consider corticosteroid therapy. Analgesics and antiemetics such as haloperidol are effective.

Hiccoughs

Try a starting dose of
> chlorpromazine 25 mg tds
> > or
> haloperidol 2.5 mg bd

Palpitations

Palpitations are defined as an unpleasant awareness of beating of the heart, including skipped heartbeat, irregular heartbeat, rapid or slow heartbeat. The symptoms are suggestive of cardiac arrhythmia but may have a non-cardiac cause. The commonest presenting cause is the symptomatic premature ventricular beat (ventricular ectopic).

Table 47 *Palpitations: diagnostic strategy model (modified)*

Q.	*Probability diagnosis*
A.	Anxiety
	Premature beats (ectopics)
	Sinus tachycardia
Q.	*Serious disorders not to be missed*
A.	Myocardial infarction/angina
	Arrhythmias
	• ventricular tachycardia
	• bradycardia
	• sick sinus syndrome
	• supraventricular arrhythmias
	WPW syndrome
	Electrolyte disturbances
	• hypokalaemia
	• hypomagnesaemia
	Thyrotoxicosis
Q.	*Pitfalls (often missed)*
A.	Fever/infection
	Pregnancy
	Menopause
	Drugs
	• social, e.g. caffeine, cocaine, amphetamines, alcohol, nicotine
	• prescribed, e.g. sympathomimetics
	Mitral valve prolapse
	Hypoglycaemia

Management strategies

- Treat the underlying cause.
- Give appropriate reassurance.
- Provide clear patient education.
- Explain about the problems of fatigue, stress and emotion.
- Advise moderation in consumption of tea, coffee, caffeine-containing soft drinks and alcohol.
- Advise about cessation of smoking and other drugs.
- Avoid drugs for atrial and ventricular premature beats and sinus tachycardia but give a beta-blocker (atenolol or metoprolol) if patient disturbed by symptoms.
- Most arrhythmias require referral.

Table 48 Summary of treatment of arrhythmias

Arrhythmia	First line	Second line
Sinus tachycardia	Treat cause	If no cause: metoprolol or atenolol or verapamil
Bradycardias		
Sick sinus syndrome	Permanent pacing if symptomatic	
AV block		
first degree	No treatment	
second degree		
Mobitz I:	No treatment	
Mobitz II:	Consider pacing	
third degree		
• acute, e.g. MI	Temporary pacing	
• chronic	Permanent pacing	
Atrial tachyarrhythmias*		
PSVT	Valsalva Carotid sinus massage	Verapamil IV or Adenosine
Atrial fibrillation* } Atrial flutter	Digoxin (to control rate) and/or Verapamil	add beta-blocker (with care—to control rate)
Atrial premature beats	Treat cause Check lifestyle	Metoprolol or atenolol or verapamil

(continues)

Table 48 (continued)

*Ventricular tachyarrhythmias***		
Ventricular premature beats	Treat cause Check lifestyle	Beta-blocker (especially mitral valve prolapse)
Ventricular tachycardia non-sustained	Lignocaine IV	Procainamide or Class III drug
sustained	Lignocaine IV if stable — if not: DC shock	Class III drug
Ventricular fibrillation	DC cardioversion	IV Adrenaline if fine VF, then DC cardioversion

* Consider anti coagulation with warfarin or aspirin
** Third line treatment may be required, usually DC cardioversion or Class III anti-arrhythmics (sotolol, flecainide or amiodarone)

Panic attack

- general support, explanation and reassurance
- stress management
- rebreathe into a paper bag if hyperventilating
- initial treatment
     oxazepam 15–30 mg (o)
          or
     alprazolam 0.25–0.5 mg (o)

Prophylaxis

Consider:

- tricyclic antidepressants
     or
- alprazolam 0.25–6 mg (o) in 2–4 divided doses

Parkinson's disease

The classic triad of Parkinson's disease
— tremor (pill-rolling at rest)
— rigidity
— bradykinesia (poverty of movement)

Power, reflexes and sensation usually normal.

Pharmacological management

Don't postpone—commence ASAP.

Mild

(minimal disability):

- levodopa preparation (low dose)
  e.g. levodopa 100 mg + carbidopa 25 mg bd (pc)—increase as necessary

Alternative

- start with amantadine 100 mg bd (up to 400 mg/day) prior to levodopa

Moderate

(independent but disabled, e.g. writing, movements, gait):

- levodopa preparation
- add if necessary—bromocriptine (or pergolide) or selegiline

Severe

(disabled, dependent on others):

- levodopa (to maximum tolerated dose) + bromocriptine or selegiline
- consider antidepressants

Note: Education and support of both patient and family essential.

Apomorphine (+ antiemetic) effective for severe rigidity.

Paronychia

Acute

Uncomplicated with localised pus:
(use digital anaesthetic blocks)

1. lateral focus of pus:
   incise, probe and drain, insert small wick
2. pus adjacent to nail:
   pack wisp cotton wool between nail and apply povidone-iodine, dry and repeat (as necessary)
3. central focus of pus:
   simple elevation of nail fold (see figure below) or puncture the fold close to the nail to drain pus
   - advice on hygiene
   - antibiotics rarely necessary
   - exclude diabetes

Chronic

- usually due to a secondary invading organism
- culture organisms
- exclude diabetes

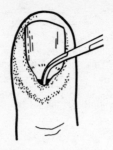

Treatment of paronychia by elevating the nail fold

Attend to causation
- Minimise contact with water, soap, detergents, lipid solvents and other irritants.
- Keep hands dry (avoid wet work if possible).
- Wear cotton lined gloves for maximum of 15 minutes.

Topical medications to nail folds
> 2% thymol in alcohol qid
> or
> 10% sulphacetamide in alcohol

For Candida (if cultured)
> tincture Daktarin bd
> or
> clotrimazole topical preparations

Pelvic inflammatory disease (females)

There are great medical problems in the serious consequences of PID, namely tubal obstruction, infertility and ectopic pregnancy. PID can either be sexually acquired, usually with *Chlamydia trachomatis* and/or *Neisseria gonorrhoeae* or from endogenous infections due to genital manipulation, e.g. IUCD, D&C or post abortion.

Clinical features

Acute PID
- fever ≥ 38°C
- moderate to severe lower abdominal pain

Chronic PID
- ache in the lower back
- mild lower abdominal pain

Both acute and chronic
- dyspareunia
- menstrual problems (e.g. painful, heavy or irregular periods)
- intermenstrual bleeding
- abnormal, perhaps offensive, purulent vaginal discharge
- painful or frequent urination

Investigations
Definitive diagnosis is by laparoscopy but this is not practical in all cases of suspected PID.

- cervical swab for Gram stain and culture (*N. gonorrhoeae*)
- cervical swab and special techniques for *C. trachomatis*

Treatment of PID
Note: Any IUCD or retained products of contraception should be removed at or before the start of treatment.
Sex partners of women with PID should be treated with agents effective against *Chlamydia trachomatis* and *Neisseria gonorrhoeae*.

Mild infection (treated as an outpatient)
> doxycycline 100 mg (o) 12 hourly for 14 days
> plus either
> metronidazole 400 mg (o) 12 hourly with food for 14 days
> or
> tinidazole 500 mg (o) daily with food for 14 days

Where penicillinase-producing *Neisseria gonorrhoeae* (which is often tetracycline-resistant) is suspected or proven, add:
> ciprofloxacin 500 mg (o) 12 hourly for 14 days

Severe infection (treated in hospital)
With IV cephalosporins and metronidazole plus oral doxycycline

Periodic limb movement disorder (nocturnal myoclonus)
> clonazepam 1mg (o) nocte increasing to 3 mg (o) nocte
> or
> sodium valproate 60 mg (o) nocte

Perioral dermatitis

Clinical features:
- acne-like dermatitis of lower face
- usually young women
- around mouth and on chin, sparing adjacent perioral area (see figure below)
- frequently begins at the nasolabial folds

Perioral dermatitis: typical distribution

Treatment

Systemic antibiotics (first choice)
Tetracycline 250 mg bd for 8 weeks

Topical agents (consider if tolerated)
- 2–4% sulphur and 2% salicylic acid in aqueous sorbolene cream
  or
- Ketoconazole 2% cream
Avoid corticosteroids.

Perspiration: excessive

- Use an antiperspirant deodorant.
- Reduce caffeine intake.
- Avoid known aggravating factors.
- Refer for axillary wedge resection.

Photoageing/wrinkles

Prevention

- Avoid exposure to the sun.
- Use an SPF 15⁺ sunscreen during the day.
- Wash with a 'neutral' mild soap, e.g. Neutrogena (maximum twice daily) and pat dry.

Treatment

- tretinoin (Retin-A) cream
    apply once daily at bedtime (on dry skin) test for skin irritation by gradual exposure, e.g. 5 minutes at first (wash off) then 15 minutes until it can be left overnight
- Lac-Hydrin (USA)
    12% solution may be effective alternative; other lactic acid preparations may be useful

Pityriasis rosea

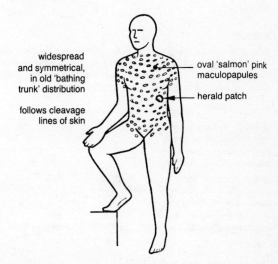

widespread and symmetrical, in old 'bathing trunk' distribution

follows cleavage lines of skin

oval 'salmon' pink maculopapules

herald patch

Pityriasis rosea: typical distribution

Management

- Explain and reassure with patient education handout.
- Bathe and shower as usual, using a neutral soap, e.g. Neutrogena, Dove.

- Use a soothing bath oil, e.g. QV bath oil, Hamilton bath oil.
- For itching: urea cream or calamine lotion with 1% phenol.
- Expose rash to sunlight (avoid sunburn).

Prognosis

A mild self-limiting disorder with spontaneous remission in 4–10 weeks. It does not appear to be contagious.

Pityriasis versicolor (tinea versicolor)

There are two distinct presentations:

1. reddish, brown, slightly scaly patches on upper trunk, which progresses to a
2. hypopigmented area that will not tan, especially in sun-tanned skin

- may involve neck, upper arms, face and groin
- scales removed by scraping show characteristic short stunted hyphae with spores on microscopy, 'spaghetti and meat balls' appearance

Treatment

- Selenium sulfide (Selsun shampoo). Wash area, leaving on for 5–10 minutes, then wash off. Do this daily for two weeks (at night), then every second day for two weeks, then monthly for 12 months. Shampoo scalp twice weekly.

or

- econazole 1% (Pevaryl) foaming solution

  apply to wet body (after shower).
  rub in from head to toe.
  do not rinse, allow to dry.
  shower off next morning.
  apply for 3 consecutive days once weekly for 3 weeks

and/or

clotrimazole, miconazole, or econazole cream/lotion applied nocte for 2–4 weeks
Ketoconazole cream for 10 days in severe or resistant cases.

Plantar warts (see page 197)

Pneumonia
Typical pneumonia

The commonest community acquired infection is with *Streptococcus pneumoniae* (majority) or *Haemophilus influenzae*.

Clinical features

- rapidly ill with high temperature, dry cough, pleuritic pain
- 1–2 days later rusty coloured sputum
- rapid and shallow breathing follows
- X-ray and examination: consolidation

The atypical pneumonias

Clinical features

- fever, malaise
- headache
- minimal respiratory symptoms, non productive cough
- signs of consolidation absent
- chest X-ray (diffuse infiltration) incompatible with chest signs

Causes

Mycoplasma pneumoniae—the commonest:
- adolescents and young adults
- treat with doxycycline 100 mg bd for 10–14 days

Legionella pneumonia (Legionnaire's disease):
- related to cooling systems in large buildings
- incubation 2–10 days

  Diagnostic criteria include:

  - prodromal influenza-like illness
  - a dry cough, confusion or diarrhoea
  - very high fever (may be relative bradycardia)
  - lymphopenia with moderate leucocytosis
  - hyponatraemia

  Patients can become very prostrate with complications—
  treat with erythromycin.

Chlamydia pneumoniae
- similar to mycoplasma

Chlamydia psittaci (psittacosis)
- treat with doxycycline (as above)

Coxiella burnetti (Q fever)
- treat with doxycycline (as above)

Antibiotic treatment according to severity

Mild pneumonia (not requiring hospitalisation)

roxithromycin 150 mg 12 hourly
    — covers most likely pathogens including mycoplasma
      and chlamydia
         or
amoxycillin/clavulanate 500/125 mg 8 hourly
    — especially if *S. pneumoniae* isolated or suspected
         or

doxycycline 200 mg loading dose then 100 mg daily
— if atypical pneumonia suspected
All courses for 5 days.

Moderately severe pneumonia (requiring hospitalisation)

Table 49 *Pneumonia: guidelines for hospitalisation*

- age over 65
- co-existing illness
- high temperature > 38°C
- clinical features of severe pneumonia
- involvement of more than one lobe
- inability to tolerate oral therapy

benzylpenicillin 600 mg IV 4–6 hourly for 5–10 days
   (drug of choice for *S. pneumoniae*)
         or
cephalothin 1 g IV 4–6 hourly for 5–10 days
(in penicillin-allergic patient)

If not so severe and oral medication tolerated can use amoxycillin/clavulanate or ceflacor or doxycycline.
If atypical pneumonia use doxycycline, erythromycin (preferable, as covers legionella) or roxithromycin.

Severe pneumoniae

The criteria for severity are presented in Table 50.

Table 50 *Guidelines for severe pneumonia*

- altered mental state
- rapidly deteriorating course
- respiratory rate > 30 per minute
- BP < 90/60 mmHg
- hypoxia PO_2 < 60 mmHg
- leucocytes < 4 × 10⁹/L or > 20 × 10⁹/L

Erythromycin 500 mg IV slowly 6 hourly
(covers myoplasma, chlamydia and legionella)
       plus
Cefotaxime 1 g IV 8 hourly
      or
Ceftriaxone 1 g IV daily

Pneumonia in children

Features

- tachypnoea, expiratory grunt
- possible focal chest signs
- diagnosis often only made by chest X-ray

Viruses are the most common cause in infants.
Mycoplasma common in children over 5.
S. pneumoniae a cause in all age groups.
Pathogens difficult to isolate—may need blood culture.

Treatment

Hospitalise, minimal handling.
Careful observations, including pulse oximetry.
Attend to hydration.
Antibiotics indicated in all cases.

Mild to moderate:
< 24 months—penicillin IV or IM initially
> 24 months—penicillin or erythromycin

Severe:
flucloxacillin IV + cefotaxime IV

Polymyalgia rheumatica and giant cell arteritis

The basic pathology of this very important disease complex is giant cell arteritis (synonyms: temporal arteritis; cranial arteritis). The clinical syndromes are polymyalgia rheumatica and temporal arteritis.

Clinical features of polymyalgia rheumatica

- pain and stiffness in proximal muscles of shoulder and pelvic girdle, cervical spine (see figure on next page)
- symmetrical distribution
- typical ages 60–70 years (rare < 50)
- both sexes: more common in women
- early morning stiffness
- may be systemic symptoms: weight loss, malaise, anorexia

Clinical features of temporal arteritis

- headache—unilateral, throbbing
- temporal tenderness
- loss of pulsation of temporal artery
- jaw claudication
- biopsy of artery (5 cm) is diagnostic

Investigation

- no specific test for polymyalgia rheumatica
- ESR—extremely high, around 100
- mild anaemia (normochromic, normocytic)

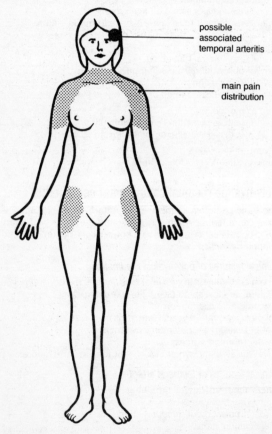

possible associated temporal arteritis

main pain distribution

Polymyalgia rheumatica: typical sites of areas of pain and stiffness

Treatment

Prednisolone

- Starting dose
  - —temporal arteritis   60–100 mg
  - —polymyalgia rheumatica   15 mg
- Taper down gradually to the minimum effective dose (often < 5 mg daily) according to the clinical response and the ESR. Aim for treatment for 2 years: relapses are common.

Premenstrual tension syndrome

Management

- explanation and reassurance
- advise recording a daily symptom diary for 2–3 months
- attend to lifestyle factors
  - — diet
  - — exercise
  - — relaxation
- medication

  moderate dose COC with 50 µg ethinyl oestradiol (ideal first choice)

  otherwise

  pyridoxine 100 mg/day

  or

  evening primrose oil capsules 1 g bd (day 12 to day 1 of next cycle)
- severe PMT

  fluoxetine 20 mg daily, 10 days before menstruation

Prickly heat (miliaria/heat rash)

- Keep the skin dry and cool, e.g. fan, air conditioner.
- Dress in loose-fitting cotton clothing.
- Reduce activity.
- Avoid frequent bathing and overuse of soap.

Rx: Lotion: salicylic acid 2%, menthol 1%, chlorhexidine 0.5% in alcohol.

Prostate disorders

Prostatitis syndromes

Includes conditions causing pain in the prostate which may develop acute or chronic bacterial infection, usually caused by *E. coli.*

Prostatodynia means the presence of symptoms typical of prostatitis but without objective evidence of inflammation or infection.

Treatment

Acute prostatitis

amoxycillin (or ampicillin) 1 g IV 6 hourly
+
gentamicin 120–160 mg IV 12 hourly to maximum 5 mg/kg/day until there is substantial improvement, when therapy may be changed to an appropriate oral agent, based on the sensitivity of the pathogen(s) isolated, for the remainder of 14 days.

For milder infection, oral treatment with amoxycillin/potassium clavulanate, trimethoprim or norfloxacin is suitable.

Chronic bacterial prostatitis

Treatment of this condition is difficult.
Advise hot baths, normal sexual activity, no caffeine, good diet.

doxycycline 100 mg (o) daily for 1 month
or
trimethoprim 300 mg (o) daily for 1 month
or
norfloxacin 400 mg (o) 12 hourly for 1 month
or
ciprofloxacin 500 mg (o) 12 hourly for 1 month

Non-bacterial prostatitis/prostatodynia

Advice as above.
Empirical trial of doxycycline 100 mg (o) for 14 days.
Prazosin 0.5 mg bd.
Consider diazepam.

Benign prostatic hyperplasia

Investigations

These include:

- urine culture
- prostate specific antigen
- prostatic needle biopsy (with or without transrectal ultrasound) if carcinoma suspected
- voiding flow rate to confirm that the symptoms reflect obstruction and not bladder irritability
  — measure time to pass 200 mL
  — significant obstruction if < 10 mL/second

Management

General advice:

- Avoid caffeine, esp. coffee.
- Reduce alcohol.
- Avoid fluids before bed-time.
- Urinate when you need to (do not hang on).
- Wait 30 seconds after voiding to ensure your bladder is empty.

Medical treatment

For milder problems:

- adrenergic blocking agents (terazosin and prazosin)
  e.g. prazosin 0.5 mg (o) nocte for 3 days, then 0.5 mg bd for 14 days (watch for postural hypotension) then increase as necessary to maximum of 2 mg bd (may postpone surgery for up to 2–5 years)

  or

  $5 \propto$ reductase inhibitors
  e.g. finasteride 5 mg (o) daily for at least 6–12 months

Surgical treatment

Transurethral resection is currently the gold standard of treatment.

Carcinoma of the prostate

Digital rectal examination (DRE), which is a vital guide, may reveal a hard nodule (50% are not carcinoma).

Investigations to detect carcinoma

Blood analysis

- prostate specific antigen (PSA)
  — normal level less than 4 ng/mL
  — can be elevated without cancer
  — levels between 4 and 10 are equivocal
  — levels > 10 are only suggestive of cancer

Biopsy

Consider biopsy (with or without transrectal ultrasound) if the DRE is positive or if the PSA is elevated.

Treatment

Many patients, particularly the elderly, have no symptoms and require no treatment. The treatment depends on the age of the patient and the stage of the disease.

For tumours that are potentially curable, radical prostatectomy or radiotherapy are the options.

For metastatic or locally advanced disease, androgen deprivation is the cornerstone of treatment, the options being:

- bilateral orchidectomy
          or
- daily antiandrogenic tablets
  e.g. cyproterone acetate (Androcur)
       flutamide (Eulexin)
          or
- monthly depot injections of luteinising hormone releasing hormone (LHRH) agonists
  e.g. goserelin (Zolodex)
       leuprorelin acetate (Lucrin)
       buserelin

Pruritus (generalised)

The broad differential diagnoses of pruritus are:

- skin disease
- systemic disease
- psychological and emotional disorders

Table 51 *Generalised pruritus: diagnostic strategy model*

Q.	*Probability diagnosis*
A.	Psychological/emotional
	Old dry skin
Q.	*Serious disorders not to be missed*
A.	Neoplasia
	• lymphoma/Hodgkin's
	• leukaemia: CLL
	• other carcinoma
	Chronic renal failure
	Primary biliary cirrhosis
Q.	*Pitfalls*
A.	Pregnancy
	Tropical infection/infestation
	Polycythaemia
	Generalised sensitivity, e.g. fibre glass, bubble bath
	Scabies
Q.	*Seven masquerades checklist*
A.	Depression ✓
	Diabetes ✓
	Drugs ✓
	Anaemia ✓ iron deficiency
	Thyroid ✓ hyper and hypo
	Spinal dysfunction —
	UTI —
Q.	*Is the patient trying to tell me something?*
A.	Quite likely: consider anxiety, parasitophobia.

Treatment

The basic principle of treatment is to determine the cause of the itch and treat it accordingly. Itch of psychogenic origin responds to appropriate therapy, such as antidepressants for depression.

If no cause is found:

- apply cooling measures, e.g. air-conditioning, cool swims
- avoid rough clothes
- avoid known irritants
- avoid overheating
- avoid vasodilatation, e.g. alcohol, hot baths/showers
- treat dry skin with appropriate moisturisers, e.g. propylene glycol in aqueous cream
- topical treatment
  — emollients to lubricate skin
  — local soothing lotion such as calamine, including menthol or phenol (avoid topical antihistamines)
- sedative antihistamines (not very effective for systemic pruritus)
- non-sedating antihistamines during day
- antidepressants or tranquillisers (if psychological cause and counselling ineffective)

Pruritus ani

Treat cause

The generalised disorders causing pruritus may cause pruritus ani. However, various primary skin disorders such as psoriasis, dermatitis, contact dermatitis and lichen planus may also cause it, in addition to local anal conditions.

General measures

- Stop scratching.
- Bathe carefully: avoid hot water, excessive scrubbing and soaps.
- Use bland aqueous cream, Cetaphil lotion or Neutrogena soap.
- Keep area dry and cool.
- Keep bowels regular and wipe with cotton wool soaked in warm water.
- Wear loose-fitting clothing and underwear.
- Avoid local anaesthetics and antiseptics.

If still problematic and a dermatosis probably involved use:

    hydrocortisone 1% cream

                or

    hydrocortisone 1% cream with clioquinol 0.5 to 3% (most effective)

If isolated area and resistant:
infiltrate 0.5 mL triamcinolone intradermally

If desperate:
fractionated X-ray therapy

Pruritus vulvae

Management depends on cause, e.g. candidiasis, anal conditions.

General measures
- Attend to hygiene and excessive sweating.
- Keep genital area dry and wash thoroughly at least once a day.
- Avoid overzealous washing.
- Do not wear pantyhose, tight jeans or tight underwear, or use tampons.
- Do not use vaginal douches, powders or deodorants.
- Use aqueous cream or Cetaphil lotion rather than toilet soap.

Psoriasis

Psoriasis is a chronic skin disorder of unknown aetiology which affects 2–3% of the population. It appears most often between the ages of 10 and 30, although its onset can occur any time from infancy to old age.

Principles of management
- Provide education, reassurance and support.
- Promote general measures such as rest, and holidays preferably in the sun.
- Advise prevention, including avoidance of skin damage and stress if possible.
- Tailor treatment (including referral) according to the degree of severity and extent of the disease.

Treatment options
1. Topical therapy

   General adjunctive therapy
   - tarbaths, e.g. Pinetarsol or Polytar
   - tar shampoo, e.g. Polytar, Ionil-T
   - sunlight (in moderation)

   For chronic stable plaques on limbs or trunks
   Combined method:
   - dithranol 0.1%
     salicylic acid 3% } in white soft paraffin
     LPC (tar) 10%

Leave overnight—(warn about dithranol stains—use old
pyjamas and sheets).
Review in 3 weeks then gradually increase strength of
dithranol to 0.25%, then 0.5%, then 1%.
Can cut down frequency to 2 to 3 times per week.
• Shower in morning and then apply topical fluorinated
corticosteroid.

Note: facts about diathranol:
• Stains light coloured hair purple so don't use on the scalp.
• Start in low concentration and build up according to tol-
erance and response.
• Use in strengths 0.1%, 0.25%, 0.5%, 1.0% and 2.0%.
• Can use a higher strength of 0.25% to start but for short
contact therapy (30 minutes before shower).
• Irritates skin causing a burning sensation.
• Don't use it on the face, genitalia or flexures.

Note: corticosteroids: the mainstay of therapy for small
plaques and the control of eruption; use 1% hydrocortisone on more sensitive areas (genitals, groin,
face) and perhaps stronger types elsewhere
• bland preparations and emollients: these can be used for
dryness, scaling and itching, e.g. liquor picis carbonis and
menthol (or salicylic acid) in sorbolene base
• 5-fluorouracil (sometimes used)

New method (adults only):
• Calcipotriol ointment, apply bd.

Note: Tends to irritate face and flexures—wash hands after
use.

For milder stabilised plaques

• Egopsoryl TA—apply bd or tds
                 or
• topical fluorinated corticosteroids

For resistant plaques

• topical fluorinated corticosteroids (higher strength II–III
class) with occlusive dressing
• intralesional injection of triamcinolone mixed (50:50)
with LA or normal saline

For failed topical therapy

• Refer for PUVA or other effective therapy.
2. Systemic therapy
• methotrexate: can have dramatic results in severe cases
• etretinate: effective in severe intractable psoriasis (never
used in females of child-bearing age)
• cyclosporin

3. Physical therapy
   • phototherapy (UVB ultraviolet light)
   • UVB plus coal tar (Goeckerman regimen): reserved for severe psoriasis.
   • photochemotherapy (PUVA = psoralen + UVA)—reserved for non-responders to UVB treatment or other therapies. A variation is REPUVA = retinoid + psoralen + UVA
   • intralesional corticosteroids——an excellent and effective treatment for isolated small or moderate-sized plaques that can be readily given by the family doctor

   Method of injection

   Mix equal parts of triamcinolone acetonide 10 mg/mL (or other steriod) and plain local anaesthetic or normal saline and, using a 25 g or 23 g needle, infiltrate the psoriatic plaque intradermally to cover virtually all of the plaque.

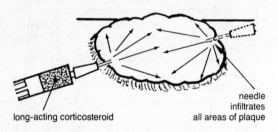

long-acting corticosteroid

needle
infiltrates
all areas of plaque

Intralesional corticosteroid injection technique
for psoriatic plaque (requiring double
injection—small plaques need only one
infiltration)

R

Rectal bleeding

Patients present with any degree of bleeding from a smear on the toilet tissue to severe haemorrhage. Various causes are presented in the figure below.

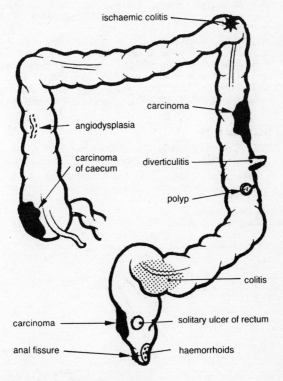

Various causes of rectal bleeding

Local causes of bleeding include excoriated skin, anal fissure, a burst perianal haematoma and anal carcinoma. A characteristic pattern of bright bleeding is found with haemorrhoids. It is usually small non-prolapsing haemorrhoids that bleed.

Black tarry (melaena) stool indicates bleeding from the upper gastrointestinal tract and is rare distal to the lower ileum.

Frequent passage of blood and mucus indicates a rectal tumour or proctitis, whereas more proximal tumours or extensive colitis present different patterns.

Substantial haemorrhage, which is rare, can be caused by diverticular disease, angiodysplasia or more proximal lesions such as Meckel's diverticulum and even duodenal ulcers. Angiodysplasias are identified by technetium-labelled red cell scan.

The examination includes a general assessment, anal inspection, digital rectal examination and proctosigmoidoscopy. Even if there is an anal lesion, proximal bleeding must be excluded in all cases by sigmoidoscopy and by colonoscopy if there are any bowel symptoms or no obvious anal cause or a doubt about a lesion causing the symptoms.

Restless legs

Exclude diabetes, uraemia, hypothyroidism, anaemia.

It is mainly a functional disorder affecting the elderly.

- diet: eliminate caffeine and follow a healthy diet
- exercises: gentle stretching of legs, particularly of hamstrings and calf muscles, for at least five minutes before retiring (see figure below)

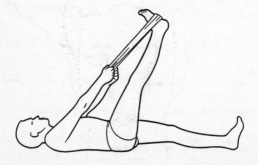

Stretching exercise for restless legs

Medication

1st choice: clonazepam 1 mg, one hour before retiring
2nd choice: diazepam
May help: codeine, levodopa, baclofen, propranolol
Generally unhelpful: carbamazepine, quinine, antipsychotics
                    and antidepressants

Reye syndrome and aspirin

- A rare complication of influenza, chickenpox and other viral diseases, e.g. Coxsackie virus.
- Suspected causal relationship between aspirin for a febrile illness in children.
- Rapid development of:
  — encephalopathy ⎫ seizures
  — hepatic failure ⎬ and
  — hypoglycaemia ⎭ coma
- 30% fatality rate and significant morbidity.
- Treatment is supportive and directed at cerebral oedema.

Recommendation

Avoid aspirin for fever in young children
— use paracetamol.

Rosacea

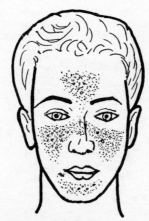

Rosacea: typical facial distribution

Management

- Apply cool packs if severe.
- Avoid factors that cause facial flushings, e.g. excessive sun exposure, heat, alcohol, spicy foods, hot drinks.

Systemic antibiotics (first choice)

Tetracycline (first choice)
>Tetracycline 1 g daily in divided doses
>then 250 mg daily when controlled for at least 8–10 weeks
>or
>Doxycycline 100 mg, then 50 mg daily

>Repeat for recurrences.
>Avoid maintenance.

Erythromycin (second choice)
>500–1000 mg daily in divided doses,
>then 250 mg daily for at least 8–10 weeks

Metronidazole (for resistant cases)
>200 mg bd for 10 days

Topical agents

Milder cases
>2% sulphur in aqueous cream
>apply lightly tds

More severe cases
>metronidazole gel or cream
>apply thin film bd

Note: Hydrocortisone 1% cream is effective, but steroids are best avoided and strong topical steroids should not be used because of severe rebound vascular changes.

Roundworms (acariasis)

- pyrantel (various preparations)
>10 mg/kg as single dose

S

Scabies

Clinical features
- intense itching (worse with warmth and at night)
- erythematous papular rash
- usually on hands and wrists
- common on male genitalia
- also occurs on elbows, axillae, feet and ankles, nipples of females

Treatment: for all types of scabies
- Permethrin 5% cream
  Apply to clean, dry cool skin of whole body from jawline down (preferably at night time).
  Leave overnight and wash off.
  Use single application.
  Complete change of clothes and bed linen and wash after treatment.
  Treat all family members and contacts.
  A topical antipruritic, e.g. crotamiton cream can be used for persistent itch.
- Use benzyl benzoate 25% in children under 2 years

Note: Lindane 1% lotion is an alternative, especially for genital scabies.

Scrotal pain

Serious problems include testicular torsion, strangulation of an inguinoscrotal hernia, a testicular tumour and a haematocele, all of which require surgical intervention.

Torsion of the testis v epididymo-orchitis

With torsion of the testicle there is pain of sudden onset, described as severe aching sickening pain in the groin that may be accompanied by nausea and vomiting. With epididymo-orchitis the attack usually begins with malaise and fever. The testicle soon becomes swollen and acutely tender; however, elevation of the scrotum usually relieves pain in this condition while tending to increase it with a torsion.

Key facts about torsion of the testis

- Is commonest cause of acute scrotal pain in childhood.
- Is the diagnosis, until proved otherwise, of a boy or young man with intense inguinal pain and vomiting.
- Must be corrected within four hours to prevent gangrene of the testis.
- Ultrasound and a scan is helpful but time usually precludes this and surgical exploration is safest.

Acute epididymo-orchitis

Guidelines only

< 30 years: usually STD pathogens
> 30 years: urinary tract pathogens

Treatment

- bed rest
- elevation and support of the scrotum
- analgesics
- antibiotics (all doses for 10–14 days)

Sexually acquired:
  ciprofloxacin 500 mg (o) bd
              or
  amoxycillin/clavulanate 500/125 mg (o) tds
              plus
  doxycycline 100 mg (o) bd

Associated with urinary infection:

  amoxycillin/clavulanate 500/125 mg (o) tds
              or
  trimethoprim 300 mg (o) daily
              or
  cephalexin 500 mg (o) qid
              or
  norfloxacin 400 mg (o) bd

Seborrhoeic dermatitis

Seborrhoeic dermatitis is common in hair-bearing areas of the body, especially the scalp and eyebrows. It can also affect the face, neck, axilla and groins, eyelids (blepharitis), external auditory meatus and nasolabial folds. The presternal area is often involved.

Principles of treatment

- Topical sulphur, salicylic acid and tar preparations are first-line treatment: they kill the yeast responsible.
- Ketoconazole is most effective as topical (preferred) or oral treatment.

- Topical corticosteroids are useful for inflammation and pruritus and best used in combination. Avoid corticosteroids if possible.

Medication: children
Scalp
- 1% sulphur and 1% salicylic acid in sorbolene cream.
- Apply overnight to scalp, shampoo off next day with a mild shampoo.
- Use 3 times a week.

Face, flexures and trunk
- 2% sulphur and salicylic acid in aqueous or sorbolene cream
- hydrocortisone 1% (for irritation on face and flexures)
- betamethasone 0.02–0.05% (if severe irritation on trunk)

Napkin area
- Mix equal parts 1% hydrocortisone with nystatin or ketoconazole 2% or clotrimazole 1% cream.

Adults
Scalp
- ketoconazole shampoo (immediately after using medicated shampoo) twice weekly
- dexamethasone gel to scalp (if very itchy)

Face and body
- Wash regularly with bland soap.
- ketoconazole 2% cream, apply once daily
- hydrocortisone 1% bd (if inflamed and pruritic)

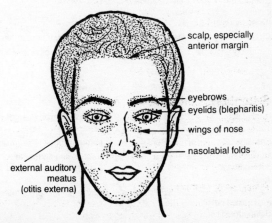

Seborrhoeic dermatitis: facial distribution in adults

Sexually transmitted diseases

Table 52 *Sexually transmitted diseases: causative organisms and treatment*

STD	Causative organism/s	Treatment
Bacterial		
Gonorrhoea	*Neisseria gonorrhoeae*	Ciprofloxacin (o) or ceftriaxone IM or spectinomycin IM + Doxycycline
Non-specific urethritis	*Chlamydia trachomatis* *Ureaplasma urealyticum* *Mycoplasma hominis*	Doxycycline
Cervicitis and PID	*Neisseria gonorrhoeae* *Chlamydia trachomatis* mixed 'vaginal' flora	Mild: doxycycline + metronidazole or tinidazole Severe: add cephalosporins (IV use in hospital)
Syphilis	*Treponema pallidum*	Benzathine penicillin: best to refer
Bacterial vaginosis	*Gardnerella vaginalis* other anaerobes	Tinidazole or metronidazole + clindamycin 2% cream
Granuloma inguinale (Donovanosis)	*Calymmatobacterium granulomatis*	Doxycycline
Chancroid	*Haemophilus ducreyi*	Erythromycin: best to refer
Lymphogranuloma venerum	*Chlamydia trachomatis*	Doxycycline: best to refer
Viral		
AIDS	HIV_1, HIV_2	Zidovudine
Genital herpes	Herpes simplex virus	Acyclovir
Genital warts	Papilloma virus	Podophyllotoxin paint or other
Hepatitis	HBV, HCV	Immunoglobulin/interferon
Molluscum contagiosum	Pox virus	Various simple methods, e.g. deroofing with needle
Fungal		
Vaginal thrush (possible STD) Balanoposthitis	*Candida albicans*	Any antifungal preparation

(continues)

Table 52 *(continued)*

Protozoal		
Vaginitis, urethritis	*Trichomonas*	Tinidazole or
Balanoposthitis	*vaginalis*	metronidazole

Arthropods		
Genital scabies	*Sarcoptes scabiei*	Permethrin 5% cream
Pediculosis pubis	*Phthirus pubis*	Maldison 0.5% lotion

Syphilis

Syphilis usually presents either as a primary lesion or through chance finding on positive serology testing (latent syphilis).

It is important to be alert to the various manifestations of secondary syphilis.

Management

The management of syphilis has become quite complex and referral of the patient to a specialist facility for diagnosis, treatment and follow-up is recommended.

Recommended anti-microbial therapy

Early syphilis (primary, secondary or latent) of not more than one year's duration:

benzathine penicillin 1.8 g IM as a single dose
For patients hypersensitive to penicillin
doxycycline 100 mg (o) 12 hourly for 14 days
or
erythromycin 500 mg (o) 6 hourly for 14 days

Late syphilis: more than one year or indeterminate duration
benzathine penicillin 1.8 g IM once weekly for 3 doses

Shoulder pain

Tendinitis syndromes, subacromial bursitis and adhesive capsulitis

Guidelines

- Most of these disorders become chronic and persist for at least 12 months.
- The tendinitis syndromes usually have unrestricted active movements but resisted movements (e.g. abduction for supraspinatus tendinitis) are painful.
  Treatment: rest during acute phase
  analgesics
  peritendon injection (1 mL corticosteroid with 2–5 mL 1% lignocaine)

- Subacromial bursitis presents in varying degrees from a 'frozen shoulder' to limited abduction (painful arc).
  Treatment: injection of 5 mL LA then 1 mL corticosteroid into and around the bursa.
- Adhesive capsulitis or traumatic arthritis of the gleno-humeral joint is a very painful condition with painful limitation of several active and passive movements, especially rotation.
  Treatment is with intraarticular steroids or hydro-dilation of the joint. Referral to a consultant is advisable as modern treatments give excellent results.

Table 53 *Shoulder pain: diagnostic strategy model (excluding trauma)*

Q.	*Probability diagnosis*
A.	Cervical spine dysfunction
	Supraspinatus tendinitis/other rotator cuff lesions
	Adhesive capsulitis (gleno-humeral joint)
Q.	*Serious disorders not to be missed*
A.	Cardiovascular
	• angina
	• myocardial infarction
	Neoplasia
	• Pancoast's tumour
	• primary or secondary in humerus
	Severe infections
	• septic arthritis (children)
	• osteomyelitis
	Rheumatoid arthritis
Q.	*Pitfalls (often missed)*
A.	Polymyalgia rheumatica
	Cervical dysfunction
	Osteoarthritis of acromioclavicular joint
	Subacromial bursitis

Sinusitis

Acute

Management

- look for nasal pathology such as polyposis and dental problems
- analgesics
- steam inhalations (see figure on page 269)
- pseudoephedrine tablets
- antibiotics (1st choice)—for 7–10 day course
      amoxycillin
            or

amoxycillin/potassium clavulanate (if amoxycillin-resistant)
> or

doxycycline

Chronic

Sinusitis persisting longer than two weeks, despite repeated antibiotic and decongestant therapy, is common in general practice. Postnasal drip with cough, especially at night, is a feature. An empirical treatment that is effective is:

• steam inhalations with Friar's balsam or menthol (best is menthol Co APF inhalation)
• vitamin C (sodium ascorbate) 2–4 g daily (a powder can be obtained and mixed with orange juice)

Skin cancer

The three main skin cancers are the non-melanocyctic skin cancers (basal cell carcinoma—BCC; squamous cell carcinoma—SCC) and melanoma. The approximate relative incidence is BCCs 80%, SCCs 15–20%, and melanomas less than 5%. About 80% of skin cancer deaths are due to melanoma and the rest mainly due to SCC.

Types

• basal cell carcinoma (BCC)
• squamous cell carcinoma (SCC)
• Bowen's disease
• malignant melanoma
• Kaposi's sarcoma
• secondary tumour (lung, bowel, melanoma)

Basal cell carcinoma (BCC)

• mostly on sun-exposed areas: face (mainly), neck, upper trunk, limbs (10%)
• may ulcerate easily = 'rodent ulcer'
• slow-growing over years
• has various forms: nodular, pigmented, ulcerated, etc.
• can spread deeply if around nose or ear

Management

• excision (3–5 mm margin) is best
• if not excision, do biopsy before other treatment
• radiotherapy is an option
• Moh's chemotherapy—a new form of treatment where the tumour removal is microscopically controlled.

Squamous cell carcinoma (SCC)

SCC tends to arise in premalignant areas such as solar keratoses, burns, chronic ulcers, leukoplakia and Bowen's disease, or it can arise *de novo*.

SCCs of ear, lip, oral cavity, tongue and genitalia are serious and need special management.

Management
• Early excision of tumours < 1 cm with 5 mm margin.
• Referral for specialised surgery and/or radiotherapy if large, in difficult site or lymphadenopathy.

Bowen's disease

Management
• biopsy first for diagnosis
• wide surgical excision if small
• skin grafting may be required

Note: Biopsy a single patch of suspected psoriasis or dermatitis not responding to topical steroids.

Malignant melanoma (see page 254)

Skin eruptions

Acute skin eruptions in children

The following skin eruptions (some of which may also occur in adults) are outlined in common childhood infectious diseases (see page 96).

• measles
• rubella
• viral exanthem (fourth disease)
• erythema infectiosum (fifth disease)
• roseola infantum (sixth disease)
• Kawasaki's disease
• varicella
• impetigo

Secondary syphilis

The rash usually appears 6–8 weeks after the primary chancre. It is relatively coarse and asymptomatic. It can involve the whole body including the palms and soles.

Table 54 *Important causes of acute skin eruptions*

Maculopapular
- measles
- rubella
- scarlet fever
- viral exanthem (fourth disease)
- erythema infectiosum (slapped face syndrome or fifth disease)
- roseola infantum (sixth disease)
- Epstein-Barr mononucleosis (primary or secondary to drugs)
- primary HIV infection
- secondary syphilis
- pityriasis rosea (see page 289)
- guttate psoriasis
- urticaria
- erythema multiforme (may be vesicular)
- drug reaction
- scabies

Maculopapular vesicular
- varicella
- herpes zoster
- herpes simplex
- eczema herpeticum
- impetigo
- hand, foot and mouth disease
- drug reaction

Maculopapular pustular
- pseudomonas folliculitis
- staphylococcus aureus folliculitis
- impetigo

Purpuric (haemorrhagic) eruption
- purpura, e.g. drug-induced purpura, severe infection
- vasculitis (vascular purpura)
  — Henoch-Schoñlein purpura
  — polyarteritis nodosa

Primary HIV infection

A common manifestation of the primary HIV infection is an erythematous, maculopapular rash. If such a rash, accompanied by an illness like glandular fever occurs, HIV infection should be suspected and specific tests ordered.

Guttate psoriasis

Guttate psoriasis is the sudden eruption of small (less than 5 mm) round, very dense, red papules of psoriasis on the trunk. The rash may extend to the limbs.

It is usually seen in children and adolescents. The rash soon develops a white silvery scale. It may undergo spontaneous resolution or enlarge to form plaques and tends to last 6 months. Treatment is with UV light and tar preparations.

Drug eruptions

A rash is one of the most common side effects of drug therapy, which can precipitate many different types of rash; the most common is toxic erythema.

Erythema multiforme

Erythema multiforme is an acute eruption affecting the skin and mucosal surfaces, mainly backs of hands, palms and forearms; also feet, toes, mouth. It is a vasculitis, the causes of which are many but mainly unknown (50%) and herpes simplex virus.

Stevens-Johnson syndrome

A very severe and often fatal variant. Sudden onset with fever and constitutional symptoms.

Treatment

Identify and remove cause, e.g. withdraw drugs.
Symptomatic treatment, e.g. antihistamines for itching.
Refer severe cases—usually need hospitalisation and high doses of steroids.

Erythema nodosum

Erythema nodosum is characterised by the onset of bright red, raised, tender nodules on the shins and sometimes thighs and arms.

Causes/associations

• sarcoidosis (commonest known cause)
• infections, e.g. tuberculosis, streptococcal
• inflammatory bowel disorders
• drugs, e.g. sulphonamides
• unknown

Investigations

Tests include FBE, ESR, chest X-ray (the most important), Mantoux test.

Treatment

Identify the cause if possible. Rest and analgesics or NSAIDs for the acute stage. Systemic corticosteroids speed resolution if severe episodes.

Prognosis

There is a tendency to settle spontaneously over 3–4 weeks.

Hand, foot and mouth disease

HFM disease affects both children and adults but typically children under the age of ten. The lesions develop on hands, palms and soles (usually lateral borders) and vesicles lead to shallow ulcers on buccal mucosa, gums and tongue. It is caused by a Coxsackie A virus.

Management

• reassurance and explanation: lesions resolve in 3–5 days
• symptomatic treatment

Smoking/nicotine

Tobacco smoking is the largest single, preventable cause of death and disease in Australia.

Getting patients to quit

Several studies have highlighted the value of opportunistic intervention by the family doctor. Not only is it important to encourage people to quit but also to organise a quitting program and follow-up.

Methods

• Educate patients about the risks to their health and the many advantages of giving up smoking, with an emphasis on the improvement in *health*, *longevity*, *money savings*, *looks* and *sexuality*.
• Ask them to keep a smoker's diary.
• If they say no to quitting, give them motivational literature and ask them to reconsider.
• If they say yes, make a contract (example below).

A contract to quit

'I ....*agree to stop smoking on* ....
I understand that stopping smoking is the single best thing I can do for my health and that my doctor has strongly encouraged me to quit.'
....................................(*Patient's signature*)
....................................(*Doctor's signature*)

- Arrange follow-up (very important), especially during first 3 months (at least every month).
- *Nicotine education* Nicotine can be used to help withdrawal from cigarette nicotine dependence. It is a temporary measure and should not be used for longer than 6 months.
  Formulations Nicotine gum (Nicorette)
  Nicotine polacrix
  Nicotine transdermal patches (probably best method)—aim for about 16 hours a day

  Note: Ongoing support and counselling (including anticipatory guidance) is essential.

- Support group recommended.
- *Going 'cold turkey'* Stopping completely is preferable but before making the final break it can be made easier by changing to a lighter brand, inhaling less, stubbing out earlier, reducing the number. Changing to cigars or pipes is best avoided.

Quitting tips (advice to patient)

- Make a definite date to stop (e.g. during a holiday).

After quitting

- Eat more fruit and vegetables (e.g. munch carrots, celery and dried fruit).
- Foods such as citrus fruit can reduce cravings.
- Chew low-calorie gum and suck lozenges.
- Increase your activity (e.g. take regular walks instead of watching TV).
- Avoid smoking situations and seek the company of non-smokers.
- Be single-minded about not smoking—be determined and strong.
- Take up hobbies that make you forget smoking (e.g. water sports).

Withdrawal effects

The initial symptoms are restlessness, irritability, poor concentration, headache, tachycardia, insomnia, increased cough, tension, depression, tiredness and sweating. After about 10 days most of these effects subside.

Snapping or clicking hip

Some patients complain of a clunking, clicking or snapping hip. This represents a painless, but annoying problem.

The usual causes are a taut iliotibial band (tendon or tensor fascia femoris) slipping backwards and forwards over the prominence of the greater trochanter or joint laxity.

Treatment

The two basics of treatment are:

- explanation and reassurance
- exercises to stretch the iliotibial band.

Snoring

If abnormal, refer to a sleep laboratory for assessment and management of obstructive sleep apnoea syndrome and other abnormalities.

If functional, give the following advice to consider:

- Obtain and maintain ideal weight.
- Avoid drugs, e.g. sedatives, hypnotics.
- Avoid sleeping on the back—consider sewing tennis balls on back of nightwear or wear bra (with tennis balls) back to front.
- Keep neck extended with a soft collar at night.
- Provide partner with appropriate ear plugs!

Sore throat

Table 55 *Sore throat: diagnostic strategy model (modified)*

Q.	*Probability diagnosis*
A.	Viral pharyngitis (main cause)
Q.	*Serious disorders not to be missed*
A.	Cardiovascular
	• angina
	• myocardial infarction
	Neoplasia
	• carcinoma of oropharynx, tongue
	Blood dyscrasias, e.g. agranulocytosis
	acute leukaemia
	Severe infections
	• acute epiglottitis (children < 4)
	• peritonsillar abscess (Quinsy)
	• pharyngeal abscess
	• diphtheria (very rare)
	• HIV/AIDS
Q.	*Pitfalls (often missed)*
A.	Foreign body
	Epstein-Barr mononucleosis
	Monilia
	• common in infants
	• steroid inhalers

(continues)

Table 55 *(continued)*

> STDs
> • gonococcal pharyngitis
> • herpes simplex (type II)
> • syphilis
> Irritants, e.g. cigarette smoke
>   chemicals
> Mouth breathing
> Thyroiditis

Symptomatic treatment of sore throat

- adequate soothing fluids, including icy poles
- analgesia: adults—2 soluble aspirin
                   children—paracetamol elixir (not alcohol base)
- rest with adequate fluid intake
- soothing gargles, e.g. soluble aspirin used for analgesia
- advice against overuse of OTC throat lozenges and topical sprays which can sensitise the throat

Streptococcal tonsillopharyngitis

Throat swabs are about 90% effective in isolating GABHS from the infected throat.

It should be treated with penicillin or an alternative antibiotic (Table 56).

Table 56 *Treatment for streptococcal throat (proven or suspected)*

Children
> phenoxymethyl penicillin 25 to 50 mg/kg/day (o) in
> 2 to 3 divided doses for 10 days (to maximum 1 g/day)
>   or
> erythromycin 25 to 50 mg/kg/day (o) in
> 2 to 3 divided doses for 10 days (to maximum 1 g/day)

Adults
> phenoxymethyl penicillin 500 mg (o) 12 hourly for 10 days
> (can initiate treatment with one injection of procaine penicillin)
>   or
> erythromycin 500 mg (o) 12 hourly for 10 days

In severe cases:
> *Procaine penicillin 1–1.5 mg IM daily for 3–5 days*
>   *plus*
> *Phenoxymethyl penicillin (as above) for 10 days*

Note: Although symptoms and most evidence will disappear within 1 to 2 days of treatment, a full course of 10 days should be given to provide an optimal chance of eradicating *Streptococcus pyogenes* from the nasopharynx and thus minimising the risk of recurrence or complications such as rheumatic fever.

Quinsy

For a peritonsillar abscess treat with antibiotics, e.g. procaine penicillin IM or clindamycin plus drainage under local anaesthetic if it is pointing. Oral penicillin treatment is likely to fail. Subsequent tonsillectomy is recommended.

Diphtheria

Management

- throat swabs
- antitoxin
- penicillin or erythromycin 500 mg qid for 10 days
- isolate patient

Candida *pharyngitis*

Management

- Determine underlying cause
  e.g. diabetes, HIV infection, corticosteroids.
- Nystatin suspension, rinse and swallow qid.

> *Note:* Don't forget to consider the often misdiagnosed Epstein-Barr mononucleosis.

Spinal dysfunction

Spinal or vertebral dysfunction can be regarded as a masquerade mainly because the importance of the spine as a source of various pain syndromes has not been emphasised in medical training.

If a patient has pain anywhere it is possible that it could be spondylogenic and practitioners should always keep this in mind.

Cervical spinal dysfunction

If the cervical spine is overlooked as a source of pain (such as in the head, shoulder, arm, upper chest—anterior and posterior—and around the ear or face) the cause of the symptoms will remain masked and mismanagement will follow.

Thoracic spinal dysfunction

The most common and difficult masquerades related to spinal dysfunction occur with disorders of the thoracic spine (and also the low cervical spine) which can cause vague aches and pains in the chest, including the anterior chest.

Such referred pain can mimic symptoms of visceral disease such as angina and biliary colic.

Lumbar spinal dysfunction

The association between lumbar dysfunction and pain syndromes is generally easier to correlate. The pain is usually located in the low back and referred to the buttocks or the backs of the lower limbs. Problems arise with referred pain to the pelvic area, groin and anterior aspects of the leg.

Typical examples of referral and radicular pain patterns from various segments of the spine are presented in the figure below.

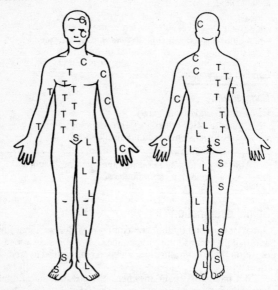

C = cervical; T = thoracic; L = lumbar; S = sacral

Examples of referred and radicular pain patterns from the spine (one side shown for each segment)

Sprained ankle

The treatment of ankle ligament sprains depends on the severity of the sprain. Most grade I (mild) and II (moderate) sprains respond well to standard conservative measures and regain full, pain-free movement in 1–6 weeks, but controversy surrounds the most appropriate management of grade III (complete tear) sprains (surgery or plaster immobilisation).

Grades I and II sprains

R rest the injured part for 48 hours, depending on disability

I ice pack for 20 minutes every 3–4 hours when awake for the first 48 hours

C compression bandage, e.g. crepe bandage

E elevate to hip level to minimise swelling

A analgesics, e.g. paracetamol

R review in 48 hours, then 7 days

S special strapping

Use partial weight bearing with crutches for the first 48 hours or until standing is no longer painful, then encourage early full weight bearing and a full range of movement with isometric exercises. Use warm soaks, dispense with ice packs after 48 hours. Aim towards full activity by 2 weeks.

Stinging fish

Injury due mainly to sharp spines, e.g. stone fish.

• Bathe or immerse part in very warm to hot water (40°C).
• Consider infiltration with local anaesthetic.

Stitch in side

A stitch in the epigastric or hypochondrium is sharp pain due to cramping in the diaphragm.

• Stop and rest when the pain strikes during activity. Then walk—don't run.
• Apply deep massage to the area with the pulps of the middle three fingers.
• Perform slow deep breathing.

Prophylaxis

• Undertake a program of abdominal breathing prior to activity.

Stroke and TIAs

Definitions

A *stroke* is a focal neurological deficit lasting longer than 24 hours and is caused by a vascular phenomenon.

A *transient ischaemic attack (TIA)* is a focal neurological deficit, presumably due to ischaemia, lasting less than 24 hours.

A *stroke in evolution* is an enlarging neurological deficit, presumably due to infarction, that is increasing over 24 to 48 hours.

Stroke

Practice tips

- Treat all TIAs and strokes as emergencies.
- Order a CT scan on all these patients: if normal repeat in 7–10 days (MRI may replace the CT scan).

Management

- investigation
- treat hypertension and other risk factors
- IV fluid, electrolyte and nutritional support
- physiotherapy and speech therapy
- vigorous rehabilitation
- intracerebral haemorrhage
    consider surgical evacuation for cerebellar and cerebral white matter haemorrhage
- SAH
    nimodipine ± surgery
- infarction
    ? no drug treatment
    Streptokinase/rtPA—awaiting trials (unconvincing so far)
- stroke in evolution
    heparin for 10 days

Transient ischaemic attacks

Some ischaemic syndromes

- transient monocular blindness (amaurosis fugax)
- transient hemisphere attacks
- the 'locked in' syndrome
- vertebrobasilar, e.g.
    — bilateral motor loss
    — crossed sensory and motor loss
    — diplopia
    — bilateral blurring or blindness

Investigations

- full blood count
- blood glucose, creatinine and cholesterol
- thyroid function tests
- carotid duplex doppler (the investigation and choice)
- ? ECG
- transoeophageal echocardiography
- CT scan (non contrast)

Management

- Aim to minimise the risk of a major stroke.
- Determine cause and correct (if possible).

- Cease smoking and treat hypertension (if applicable).
- Antiplatelet therapy
    aspirin 100–300 mg daily (gives 30% protection from stroke or death after TIA)
        or
    ticlopidine 250 mg bd (concern about neutropenia)
- Anticoagulation therapy
    warfarin — for failed antiplatelet therapy
             — atrial fibrillation (selected cases)
- Carotid endarterectomy: although its efficacy is uncertain it does appear to have a place in the management of carotid artery stenosis and the decision depends on the expertise of the unit. There is no evidence that surgery is appropriate for the asymptomatic patient with a stenosis < 60% or the symptomatic patient with a stenosis less than 30%, but there is a significant benefit for a stenosis greater than 70% (and possibly > 60% in asymptomatic patients).

Atrial fibrillation and TIAs

Management
- valvular disease: warfarin
- nonvalvular AF
    — no risk factors: aspirin 100–300 mg/day
    — risk factors: warfarin: INR 1.5–2.5
    — if warfarin contraindicated: aspirin

Indications for carotid duplex studies
- bruit in neck, because of significant stroke rate
- TIAs
- crescendo TIAs (more frequent and longer lasting)
- vertebrobasilar insufficiency symptoms
- hemispheric stroke
- prior to major vascular surgery, e.g. CABG

When to refer
- consider referral most cases
- suspicion of SAH
- carotid artery stenosis
- cerebellar haemorrhage on CT scan
- stroke in a young patient < 50 years
    consider patent foramen ovale and other rare causes

Stuttering

Recommend medical hypnotherapy if no contraindications.

Stye in eye

- Apply heat with direct steam from a thermos (see figure below) onto the closed eye or by a hot compress (helps spontaneous discharge).
- Perform lash epilation to allow drainage (incise with a D_{11} blade if epilation doesn't work).
- Only use topical antibiotic ointment, e.g. chloramphenicol, if infection spreading locally, and systemic antibiotics if distal spread noted by preauricular adenitis.

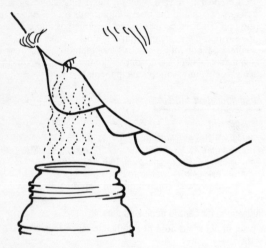

Steaming a painful eye

Subconjunctival haemorrhage

- Patient explanation and reassurance is necessary.
- It absorbs over two weeks.
- Although no local therapy is necessary, bathing with a weak salt solution twice daily helps.

Sudden infant death syndrome (SIDS)

Preventive advice

- Place babies to sleep on their sides or back (unless special reasons for placing them on their stomachs.
- Breast-feed babies.

- Ensure babies are not exposed to cigarette smoking.
- Ensure that babies do not get overheated (the sign of sweating around the head and neck indicates the baby is too hot).

Management of SIDS

- Allow parents to see or hold baby.
- Give explanations including reasons for coroner's involvement.
- Provide bereavement counselling.
- Provide early contact and continuing support.
- Revisit home.
- Provide hypnotics (limited).
- Offer advice on lactation suppression.
- Remember siblings can experience grief reactions.

Apparent life threatening episode (ALTE)

ALTE or 'near-miss SIDS' is defined as a 'frightening' encounter of apnoea, colour change or choking. At least 10% will have another episode. Management includes admission to hospital for investigation and monitoring.

Guidelines for home apnoea monitoring:

- ALTE
- subsequent siblings of SIDS victims
- twins of SIDS victims
- extremely premature infants

Sunburn

Treatment

- aspirin (for pain)
- promethazine (for sedation/itching) only if necessary

Topical:

- hydrocortisone 1% ointment or cream for unblistered severe cases (early)
    repeat in 2–3 hours, then next day (not after 24 hours)
                or
- bicarbonate of soda paste, applied 2 hourly
                or
- oily calamine lotion

Prevention

Avoid exposure to summer sunlight 10 am to 2 pm (or 11 am to 3 pm summer time saving). Use natural shade—beware of reflected light from sand or water and light cloud. Use a sunscreen with a minimum of SPF 15 +. Wear broad-brimmed hats and protective clothing.

Sweating (excessive)

General hyperhidrosis

- explanation and reassurance
- trial of probanthine aluminium chloride 20% in alcohol solution if localised area

Axillary hyperhidrosis

Treatment:

- explanation and reassurance
- *see* treatment of body odour
- aluminium chloride 20% in alcohol solution (Driclor, Hidrosol); apply nocte for one week, then 1–2 times weekly or as necessary

Surgery

Wedge resection of a small block of skin and subcutaneous tissue from axillary vault. Define sweat glands with codeine starch powder. The area excised is usually about 4 cm × 2.5 cm.

Syphilis (see page 311)

Tampon toxic shock syndrome

Caused by staphylococcal exotoxin associated with tampon use. The syndrome usually begins within five days of the onset of the period.

The *clinical features* include sudden onset fever, vomiting and diarrhoea, muscle aches and pains, skin erythema, hypotension progressing to confusion, stupor and sometimes death.

Management

Active treatment depends on the severity of the illness. Cultures should be taken from the vagina, cervix, perineum and nasopharynx. The patient should be referred to a major centre if 'shock' develops. Otherwise the vagina must be emptied, ensuring there is not a forgotten tampon, cleaned with a povidone iodine solution tds for two days, and methicillin or cloxacillin antibiotics administered for 8–12 days.

Tearduct (nasolacrimal duct) blockage in child

- if conjunctivitis present
      chloramphenicol eye drops
- perform regular massage from inner canthus to base of nose (teach mother) at least twice daily
- if persistent in infant: requires nasolacrimal probing at 4 months—otherwise leave to 6 months or so as it may resolve

Teething

Precautions: exclude other possible causes of irritability in a teething child, e.g. UTI, meningitis, otitis media. Teething doesn't cause fever.

Treatment

- paracetamol
- trimeprazine or antihistamine (o) nocte
                  or
- combined mixture, e.g. Polaramine Infant Co

Chewing

- teething ring (kept cold in the refrigerator)
                  or

- baby can chew on a clean, cold, lightly moistened face-washer (a piece of apple can be placed in the facewasher)
  or
- parent can massage gum with forefinger wrapped in a soft cloth or gauze pad (Orosed gel can be massaged into gums every 3 hours if extremely troublesome)

Temporomandibular joint dysfunction

Refer to the techniques on page 184. Most effective and simplest method is placing a piece of soft wood, e.g. carpenter's pencil, firmly against back molars and biting rhythmically on the object with a grinding movement for 2–3 minutes at least 3 times a day.

Tennis elbow

(see page 39)

Tension headache

(see page 208)

Testicular tumours

A mass that is part of the testis, and solid, is likely to be a tumour.

Table 57 *Testicular tumours*

Tumour	Incidence (%)	Peak incidence (years)
Seminoma	40	30–40
Teratoma	32	20–30
Mixed seminoma/teratoma	14	20–40
Lymphoma	7	60–70
Other tumours e.g. interstitial (Leydig) gonadoblastoma	uncommon	variable

Clinical features

- young men 20–40 years
- painless lump in body of testis (commonest feature)
- loss of testicular sensation
- associated presentations (may mask tumour) e.g. hydrocele; epididymo-orchitis

Golden rules

- All solid scrotal lumps are malignant until proved otherwise and must be surgically explored.
- Beware of hydroceles in young adults.

Prognosis is good for most testicular tumours with five year cure rates of 85–90%.

Tetanus

Up to 20% of patients have no observable entry wound.

Clinical features

- prodrome: fever, malaise, headache
- trismus (patient cannot close mouth)
- risus sardonicus (a grin-like effect from hypertonic facial muscles)
- opisthothonus (arched trunk with hyperextended neck)
- spasms, precipitated by minimal stimuli

Differential diagnosis: phenothiazine toxicity, strychnine poisoning, rabies.

Refer immediately to expert centre.

Intubate and ventilate if necessary.

Prophylaxis

Immunisation of adults
- 2 doses 6 weeks apart
- 3rd dose 6 months later

Boosters every 10 years or 5 years if major wound

In wound management (see Table 58).

Table 58 Guide to tetanus prophylaxis in wound management

History of active tetanus immunisation	Clean, minor wounds		All other wounds	
	Tetanus toxoid[1]	Tetanus immune globulin	Tetanus toxoid[1]	Tetanus immune globulin
Uncertain, or less than 3 doses	yes	no	yes	yes
3 doses or more	no[2]	no	no[3]	no[4]

1. Adult or child 8 years and over—use tetanus toxoid or ADT. Child 7 years or less, CDT or DTP (if due).
2. Yes, if more than 10 years since last dose.
3. Yes, if more than 5 years since last dose.
4. Yes, if more than 10 years since last dose and tetanus-prone wound.

Threadworms

- explanation and reassurance
- pyrantel (various oral preparations)
    10 mg/kg as a single dose

Thrush (moniliasis) of mouth

In infants: nystatin oral drugs 1 mL held in mouth as long as possible 4 times daily

In adults: amphotericin, 1 lozenge (10 mg) dissolved slowly in mouth, 6 hourly for 10 days

or

nystatin, 1 lozenge (100 000 units) dissolved slowly in mouth, 6 hourly for 10 days

Thumb sucking

A behaviour disorder.

Only causes damage from time onset of permanent teeth (6–7).

Usually spontaneous cessation if not an issue between child and parent.

Management

- no medication
- avoid drawing attention to it
- give child extra attention
- help child explore other solutions/distractions
- refer if prolonged and excessive

Thyroid disorders

Thyroid disorders can be a diagnostic trap in family practice. Guidelines for ordering thyroid function tests are:

- if hypothyroidism suspected: TSH + T_4
- if hyperthyroidism suspected: TSH + T_3

The relative values are summarised in Table 59.

Hypothyroidism (myxoedema)

- typically physical and mental slowing, lethargy, constipation, cold intolerance and characteristic signs, e.g. dry, cool skin
- T_4—subnormal, TSH elevated

Thyroid medication

thyroxine 100–150 µg daily (once daily)

Table 59 *Summary of thyroid function tests*

	TSH thyroid stimulating hormone	T_4 free thyroxine	T_3 tri-iodothyronine
Hypothyroidism			
• primary	↑ *	↓ *	N or ↓
• secondary (pituitary dysfunction)	N or ↓	↓	N or ↓
Hyperthyroidism	↓ *	↑	↑ *
Sick euthyroid	N or ↓	N or ↓	N or ↓

Note: Results similar to hyperthyroidism can occur with acute psychiatric illness.
   * Main tests

Note: Start with low doses (25–50 µg daily) in elderly and ischaemic heart disease.

Monitor T_4 and TSH levels monthly at first, then 2–3 monthly and when stable on optimum dose of T_4, every 2 to 3 years.

Hashimoto's disease

Commonly presents as postpartum hypothyroidism (thyroiditis).

• bilateral goitre, firm and rubbery
• may be hypothyroid or euthyroid

Neonatal hypothyroidism

This demands early diagnosis to avoid intellectual disability (cretinism): thyroxine replacement should be started by the 14th day.

Hyperthyroidism (thyrotoxicosis)

Classic symptoms of hyperactive metabolism including heat intolerance, agitation, restlessness, warm and sweaty hands may be absent in elderly patients. Avoid dismissing it as anxiety.

• T_3 (and T_4) elevated, TSH suppressed
• Radioisotope scan a very useful test

Refer to endocrinologist for treatment.

Subacute thyroiditis

Usually transient and often follows a viral-type illness. May be pain over goitre and fever.

Tick bites

Some species of ticks are very dangerous so it is mandatory to remove the embedded tick which should be totally removed, including the mouthparts. Do not attempt to grab the tick by its body and tug.

First aid outdoor removal method

- Saturate the tick with petrol or kerosene and leave for three minutes.
- Loop a strong thin thread around the head as close to the skin as possible then pull sharply with a twisting motion.

Office procedure

- Infiltrate a small amount of LA in the skin around the site of embedment.
- With a number 11 or 15 scalpel blade make the necessary very small excision, including the mouth parts of the tick, to ensure total removal (see figure below).
- The small defect can usually be closed with a bandaid (or Steri-strips).

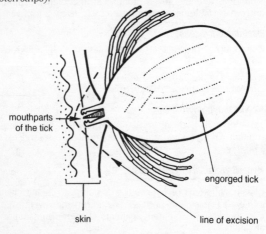

Removing the embedded tick

Tinea infections

Tinea, or ringworm infections, are caused mainly by three major classes of dermatophytic organisms. It is most useful to perform skin scrapings and microscopy to look for encroaching septate hyphae. Confirm the diagnosis by fungal culture.

Tinea capitis

Clinical features
- usually in children
- patches of partial alopecia
- scaly patches
- small broken-off hair shafts
- hairs usually fluoresce yellow-green with Wood's light

Treatment
- griseofulvin (o) Adults: 500 mg daily
  - Children: 10 mg/kg/day (max. 250 mg)
  - 4–8 week course
- Also — take hair plucking and scale for culture
  - — Selsun shampoo twice weekly
  - — topical clotrimazole or miconazole

Tinea cruris (jock itch)

- related to chafing in groin, e.g. tight pants, and especially nylon 'jock straps'
- scaling, especially at margin
- well-defined border

Diagnostic aids
- Skin scrapings should be taken from the scaly area for preparation for microscopy.
- Wood's light may help the diagnosis, particularly if erythrasma is suspected.

Treatment
- Soak the area in a warm bath and dry thoroughly.
- Apply clotrimazole 1% or miconazole 2% or ketoconazole 2% cream; rub in a thin layer bd for 3–4 weeks.
- When almost healed, apply tolnaftate dusting powder bd for 3–4 weeks.
- If itch severe: add 1% hydrocortisone cream.
- If weeping: apply Burow's solution compresses.
- For persistent or recurrent eruption, use oral griseofulvin for 6–8 weeks, or terbinafine for 2–4 weeks.

Tinea pedis (athlete's foot)

Symptoms
The commonest symptoms are itchiness and foot odour. There is scaling, maceration and fissuring of the skin between the fourth and fifth toes and also third and fourth toes.

Management

- Patient education.
- Keep feet clean and dry.
- Use antifungal powder between toes after drying.
- Wear socks of natural absorbent fibres (avoid synthetics).
- Wear open sandals and shoes with porous soles and uppers (if possible).
- Use thongs in public showers.
- Keep toe spaces separated if interdigital.

Rx: clotrimaxole 1% or miconazole 2% cream or lotion; apply bd or tds for 2–3 weeks

or

ketoconazole 2% cream bd
If widespread or smelly vesiculobullous (take scrapings), use griseofulvin (Griseostatin) 330 mg (o) daily for 6 weeks or terbinafine for 2–6 weeks.

Tinea of toe nails and fingernails (tinea unguium)

- usually associated with tinea pedis
- nails show white spots; may be yellow and crumbling
- starts at the edge of periphery and spreads towards base

Treatment

- terbinafine (Lamisil) 250 mg (o) daily
  - — fingernails 4 weeks
  - — toe-nails 12 weeks

Tinea corporis

Management

- take skin scrapings
- clotrimazole 1% or miconazole 2% cream or ketoconazole 2% cream, applied bd for 3–4 weeks
- oral terbinafine or griseofulvin if no response

Tinea incognito

This is the term used for unrecognised tinea infection due to modification with corticosteroid treatment. The lesions are enlarging and persistent, especially on the groins, hands and face.

The sequence is initial symptomatic relief of itching, stopping the ointment or cream and then relapse.

Tinnitus

Precautions:

- exclude wax, drugs including marijuana, vascular disease, depression, aneurysm and vascular tumours
- beware of lonely elderly people living alone (suicide risk)

Management

- full ENT examination including hearing
- educate and reassure the patient/counselling
- relaxation techniques
- background 'noise', e.g. music playing during night or
- tinnitus maskers or
- hearing aids

Drug trials to consider (limited efficacy)

- betahistine (Serc) 8–16 mg daily (max. 32 mg)
- carbamazepine
- antidepressants
- sodium valproate

Acute severe tinnitus

Slow IV injection of 1% lignocaine. Up to about 5 mL can be very effective.

Those for investigation

- asymmetrical with hearing loss (? acoustic neuroma)
- true pulsatile tinnitus
- severe hearing loss

Tiredness/fatigue

Tiredness can be a symptom of a great variety of serious and uncommon diseases including malignant disease. The most probable diagnoses to consider are:

- tension, stress and anxiety
- depression
- viral or postviral infection
- sleep-related disorders

It is important not to overlook drugs whether self-administered or iatrogenic as a cause.

Sleep-related disorders

An important cause of daytime tiredness is a sleep disorder such as obstructive sleep apnoea which results in periodic hypoventilation during sleep. It occurs in 2% of the general population in all age groups and in about 10% of middle-aged men. A history of snoring is a pointer to the problem.

Referral to a comprehensive sleep disorder centre is appropriate if this disorder is suspected.

Narcolepsy

Narcolepsy is a condition where periods of irresistible sleep occur in inappropriate circumstances and consists of a tetrad of symptoms:

- sudden brief sleep attacks (15–20 minutes)
- cataplexy—a sudden loss of muscle tone in the lower limbs—may slump to floor
- sleep paralysis.
- hypnagogic (terrifying) hallucinations on falling asleep

Treatment
Methylphenidate (Ritalin) or amphetamines
Tricyclic antidepressants (small doses) for cataplexy

Chronic fatigue syndrome

Chronic fatigue syndrome (CFS) is defined as debilitating fatigue, persisting or relapsing over six months, associated with a significant reduction in activity levels of at least 50% and for which no other cause can be found.

It does appear to be a real illness, probably caused by a virus.

Management
- recognition of CFS, education and reassurance
- ongoing support
- rest and pacing activity
- a supervised self management action plan
- cognitive therapy, meditation and group support

Medication options:

- antidepressant trial (if signs of depression)
  consider evening primrose oil

Tongue problems
- geographical tongue: reassurance and Cepacaine gargles 10 mL tds if tender
- black or hairy tongue: this is basically a harmless condition related to smoking and antibiotic treatment
  Rx (if patient pressure):

— brush with toothbrush using sodium bicarbonate paste
       or
— suck fresh pineapple pieces

Torticollis (acute wry neck)

Muscle energy therapy, which is simple to use and highly effective, is recommended.

Travel medicine and tropical infections

- The main diseases facing the international traveller are traveller's diarrhoea (relatively mild) and malaria, especially CRFM.
- Infections transmitted by mosquitoes include malaria, yellow fever, Rift Valley fever, Japanese encephalitis and dengue fever. Preventing their bites is excellent prevention.
- STDs including HIV of concern in certain areas.

Traveller's diarrhoea

The illness is usually mild and lasts only two or three days. It is unusual for it to last longer than five days. Mainly caused by an *E. coli* strain.

Treatment

Mild diarrhoea

- maintain fluid intake—cordial or diluted soft drink
- antimotility agents (judicious use: if no blood in stools) loperamide (Imodium) 2 caps statim then 1 after each unformed stool (max: 8 caps/day)

Moderate diarrhoea

- attend to hydration
- patient can self-administer antibiotic—e.g. norfloxacin 400 mg bd for 3 days, or ciprofloxacin; use co-trimoxazole in children
- avoid Lomotil or Imodium

Severe diarrhoea (patient toxic and febrile)

- ? admit to hospital
- attend to hydration—use an oral hydrate solution, e.g. Gastrolyte or WHO formulation
- avoid Lomotil and Imodium
- antibiotic: norfloxacin or ciprofloxacin

Persistent diarrhoea

Consider giardiasis or amoebiasis.

Treatment

Giardiasis: tinidazole or metronidazole
Amoebiasis: metronidazole or tinidazole

Preventive advice (countries at risk)

- Purify all potentially contaminated water by boiling for 10 minutes. 2% tincture of iodine is useful
- Do not use ice or salads.
- Drink hot drinks or reputable bottled soft drinks.

Malaria

Malarial prevention

Following two simple rules:

- avoid mosquito bites; and
- take antimalarial medicines regularly.

Consider:
- smearing an insect repellent on exposed parts of the body
- using mosquito nets
- impregnating nets with permethrin (Ambush) or deltamethrin.

Drug prophylaxis

> *Summary of recommendations*
>
> 1. CSFM area: chloroquine 300 mg/week
> 2. CRFM area:
>   mefloquine 250 mg/week
>   or
>   doxycycline 100 mg/day
> 3. Multi-drug resistant area
>   doxycycline 100 mg/day
>
>   For stays > 8 weeks in areas 2 and 3
>   chloroquine 300 mg/week
>   +
>   doxycycline 50 mg/day
> CSFM = chloroquine-sensitive falciparum malaria
> CRFM = chloroquine-resistant falciparum malaria

Table 60 *Common drugs used for malarial prophylaxis*

	Adult dosage	**Children's dose**
Chloroquine	300 mg base (2 tabs) same day each week 2 wk before, during 4 wk after exposure	5 mg base/kg up to maximum adult dose

(continues)

Table 60 *(continued)*

| *Doxycycline* | 100 mg each day, 1 to 2 days before, during, 4 weeks after | > 8 years only 2 mg/kg/day up to 100 mg |
| *Mefloquine (Lariam)* | 250 mg (1 tab) same day each week, 1 week before, during, 4 weeks after | Not recommended < 45 kg > 45 kg as for adults |

Treatment of breakthrough malaria during travel (where medical care unavailable)

  Mefloquine 500 mg (2 tabs) statim
        Repeat after 8–12 hours

Table 61 *Summary of preventive measures and vaccinations*

All travellers, all destinations

Tetanus toxoid booster

if > 10 years since last dose
if > 5 years for Third World travel

All travellers to developing countries free of malaria

Tetanus toxoid booster

Polio immunisation, if > 10 years

Measles immunisation

Yellow fever and cholera vaccine (if compulsory)

Preventive measures against:
• gastrointestinal infections
• sexually transmitted diseases
• mosquito bites

Travellers to developing and other countries at high risk of infection

As above plus:

Malaria prophylaxis

Hepatitis A—vaccine or immunoglobulin

Tuberculosis

Typhoid

Other vaccinations: consider
• hepatitis B
• meningococcus
• Japanese B encephalitis
• rabies
• typhus
• plague

Management of specific acquired infections

Typhoid fever

Incubation period 10–14 days.

Diagnosis on suspicion → blood culture

Treatment ciprofloxacin

Japanese B encephalitis and meningococcal meningitis

Consider these serious infections in a patient presenting with headache, fever and malaise before neurological symptoms such as delirium, convulsions and coma develop.

Tropical infections

Dengue fever

Also known as 'breakbone' fever.
Febrile illness with severe aching of muscles and joints.

Diagnosis
Clinical suspicion → isolation of virus

Treatment
Is symptomatic with supportive follow-up. Depression a worry.

Melioidosis

Caused by a Gram-negative bacillus. It may manifest as a focal infection or as septicaemia with abscesses in the lung, kidney, liver or spleen. It presents with fever, cough and myalgia.

Diagnosis
Blood culture, swabs from focal lesions, haemagglutination test

Treatment
Ceftazidime IV

Malaria

- incubation period: *P. falciparum* 7–14 days; others 12–40 days
- most present within 2 months of return from tropics
- can present up to 2 or more years

Symptoms
- high fever, chills, rigor, sweating, headache
- usually abrupt onset
- can have atypical presentations, e.g. diarrhoea, abdominal pain, cough

Other features
- beware of modified infection
- must treat within 4 days
- typical relapsing patterns often absent
- thick smear allows detection of parasites
- thin smear helps diagnose malaria type

If index of suspicion high, repeat the smear ('No evidence of malaria' = 3 negative daily thick films). Monocytosis is a helpful diagnostic clue. Cerebral malaria and blackwater fever are severe and dramatic.

Treatment
- admit to hospital with infectious disease expertise
- supportive measures including IV fluids
- *P. vivax, P. ovale, P. malariae*
     chloroquine + primaquine: 14 days (check G6PD first)
  P. falciparum
     uncomplicated: quinine (o) + doxycycline
     or mefloquine (alone)
     complicated: quinine IV
                  then
                  quinine + Fansidar (o)

Note: Check for hypoglycaemia.
        Beware if antimalarial use in previous 48 hours.

Prevention
(see page 340)

Schistosomiasis (bilharzia)
- first sign is local skin reaction ('swimmer's itch')
- generalised allergic reaction (fever, malaise, urticaria) some days later
- other symptoms, e.g. nausea, vomiting, cough

Diagnosis
Specific serology: also eggs in excreta.

Treatment
Praziquantel.

Prevention
Travellers should be warned against drinking from, or swimming and wading in dams, watercourses or irrigation channels especially in Egypt and Africa.

African trypanosomiasis (sleeping sickness)

- fever, headache and a skin chancre or nodule
- lymphadenopathy, hepatosplenomegaly

Diagnosis: on blood smear or chancre aspirate
Treatment: suramin IV
Prevention: avoid bites of the tsetse fly

Hookworm and strongyloidiasis

- first sign—'creeping eruption' at entry point on feet
- 1–2 weeks later—respiratory symptoms like pneumonia
- anaemia follows

Diagnosis: larvae or ova in stool
Treatment: special drugs for each parasite
Prevention: use footwear in endemic areas

Cutaneous myiasis

Consider infestation of body tissues by larvae (maggots) of flies
if traveller presents with 'itchy boils', e.g. tumbu fly, New World
screw worm.
Treatment: pressure and tweezer extraction of maggot.

Travel sickness

Oral preparations:

- dimenhydrinate (Andrumin, Dramamine, Travacalm)
  or
- promethazine theoclate (Avomine)
  or
- hyoscine (Kwells)

Take 30–60 minutes before the trip.
Repeat 4–6 hourly during trip (maximum 4 doses in 24 hours).

Dermal:

- hyoscine dermal disc (Scop)
  Apply to dry hairless skin behind ear 5–6 hours before
  travel, leave on for 3 days.

Tremor

Tremor is an important symptom to evaluate correctly. A
common mistake is to misdiagnose the tremor of essential
tremor for that of Parkinson's disease.

Classification

Resting tremor—Parkinsonian

The tremor of Parkinson's disease is present at rest. The hand tremor is most marked with the arms supported on the lap and during walking. The characteristic movement is 'pill-rolling'.

Action or postural tremor

This fine tremor is noted by examining the patient with the arms outstretched and the fingers apart.

Causes include:

- essential tremor (also called familial tremor or benign essential tremor)
- senile tremor
- physiological
- anxiety/emotional
- hyperthyroidism
- alcohol
- drugs, e.g. drug withdrawal (e.g. heroin, cocaine, alcohol), dexedrine, lithium

Intention tremor (cerebellar disease)

This coarse oscillating tremor is absent at rest but exacerbated by action and increases as the target is approached. It is tested by 'finger-nose-finger' touching.

Flapping (metabolic tremor)

A flapping or 'wing-beating' tremor is observed when the arms are extended with hyperextension of the wrists. Typically caused by metabolic disorders such as uraemia, hepatic failure and respiratory failure.

Essential tremor

Called benign, familial, senile or juvenile tremor.

Triad of features

- positive family history
- tremor with little disability including head movement
- normal gait

Management

- explanation and reassurance
- drugs usually not needed

If necessary:

> propranolol (first choice)
> or primidone

Tropical ear

For severe painful otitis externa in tropics:

- prednisolone (orally) 15 mg statim, then 10 mg 8 hourly for 6 doses followed by
- Merocel ear wick
- topical Kenacomb or Sofradex drops for 10 days

U

Umbilical discharge

Usually infected (fungal or bacterial) dermatitis, often with offensive discharge.

Precautions: consider umbilical fistula, carcinoma, umbilical calculus.

Management:

- swab for micro and culture
- toilet—remove all debris and clean
- keep dry and clean—daily dressings
- consider Kenacomb ointment

Umbilical granuloma in infants

Apply a caustic pencil gently daily for about 5 days.

Undescended testes

A testis that is not in the scrotum may be ectopic, absent, retractile or truly undescended.

The problem of non-descent

- testicular dysplasia
- susceptible to direct violence (if in inguinal region)
- risk of malignant change (seminoma) is 5–10 times greater than normal

Optimal time for surgery

The optimal time for orchidopexy is 12–18 months of age. The production of spermatozoa is adversely affected in undescended testes from the age of two years onwards. Exploration for the uncommon impalpable testis is worthwhile.

Hormone injections

Injections of chorionic gonadotrophic hormones are generally not recommended. They are ineffective except for borderline retractile testes.

Urethritis

The important STDs that cause urethritis are gonorrhoea and non-specific urethritis.

Collection of specimens

Take two swabs:

- standard swab for *Gonococcus* (into the urethral meatus): place into Stuart's transport medium
- wire swab for *Chlamydia* (2–4 cm into the urethra and twist around), after wiping away frank pus and exudate: place into *Chlamydia* transport medium.

Take cervical swab in females.

In males direct immunofluorescence or ELISA is diagnostic of *Chlamydia*.

Non-specific urethritis

Rx: Doxycycline 100 mg (0) 12 hourly for 10 days.

A second course may be required if the symptoms persist or recur (about one in five cases). Second-line treatment is erythromycin 500 mg qid for 7 days.

- treat (same way) sexual partners (even if asymptomatic)
- avoid sexual intercourse until resolution

Gonorrhoea

Rx: ciprofloxacin 500 mg (o) statim
     plus
doxycycline 100 mg (o) bd for 10 days
If pharyngeal or anorectal infection
     ceftriaxone 250 mg (IM) as single dose
Same rules as for NSU.

Urinary tract infection

Treatment

- Treat all patients with symptomatic urinary infection.
- Treat these asymptomatic patients with bacterial UTI: neonates, preschool children, pregnant women, all those with known or presumed urinary tract abnormality and/or renal impairment, men < 60 years.

Optimal treatment includes:
— high fluid intake
— complete bladder emptying, especially at bedtime or after intercourse (women)
— urinary alkalinisation for severe dysuria, e.g. sodium citrotartrate (4 g orally 6 hourly)

Acute uncomplicated cystitis

Antimicrobial regimen

Multiple dose therapy preferred.

Single dose therapy
• trimethoprim 600 mg orally
or
• gentamicin 120 mg IM

Multiple dose therapy
use for 5 days in women (trimethoprim—3 days)
use for 10 days in women with known UT abnormality
use for 10 days in men with acute cystitis
• trimethoprim 300 mg (o) daily for 3 days
or
• cephalexin 250 mg (o) 6 hourly
or
• amoxycillin/potassium clavulanate 250/125 mg (o) 8 hourly
  (preferred agent)
or
• norfloxacin 400 mg (o) 12 hourly (if resistance to above
  agents proven)

Follow-up: MSU 3 weeks later.

Acute cystitis in children

Treatment should be continued for 7 to 10 days.

• trimethoprim 6 mg/kg (maximum 300 mg) orally, daily (suspension is 50 mg/5 mL)
or
• cephalexin 10mg/kg (maximum 250 mg) orally 6 hourly
or
• amoxycillin/potassium clavulanate 10/2.5 mg/kg (maximum
  250/125 mg) orally 8 hourly

Norfloxacin is contraindicated in children.
Check MSU in three weeks.

Urinary infections in pregnancy

Acute cystitis is treated for 10 to 14 days with any of the
following antimicrobiols: cephalexin, amoxycillin/potassium
clavulanate or nitrofurantoin (if a beta-lactam antibiotic is
contraindicated). The dosages are the same as for other groups.
Asymptomatic bacteruria should be treated with a week-long
course.

Urinary infections in the elderly

Treat uncomplicated symptomatic infections as for adults but not asymptomatic bacteruria.

Acute pyelonephritis

Mild cases: oral therapy (as for cystitis) but double dose
       except trimethoprim (same dose)
Severe: admit to hospital
      take urine for MCU and blood for culture
      amoxycillin 1 g IV 6 hourly
         plus
      gentamicin 120–160 mg IV 12 hourly for 2 to 5 days
      then use oral therapy ASAP (total 14 days treatment)
Investigate all for an underlying LIT abnormality.

Treatment of recurrent or chronic UTI

A 10 to 14 day course of
- amoxycillin/potassium clavulanate (250/125mg) (o) 8 hourly
    or
- nitrofurantoin 100 mg (o) 6 hourly
    or
- norfloxacin 400 mg (o) 12 hourly (if proven resistance to above agents)

Prophylaxis for recurrent UTI

In some female patients a single dose of a suitable agent after intercourse is adequate but, in more severe cases, courses may be taken for 6 months or on occasions longer.

- nitrofurantoin (macrocrystals) 50–100 mg (o) nocte
    or
- trimethoprim 150 mg (o) nocte
    or
- norfloxacin 200–400 mg (o) nocte (if proven resistance to others)

Investigations for UTI

Basic investigations include:
- MSU—microscopy and culture (post-treatment)
- renal function tests: plasma urea and creatinine
- intravenous urogram (IVU), and/or ultrasound

Special considerations:
- in children: micturating cystogram
- in adult males: consider prostatic infection studies if IVU normal

- in severe pyelonephritis: ultrasound or IVU (urgent) to exclude obstruction
- in pregnant women: ultrasound to exclude obstruction

Table 62 *Indications for investigation of urinary tract infection*

Patients with first UTI
- all infants and children
- all males
- those not responding to a course of an *appropriate* antibiotic

Patients with recurrent UTI
- failure to respond to a course of appropriate therapy
- those with a positive family history of vesicoureteric reflux
- renal symptoms/pyelonephritis (loin pain, fever)
- other features suggesting renal disease, e.g. hypertension, continuing haematuria, proteinuria

---

Urticaria (hives) (see page 23)

- search for cause, e.g. drugs, food, infestation
- food check: nuts, chocolate, cheese, fish, eggs

Rx: antihistamines: cyprohepadine 16–32 mg daily or astemizole or terfenadine
- lukewarm baths with Pinetarsol or similar soothing bath oil
- topical 0.5% hydrocortisone—apply every 4 hours for itching

Vaginal discharge

Table 63 *Vaginal discharge: diagnostic strategy model (modified)*

Q. *Probability diagnosis*
A. Normal physiological discharge
Vaginitis
  • bacterial vaginosis   40–50%
  • candidiasis   20–30%
  • trichomonas   10–20%

Q. *Serious disorders not to be missed*
A. Neoplasia
  • carcinoma
  • fistulas
STDs/PID
  • gonorrhoea
  • chlamydia
Sexual abuse, esp. children
Tampon toxic shock syndrome (staphylococcal infection)

Q. *Pitfalls (often missed)*
A. Chemical vaginitis, e.g. perfumes
Retained foreign objects, e.g. tampons, IUCD
Endometriosis (brownish discharge)
Ectopic pregnancy ('prune juice' discharge)
Poor toilet hygiene
Genital herpes (possible)
Papilloma virus infection
Atrophic vaginitis

Investigations

• pH test with paper of range 4 to 6

Make two slides:

• one smear for air-drying and Gram stain
• one wet film preparation, under a cover slip for direct inspection for the
   — pseudohyphae of *Candida*
   — 'clue cells' of *Gardnerella*
   — motile *Trichomonas*

A full STD workup (if relevant)
- swabs from the cervix for chlamydia, *N. gonorrhoeae*
  — swab mucus from cervix first
  — swab endocervix
  — place in transparent media
- Pap smear
- viral culture (herpes simplex)

Table 64   *Characteristics of discharge*

Infective organism	Colour	Consistency	Odour
Candida albicans	White	Thick (cream cheese)	—
Trichomonas	Yellow/green	Bubbly, profuse (mucopurulent)	Malodorous, fishy
Bacterial vaginosis	Grey	Watery, profuse, bubbly	Malodorous, fishy
Physiological	Milky white or clear (oxidises to yellow or brown)	Thin or mucoid	—
Atrophic vaginitis	Yellow (may be bloody)	Thin—slight to moderate	—

Vaginal thrush (monilial vaginitis)

- Bathe genital area bd or tds with sodium bicarbonate (especially before using treatment).
- Dry area thoroughly.
- Wear loose-fitting cotton underwear.
- Avoid wearing tight clothing or using tampons.
- Avoid vaginal douches, powders or deodorants.

Rx: can use amphotericin, clotrimazole, econazole, isoconazole, miconazole, nystatin, ketoconazole or fluconazole
Examples:
- clotrimazole 500 mg vaginal tablet statim, and clotrimazole 2% cream applied to vagina and vulva (for symptomatic relief)
      or (especially if recurrent)
- nystatin pessaries, once daily for 7 days
  and/or nystatin vaginal cream, 4 g once daily for 7 days
      or (if recalcitrant)
- ketoconazole 200 mg or fluconazole 50 mg daily (orally) for 14–21 days
- male sexual partner not treated (on current evidence)

Bacterial vaginosis

Due to overgrowth of *Gardnerella vaginalis* and other anaer-
obes such as *Mobiluncus* species.

Rx: metronidazole 400 mg (o), bd for 7 days
    or
   tinidazole 500 mg (o) daily for 7 days
    or (for resistant infections and pregnancy)
   clindamycin 300 mg (o) bd for 7 days
   ± clindamycin 2% cream

- restore pH with douches, e.g. topical Acigel or vinegar (3–4 tablespoons/L water)
- male sexual partner not treated

Trichomonas vaginalis

Rx:
- oral metronidazole 2 g as a single dose (preferable) *or* 600 mg daily for 7 days
    or
  tinidazole 500 mg qid over 1 day
- use clotrimazole 100 mg vaginal tablet daily for 6 days during pregnancy
- attention to hygiene
- the sexual partner must be treated simultaneously
- the male partner should wear a condom during intercourse
- for resistant infections a 3–7 day course of either metronidazole or tinidazole may be necessary.

Atrophic vaginitis

Rx:
- Oral hormone replacement therapy.
- Local oestrogen cream or tablet, e.g. Vagifem. The tablet is preferred as it is less messy.

Venous ulcers

The area typically affected by varicose eczema and ulceration
is shown in the figure. The secret of treating ulcers due to
chronic venous insufficiency is the proper treatment of the
physical factors, especially compression. Removal of fluid from
a swollen leg is also mandatory.

Treatment method

1. Clean the ulcer with N saline. If slough, apply Intra Site Gel.
2. Apply paraffin gauze, then pack the defect with sponge rubber or other suitable dressing, e.g. Melolin.

3. Apply a compression bandage below the knee (e.g. graduated compression stockings, Eloflex bandage, Unna's type boot).
   Alternatively, an occlusive paste bandage (e.g. Viscopaste or Icthaband) can be applied for 7 days from the base of the toe to just below the knee.
4. Prescribe diuretics if oedema is present.
5. Insist on as much elevation of the leg as is possible.

   Note: Dressings should be changed when they become loose or fall off, or when discharge seeps through. Patients may get ulcers wet and have baths.

Area typically affected by varicose eczema and ulceration (the 'gaiter' area)

Visual loss

Apart from migraine, virtually all cases of sudden loss of vision require urgent treatment.

Important causes

Amblyopia

—in children, a lazy eye with reduced vision.
   Refer strabismus early.

Retinoblastoma

—in children: white pupil and 'cat's eye' reflex.

Cataracts

- reduced visual acuity (sometimes improved with pinhole)
- diminished red reflex on ophthalmoscopy
- a change in the appearance of the lens

Advise extraction when the patient cannot cope.

Glaucoma

Acute—rapid onset over a few days
Chronic—gradual loss of outer fields of vision
Tonometry: 22 mm Hg is upper limit of normal

- medication (for life) usually selected from
  — timolol drops bd
  — pilocarpine drops qid
  — dipivefrine drops bd
  — acetazolamide (oral diuretics)
- surgery or laser therapy for failed medication

Retinitis pigmentosa

- begins as night blindness in children
- ophthalmoscopic examination—irregular patches of dark pigment

Sudden loss of vision

Amaurosis fugax

- usually due to embolus from carotid artery
- requires investigation including carotid duplex doppler scan

Retinal detachment

- sudden onset of floaters or flashes or black spots
- blurred vision in one eye becoming worse
- immediate referral for sealing of retinal tears

Vitreous haemorrhage

- sudden onset of floaters or 'blobs' in vision
- urgent referral to exclude retinal detachment
- surgical vitrectomy for persistent haemorrhage

Central retinal artery occlusion

- sudden loss of vision like a 'curtain descending'
- vision not improved with 1 mm pinhole
- classical 'red cherry spot' at macula

Management

If seen early, use this procedure within 30 minutes:

- massage globe digitally through closed eyelids (use rhythmic direct digital pressure)

- rebreathe carbon dioxide (paper bag) or inhale special CO_2 mixture (carbogen)
- intravenous acetazolamide (Diamox) 500 mg
- refer urgently

Central retinal vein thrombosis

Ophthalmoscopy shows swollen disc and multiple retinal haemorrhages.

No immediate treatment is effective.

Macular degeneration

There are two types: exudative (acute) and pigmentary (slow onset).

Acute—visual distortion then sudden fading of central vision.

Usually white exudates, haemorrhage in retina.

Urgent referral for fluorescein angiography and possible laser photocoagulation.

Temporal arteritis

- sudden loss of central vision in one eye (central scotoma)
- can rapidly become bilateral
- associated temporal headache

Management
- other eye must be tested
- immediate corticosteroids (60–100 mg prednisolone daily for at least one week)
- biopsy temporal artery

Posterior vitreous detachment

- sudden onset of floaters
- visual acuity usually normal
- flashing lights indicate traction on the retina

Refer urgently.

Optic (retrobulbar) neuritis

- usually a woman 20–40 years with multiple sclerosis
- loss of vision in one eye over a few days
- retro-ocular discomfort with eye movements
- variable visual acuity
- usually a central field loss (central scotoma)
- optic disc changes

Refer immediately. Steroids hasten recovery.

Warfarin oral anticoagulation

Warfarin actions

- antagonises vitamin K
- achieves full anticoagulation effect after 3–4 days
- prothrombin time (INR ratio) of 2 times normal control indicates therapeutic effect
- duration of effect is 2–3 days
- antidote is vitamin K

Initiation of warfarin treatment

An estimate of the patient's final steady dose is made. The patient is commenced on this dose and the INR monitored daily and the dose altered accordingly.

- Measure INR first to establish baseline.
- Generally warfarin is commenced on same day or day after heparin is commenced.
- Heparin can be ceased when INR > 2 for two consecutive days.
- Typical loading dose is 10 mg (o) daily for 2 days (avoid dose > 30 mg over 3 days without INR).
- Adjust the dosage according to the INR table (Table 65) from the third day.
- Establish the INR in the therapeutic range, usually 2–3.
- Maintenance dose usually reached by day 5.
- The INR reflects the warfarin dose given 48 hours earlier.

INR measurement schedule

before treatment
on third day
↓
daily for 1 week
↓
2 times weekly for 2 weeks
↓
weekly for 4 weeks
↓
monthly

Note: • Warfarin should be continued for 3 to 6 months and longer if major risk factors present.
- Watch for potential drug interactions.

Table 65 *Warfarin dosage adjustment[1]*

Day	INR	Dose
1	—	5 to 10 mg[2]
2	—	5 to 10 mg[2]
3	< 2	10 mg
	2.0 to 2.4	5 mg
	2.5 to 2.9	3 mg
	3.0 to 3.4	2 mg
	3.5 to 4.0	1 mg
	> 4.0	nil
4, and until stabilised	< 1.4	10 mg
	1.4 to 1.9	7 mg
	2.0 to 2.4	5 mg
	2.5 to 2.9	4 mg
	3.0 to 3.9	3 mg
	4.0 to 4.5	miss 1 day, then 2 mg
	> 4.5	miss 2 days, then 1 mg

[1] This table should be used only if the pre-treatment INR is normal.
[2] 5 mg of warfarin should be given to patients who are more likely to be sensitive to warfarin. This includes the elderly, the very ill, the malnourished and patients with abnormal liver function or significant chronic renal failure.

Warts

Types of warts

These include common warts, plane warts, filiform warts (fine elongated growths, usually on the face and neck), digitate warts (finger-like projections, usually on scalp), genital and plantar.

Treatment options for warts

Topical applications:

• salicylic acid, e.g. 5–20% in flexible collodion (apply daily or bd)
• formaldehyde 2–4% alone or in combination
• cantharadin 0.5–1% in equal parts collodion (available in USA), applied with care and occluded for 12 hours
• podophyllin 10–25% in tinct benz co *or* podophyllotoxin 0.5% (better) for anogenital warts—it is good on mucosal surfaces but does not penetrate normal keratin
• cytotoxic agents, e.g. 5-fluorouracil: very good for resistant warts such as plane warts and periungal warts

Cryotherapy

Carbon dioxide ($-56.5°C$) or liquid nitrogen ($-195.8°C$) destroys the host cell and stimulates an immune reaction.

Note: Excessive keratin must be pared before freezing.
Results often disappointing.

Curettage

Some plantar warts can be removed under LA with a sharp spoon curette. The problem is a tendency to scar so avoid over a pressure area such as the sole of the foot.

Electrodissection

A high-frequency spark under LA is useful for small, filiform or digitate warts. A combination of curettage and electro-dissection is suitable for large and persistent warts.

Vitamin A and the retinoids

- topical retinoic acid, e.g. tretinoin 0.1% cream (Retin A) is effective on plane warts
- systemic oral retinoid, etretinate (Tigason) for recalcitrant warts

Specific wart treatment

The method chosen depends on the type of wart, its site and the patient's age.

Plantar warts: refer page 197.

Genital warts: podophyllotoxin 0.5% paint (see page 201).

Filiform and digitate warts: liquid nitrogen or electrodissection.

Plane warts: liquid nitrogen; salicylic acid 20% Co, e.g. Wartkil; consider 5-fluorouracil cream or Retin-A.

Common warts: a recommended method:

1. Soak the wart/s in warm soapy water.
2. Rub back the wart surface with a pumice stone.
3. Apply the paint (only to the wart; protect the surrounding skin with Vaseline). The paint: formalin 5%, salicylic acid 12%, acetone 25%, collodion to 100%.

Do this daily or every second day. Carefully remove dead skin between applications.

Periungal warts (fingernails): consider 5-fluorouracil or liquid nitrogen. Always use a paint rather than ointment or paste on fingers.

Weight loss

Weight loss is an important symptom because it usually implies a serious underlying disorder, either organic or functional.

Table 66 *Weight loss: diagnostic strategy model (other than deliberate dieting or malnutrition)*

Q.	*Probability diagnosis*
A.	Stress and anxiety
	Non-coping elderly
Q.	*Serious disorders not to be missed*
A.	Congestive cardiac failure
	Malignant disease, e.g. stomach
	Chronic infection, e.g. tuberculosis
Q.	*Pitfalls (often missed)*
A.	Drug dependence, esp. alcohol
	Malabsorption states
	? intestinal parasites
	Other GIT problems
	Chronic renal failure
	Connective tissue disorders, e.g. SLE

Q.	*Seven masquerades checklist*	
A.	Depression	√
	Diabetes	√
	Drugs	√
	Anaemia	√
	Thyroid disease	√ hyperthyroid
	Spinal dysfunction	—
	UTI	—

Q.	*Is the patient trying to tell me something?*
A.	A possibility. Consider stress, anxiety and depression. Anorexia nervosa and bulimia are special considerations.

Eating disorders in the adolescent

Anorexia nervosa

Anorexia nervosa is a syndrome characterised by the obsessive pursuit of thinness through dieting with extreme weight loss and disturbance of body image.

Typical features

- adolescent and young adult females
- up to 1% incidence among 16 year old schoolgirls
- bimodal age of onset: 13 to 14 and 17 to 18 years
- unknown cause
- amenorrhoea

Bulimia

Bulimia is episodic secretive binge eating followed by self-induced vomiting, fasting or the use of laxatives or diuretics.

Typical clinical features

- young females
- begins at later age, usually 17–25 years
- associated psychoneurotic disorders
- fluctuations in body weight
- periods irregular—amenorrhoea rare
- physical complications of frequent vomiting, e.g. dental decay, effects of hypokalaemia

Management of eating disorders

There are often problematic family interrelationships which require exploration.

Important goals are:

- establish a good and caring relationship with the patient
- resolve underlying psychological difficulties
- restore weight to a level between ideal and the patient's concept of optimal weight
- provide a balanced diet of at least 3000 calories per day (anorexia nervosa)

Structured behavioural therapy, intensive psychotherapy and family therapy may be tried but supportive care by physicians and allied health staff appears to be the most important feature of therapy. Antidepressants may be helpful for selective patients.

Whiplash

(see page 267)

Whole person approach to management

The patient-centred consultation not only takes into account the diagnosed disease and its management but adds another dimension—that of the psychosocial hallmarks of the patient (Table 67).

Whole person diagnosis is based on two components:
1. the disease-centred diagnosis
2. the patient-centred diagnosis

The management of the whole person, or the holistic approach, is fundamental to good general practice.

Table 67 *Whole person diagnosis and management*

Disease-centred diagnosis	*Patient-centred diagnosis*
• aetiology of disease	• significance of illness to patient
	• effect on family and relationships
	• effect on work and income
	• psychological effects
	— stress and anxiety
	— abnormal illness/behaviour
	— sleep
	— depression
	• effect on sexuality
	• effect on attitudes and spirituality

Disease-centred management	*Patient-centred management*
• rest	• psychological support
• drugs	• appropriate reassurance
• intervention	• patient education
• surgery	• empowering self-responsibility
• other invasive techniques	• anticipatory guidance/special hazards
	• prevention
	• health promotion
	• lifestyle recommendations/ modifications
	— diet/nutrition
	— exercise
	— alcohol
	— smoking
	— stress management
	• family and social supports
	• self-help groups
	• alternative options
	• consultation and referral
	• follow-up
	• consideration of meditation

The general practitioner has an obligation to his or her patients to use natural healing methods wherever possible and be very discerning and conservative with investigatory medicine and drug prescribing.

Patients appreciate natural remedies and taking responsibility for their own management wherever possible and appropriate. Examples include relative rest, exercise, swimming, stress management, meditation, spiritual awareness, antioxidant therapy (e.g. vitamin C, vitamin E, selenium), weight control, optimal healthy nutrition, avoidance of toxins (e.g. illicit drugs, nicotine, caffeine and alcohol) and sexual fulfilment.

Underlying a successful outcome is motivation and the healing factor of the physician in being the motivator, teacher and facilitator should never be underestimated.

Wrinkles

(see page 289)

Writer's cramp

- education and reassurance
- avoid holding pen too tight
- clonazepan 0.5 mg bd (if persisting)

Z

Zoonoses

Zoonoses are those diseases and infections which are naturally transmitted between vertebrate animals and humans (see Table 68). There is a long list of diseases which vary from country to country and includes plague, rabies, scrub typhus, Lyme disease and tularaemia.

Table 68 *Major zoonoses in Australia*

Zoonosis	Organism/s	Animal host	Mode of transmission	Main presenting features	Diagnosis	Treatment
Q Fever	*Coxiella burnetti*	Various wild and domestic animals	Inhaled dust Animal contact Unpasteurised milk	Fever, rigors, myalgia, headache, dry cough	Serology CFT	Tetracycline
Leptospirosis	*Leptospira pomona*	Various domestic animals	Infected urine contaminating cuts or sores	Fever, myalgia, severe headache, macular rash	Serology Culture	Penicillin + tetracycline
Brucellosis	*Brucella abortus*	Cattle	Contamination of cuts or sores by animal tissues Unpasteurised milk	Fever (undulant) sweats, myalgia, headache, lymphadenopathy	Agglutination test Blood culture	Tetracycline + erythromycin or rifampicin
Lyme disease	*Borrelia burgdorferi*	Marsupials (probable)	Tick bites	Fever, myalgia, arthritis, backache, doughnut-shaped rash	Serology	Tetracycline
Psittacosis	*Chlamydia psittaci*	Birds: parrots, pigeons, ducks, etc.	Inhaled dust	Fever, myalgia, headache, dry cough	Serology	Tetracycline or erythromycin

Bovine tuberculosis	Mycobacterium bovis	Cattle	Unpasteurised milk	Fever, sweats, weight loss, cough (as for human pulmonary TB)	Culture	As for pulmonary TB
Plague	Yersinia pestis	Wild rodents	Fleas	Fever, myalgia, headache, prostration, lymphadenitis (bubo)	Smears, culture	Tetracycline + streptomycin